Wild Bird

Wild Bird

THE TRUE JAZZ AGE TALE OF
RUTH WIGHTMAN MORRIS

—

JOHN A. GREENWALD

Hawk Tower
— PRESS —

Published by Hawk Tower Press, Monterey, CA
www.johnagreenwald.com

Edited and designed by Girl Friday Productions
www.girlfridayproductions.com
Editorial: Emilie Sandoz-Voyer, Mark Steven Long, and Janice Lee
Interior design: Rachel Christenson
Cover design: Connie Gabbert
Image credits: cover photo courtesy of University of Southern California, on behalf of the USC Libraries Special Collections

ISBN-13: 978-0-9977367-0-0
ISBN-10: 0-9977367-0-4
eISBN: 978-0-9977367-1-7
Library of Congress Control Number: 2016913431

First Edition

Printed in the United States of America

To Carol, for her unwavering support of this project, her thoughtful suggestions throughout, and her good-natured acceptance of my many hours spent with the other woman.

AUTHOR'S NOTE

The story of Ruth Wightman Morris was assembled from a number of sources, including personal letters, interviews, newspaper and magazine articles, and books, among others. The sources used are listed by chapter in the notes section at the end of this book. Direct quotations from some of these sources are used in the text. The letters quoted herein, either in whole or in part, are presented exactly as they were transcribed from the originals.

CONTENTS

INTRODUCTION

There are few moments in life as sublime for a writer as stumbling upon a great, untold story. *Wild Bird: The True Jazz Age Tale of Ruth Wightman Morris* is one such untold story, and how it was discovered is a tale unto itself.

It begins in the fall of 1930. As the finishing touches were being completed on an addition to a Spanish-style mansion in Monterey, California, someone—who that might have been remains a tantalizing mystery—sealed a small safe inside one of the walls.

Roughly a year and a half later, the owners of the property, Ruth and Gouverneur Morris, were forced by economic circumstances to abandon their home, leaving the safe and its contents behind.

Subsequent owners never realized the safe even existed, and it wasn't until after the Monterey Museum of Art moved into the building in the 1990s that its hiding place was finally revealed. During the routine installation of a display case, a carpenter opened up the wall, and there it was: the little safe.

Inside were two handwritten letters, a copy of a typed letter, and a telegram. After a quick reading of the documents, museum staffers unceremoniously tucked the letters and the telegram inside an unmarked manila folder and buried them once again, this time in the back of an old filing cabinet in the museum's archive.

There they remained undisturbed for almost a decade until one Monday afternoon in January 2012. I was going through the archive files looking for information about the history of the mansion, one section of which dates back to the Spanish era of California, when I noticed an additional folder in the back. Curious, I pulled it out and opened it up.

As I began reading the first letter, which is addressed to "Govie my dear," I became engrossed. Its author categorically denies she is having an affair with someone named Alec, and her language is so infused with emotion, it drew me in. The letter is signed "Ruth."

I continued on to the second letter, which is addressed simply to "Dearest" and is clearly intended for the eyes of someone other than her husband. It includes the line "I do love you." It is also signed "Ruth."

The third document is a copy of a typed letter addressed to "Alec" and says, in essence, "Stay away from my wife." It is signed "Gouverneur Morris."

The telegram, which originated from London, is short and to the point: "Have just received your letter it shall be as you wish. Alec Waugh."

When I saw the name Alec Waugh, my eyebrows shot up. Was he in any way related to the celebrated author Evelyn Waugh? Yes, he was, I quickly discovered. Alec and Evelyn were brothers.

As I reread all four documents slowly and carefully, it dawned on me what had happened: the letter addressed to "Dearest" and intended for Alec Waugh had accidentally been sent to Ruth's husband, Gouverneur Morris. What was unfolding before me was the end of a love affair, a denouement in four documents.

It was all an irresistible tease. I had to know more. How had the affair begun? How had it played out? But more than that, I had to know more about these three people, particularly the woman in the middle of the triangle. Thus began my intense search for information that would shed light on the lives of Ruth Morris, Gouverneur Morris, and Alec Waugh and on the actions and events that had brought them to this moment.

My first major discovery came quickly. I learned that the papers of Alec Waugh, a writer like his brother, are held at the Howard Gotlieb Archival Research Center at Boston University and include letters from Ruth Morris. It turns out Alec had saved virtually every letter Ruth had ever sent to him, and taken together they provide a road map of their relationship. They even reveal that Ruth and Alec had a romantic rendezvous in the tropical paradise of Tahiti.

Soon, though, I began uncovering information about Ruth that went way beyond her love affair, as intriguing as that certainly is. I learned that Ruth Wightman (her name before marriage) had been one of America's first female race car drivers, during the brief period in 1918 when women were allowed to drive race cars, and had set the women's speed record. Before she took up auto racing, she had trained as a pilot and had become adept at performing stunts.

I also learned that Ruth had worked in Hollywood, which was where she met her future husband. With help from Charlie Chaplin, she had landed a job at Goldwyn Pictures as a secretary for Gouverneur Morris, a famous and successful writer of the era, who had been lured to Hollywood to work on movie projects as part of a group called the Eminent Authors.

Though her job title was secretary, over time Ruth learned how to write scenarios, the term then used for adapting stories for the screen, and what had begun as a secretary-boss relationship evolved into a creative partnership. Along the way, Ruth and Govie (the name everyone called him) became a couple.

When Govie's studio contract ran out, he and Ruth decided to ditch Hollywood and begin a new life in Monterey, California, a move Govie was able to easily finance, thanks to a generous inheritance that had just come his way.

Once resettled in their newly built mansion on the Monterey Peninsula, they proceeded to live a life right out of an F. Scott Fitzgerald novel. There were gin-soaked parties with their many celebrity friends like Charlie Chaplin, Pola Negri, Rudolph Valentino, and Sinclair Lewis. There were trips to Southern California to hang out at William Randolph Hearst's beach house with "Mr. Hearst and Marion," as Ruth called them. There was also extensive foreign travel by ocean liner, the 1920s version of jet setting.

The year 1925 found them living at the Ritz in Madrid and developing a keen interest in bullfighting, which led Ruth to become the only woman on record during that era to step into the ring with a bull, an act strictly forbidden under Spanish law. After training with two of Spain's most talented bullfighters, one of whom would become the model for Pedro Romero in *The Sun Also Rises*, Ruth staged a private exhibition for invited guests, thus adding bullfighter to her curriculum vitae, along with aviatrix, auto racer, and scenario writer.

Soon after, Ruth traveled to Pamplona with the US ambassador and stayed just across the square from Ernest Hemingway's hotel. To Hemingway and his buddies, the ambassador and his traveling companions were unwelcome visitors, and the author would later include uncomplimentary observations about them in his novel *The Sun Also Rises*.

Of course, Ruth's love affair with Alec Waugh played an important role in her life, and its abrupt end following the misdirected letters proved painful and unsettling. Compounding matters, the end came at about the same time that the aftereffects of the 1929 stock market crash were beginning to destabilize the Morrises' finances.

Then there was the great scandal of Ruth's life, which turned her into media fodder and all but destroyed her. In 1936 the dead body of a young man was found in Ruth and Govie's backyard in Manhattan Beach near Los Angeles, and questions of possible foul play quickly emerged. The investigation that followed grew into a nightmare for Ruth, reaching its nadir when she literally collapsed under police questioning.

Ruth Wightman Morris would die a few years later, bringing to a close a life more vivid, more daring, and vastly more interesting than the lives of Daisy Buchanan or Lady Brett Ashley or any of the fictional women who came to personify the age. More important, her story has one other quality that none of them can match: it's all true.

PROLOGUE

As the RMS *Makura* knifed its way through a tranquil stretch of the South Pacific en route to San Francisco in late February 1927, Ruth Morris gently lowered her elfin frame into a bathtub, and as the water wrapped itself around her, she reflected on her situation and considered her next move. Should she continue her seduction of the British writer who had come on board during the brief stopover in Papeete, Tahiti, or should she do the more sensible thing? Put another way, should she follow a risky, impetuous, passion-filled path or focus on preserving her marriage?

The sensible choice was never going to prevail for Ruth. Besides, she had convinced herself that she could have it both ways. And there was this: she liked the guy.

Almost from the moment twenty-eight-year-old Alec Waugh, Evelyn Waugh's brother, was seated across from her during a bridge match, Ruth lost her concentration. Maybe it was his gentle charm. Or possibly his keen intelligence. Or because he was, unlike her husband, about her own age. Whatever the reason, it was a distraction.

The most immediate consequence was that Ruth's bridge game fell apart. She threw away the wrong card here. Misplayed a hand there. It was entirely uncharacteristic of her. This was a woman for whom a chat with a celebrity or a head of state was like gossiping with a neighbor. Almost nothing could faze her, but somehow Alec Waugh had managed to do just that.

Their next encounter occurred under the stars on a warm, quiet evening and quickly evolved into a leisurely stroll along the upper deck. As the vessel gently undulated to the rhythm of the waves, Ruth and Alec found their way to a spot along the rail that afforded some privacy.

Ruth then fixed Alec with her dark eyes and with her "beautiful voice" began sharing the story of her mad fling with a ship's officer on another voyage, across the Atlantic from Europe. The details about her encounter with "the Lad," as she called him, were vivid and intimate, and Alec was transfixed.

"How long ago was this?"

"Fifteen months."

"And have you seen him since?"

"He's on the high seas nearly all the time. I've never been in San Francisco when he has."

This was Ruth's opening gambit: revelation and candor about an intimate part of her personal life. It had the intended effect. By the time Ruth and Alec parted, they both knew they would be meeting again.

Late the following evening with "the moon smaller and rising later," they both found their way back to the same spot on the upper deck by the rail. Ruth's "voice had a new and deeper tone" as she and Alec began the delicate dance of getting to know one another, and an intense, urgent attraction seemed to draw them closer together.

It was all quite lovely and romantic, save one slight complication: Ruth was married. No amount of moonlight and gentle tropical breezes was going to change that unassailable fact, so after she returned to her stateroom, she decided to put on the brakes.

When Alec Waugh returned to the upper deck the next evening, Ruth would not be there, and when they encountered one another the following afternoon at a tennis match, Ruth would greet Alec politely if a bit formally, limiting their conversation to impersonal small talk.

Then came Ruth's heart-to-heart with herself in the bathtub, and that settled it.

Sitting in the ship's bar, resplendent in a pink scarf with nail polish to match, and nursing a glass of gin, Ruth was ready when Alec walked in. She gestured for him to sit next to her and then gave him an appraising look.

"What are your plans in America?"

"To go straight to New York."

"Oh, no, you are not. Are you booked on a ship to England?"

"The *Aquitania*, tomorrow week."

"That will give you two days in San Francisco."

They would spend those two days together, she insisted, and Alec could do little more than nod in dazed agreement.

Ruth and Alec would meet once more before the ship landed in San Francisco, and their meeting would begin awkwardly. She had sent him a message via the ship's steward that she wanted to see him before retiring for the evening.

As Alec approached the bar, Ruth's husband, Gouverneur, angrily burst out the door with Ruth in pursuit.

"Leave me alone. I know when I've had enough and when I haven't, without you telling me."

"Please, Govie, please."

"Leave me alone."

Her husband then headed off to their stateroom, and Ruth redirected her attention to Alec.

"I had to say good night to you. Tomorrow; it'll all start again tomorrow. We've had so little time. We've decided nothing. You are coming back to Tahiti in the summer, aren't you?"

He paused a beat, as he digested what she had just proposed: that he travel halfway around the world to rendezvous with her in French Polynesia.

"Yes, I'll be coming back."

CHAPTER ONE

THE LITTLEST REBEL

Ruth Wightman Morris was born fearless. Either that or she developed the trait at quite a young age, because what else can explain the first public impression she made when she was all of fourteen years old and well shy of her adult height of five feet?

The setting was San Diego, California. The date was Sunday, March 10, 1912. The situation was a boisterous free speech demonstration that had clogged the streets.

As firemen deployed a fifty-foot hose and prepared to administer "the water treatment" to the protestors, Ruth Wightman (the Morris would come later) carefully and deliberately stepped forward from the crowd and "walked to the spot where the heavy stream of water was hitting the street." *Go ahead,* she seemed to be saying. *I dare you. Go ahead and drench a little creature like myself.*

The firemen flinched, quickly redirecting the stream away from her, but it was of no avail. She chased right after it. Then to the delight of the protestors, she stepped into the splashing water, her white Sunday dress and matching shoes getting soaked in the bargain.

A subhead on the front page of the *San Diego Union* the following day sums up what happened next: "Little Girl Leads Mob in Defiance of Deluge. Other Sympathizers Follow Her into Stream." First one man stepped forward. Then two women. Ruth stepped back to give them room. What followed was a struggle between three humans and a mighty blast of water.

As if on cue, prisoners held in a nearby jail broke into "La Marseillaise." One of the protest leaders, Laura Payne Emerson, leaped onto a soapbox and exhorted the crowd to join the valiant three. The water was too powerful, however, and they retreated, battered and shivering.

Emboldened, the firemen redirected their hose at Emerson, prompting one hundred protesters to form a human shield around her. The escalation continued. More fire trucks. Bigger hoses. Eventually the shield broke, and Emerson was literally blown off the soapbox.

Another protestor defiantly wrapped himself in an American flag, and the authorities responded by washing him down the street like a leaf being hosed off a patio. Then they arrested him for desecrating the flag.

Hours later the crowd was finally dispersed, ending one round in what would prove to be a months-long battle over the most basic of human rights: free speech. Because for all practical purposes free speech had been outlawed that year in downtown San Diego, particularly in an area known as Soapbox Row.

The problem was this: the city fathers and their patrons in the business community did not like what they were hearing. Socialists were spouting off about the evils of capitalism. Suffragettes were making noise about equal rights for women. And Wobblies (International Workers of the World) were demanding jobs for folks on the bottom rung of the ladder, including immigrants and minorities. It was simply more than the boys downtown could bear.

On January 8, 1912, the city council passed Ordinance 4623, a document breathtaking in its scope. In part it reads, "It shall be unlawful for any person to address any assemblage, meeting or gathering of persons or hold or conduct any public meeting or make or deliver any public speech, lecture or discourse or sing any song or songs or take part in any public debate or discussion in or upon any public street or alley within that certain district in the City of San Diego."

What happened next was all too predictable: The street speakers refused to comply. The cops made arrests. New people spoke. More arrests. Still more people spoke. Both sides became trapped in a feedback loop they couldn't break out of. The jails were filling up, the city was paralyzed, and neither side was backing down.

It was at this point Ruth had traveled with her mother, evangelist Lulu Wightman, to San Diego to provide moral support for the protestors. That Sunday around noon, Lulu stepped up on a soapbox and gave a ringing defense of free speech while castigating the authorities, calling them "brass-buttoned anarchists" and "Cossacks." The teeming crowd of five thousand "laughed, jeered and applauded," and the "water cure" soon followed.

For Lulu, this baptism by fire hose was a bit more than she had bargained for, so she retreated with her daughter to Los Angeles and devoted herself to fund-raising on behalf of the demonstrators.

Meanwhile in San Diego, vigilantes became the order of the day. The *San Diego Tribune* urged them to employ "beatings, deportations, and other tactics of terror." One former city official suggested a "horsewhip vigilance committee." Ultimately axe handles would prove the tool of choice.

One prisoner died of a beating. An International Workers of the World (IWW) member was shot and killed. Things hit bottom when Ben Reitman, lover of anarchist icon Emma Goldman, was kidnapped and brutally beaten and had the letters *IWW* burned into his rear with a cigar, a cane shoved up his rectum, and hot tar poured over his head and body.

Lulu and Ruth visited San Diego one more time in May but did not stay long. The situation had spun completely out of control, and there was little either could do to help. They headed back to Los Angeles and did not return again. By the end of the summer, the battle on the streets of San Diego had slowly burned itself out.

Thus ended mother and daughter's first foray into political direct action. It would not be their last, but the experience had to have been sobering, given that it was such a departure from the life the Wightmans had lived up to that point, indeed the life Ruth had been born into on August 15, 1897, in Falconer, New York.

That life, that very different life, was something about which Ruth rarely spoke. That her parents had been itinerant evangelists for the

Seventh Day Adventist Church. That they traveled around Upstate New York, staging tent shows. That Ruth's mother, Sister Lulu to the faithful, was one of the first women licensed as a minister. That Ruth's father, John, handled all the publicity and promotion.

This then was Ruth's young life. Tent shows. Constant moves. New towns. From Wallace to Woodhull to Silver Creek to Geneva.

Upon arriving in each new town, the Wightmans would take up residence in a small canvas tent adjacent to the larger meeting tent, and John Wightman would paper the town with flyers and contact the local newspaper, announcing a series of meetings featuring lectures by Lulu Wightman.

As the curious and the faithful gathered on warm summer evenings, the meetings would follow a pattern. Hymns interspersed with scriptural readings would lead up to the sermon or lecture. Among the topics Lulu favored were "Is the Bible True?," "Is There a Devil?," "Second Coming of Christ," "The Millennium and When Does It Begin?," and "Who Are Angels?"

Always the goal of the tent meetings was to win converts who would in turn serve as the foundation for new outposts for the church, and the Wightmans proved quite successful at winning over new members.

For young Ruth, though, this extended itinerancy prevented her from developing the kinds of enduring friendships greater permanency would have allowed, so she spent most of her time with her mother, a powerful and inspiring influence. Brilliant, charismatic, confident, and charming, Lulu Wightman rose rapidly from the choir to the front of the church to become one of the most effective evangelists in the history of her faith.

Then she went a step further, traveling across the country to reach new audiences, including the Missouri House of Representatives, as she redefined her mission and broadened her message.

Over time there was much less talk about the "Devil" and "the Second Coming" and much more about "equal and exact justice for all; special privileges for none." Phrases like "separation of church and state" started creeping into her talks. She even began suggesting that the rights of Jews and atheists deserved to be protected, and as word of Sister Lulu's drift from orthodoxy began filtering back to church headquarters, there was much furrowing of brows and muttering of concern.

It all became too much when Lulu spoke out against using the Bible in public schools and began throwing around terms like "religious despotism" and "ecclesiastical oligarchy," and Lulu's own brother delivered the coup de grâce, publicly denouncing her. Soon thereafter, Lulu, John, and Ruth Wightman were unceremoniously given the boot.

While this created a terrible breach between Lulu and her father and her siblings, all of whom were deeply committed Adventists, it also proved liberating. She no longer had to pull her punches, and with husband John acting as her agent, she began traveling around the country speaking on a range of topics that had as their common thread personal liberty.

Then came San Diego in 1912 and the messy struggle for free speech, which provided the first hint of the woman Ruth Wightman would become. A second hint came two years later under the most curious of circumstances.

During an extended family visit to San Francisco, which included encounters with writer Jack London, with whom her parents were politically simpatico, Ruth made a delightful discovery: Chinatown. She was fascinated by its intriguing and provocative smells, sights, sounds, and tastes as she wandered its dense warren of streets and alleys between Kearny, Stockton, California, and Pacific Streets, home to almost nine thousand inhabitants at the time, and poked around in shops with names like the Sing Fat Company and Chee Chong & Company, and the Shanghai bazaars. Before long, sixteen-year-old Ruth had adopted a new style of dress that spoke to her independent spirit: comfortable, loose-fitting Chinese clothing.

This became Ruth's new look, and she wore it everywhere, seemingly bothering no one. That is, until she happened to set foot in Sacramento in early 1914. Evidently the mere sight of a young Caucasian woman dressed in distinctively Chinese clothing triggered racially tinged animus in one police officer, so he arrested her.

Thus Ruth Wightman had her day in court, an occasion for which she changed into a checked wool coat, a white blouse, and a jaunty beret. "Pleading personal liberty in matters of dress, she convinced the judge that she had the same right under the law that the Chinese have and won her liberty," reported the *Sacramento Star*.

A month later, mother and daughter were back on the streets of Sacramento, this time in support of yet another cause: the Army of the Unemployed. Its leader, "General" Charles Kelly, a printer by trade from Oakland, had organized his ragtag band of down-and-outers and intended to lead them to Washington, where they would demonstrate for jobs.

Kelly's 1914 march was something of a sequel, following an attempt some twenty years earlier as part of a larger movement started by Ohio native Jacob Coxley. Coxley's 1894 Army of the Unemployed was successful in reaching Washington, but that was about it. Coxley was promptly arrested, and the protest itself achieved none of its stated goals.

Meanwhile in California, Kelly had organized a West Coast version of the Army of the Unemployed that was supposed to meet up with Coxley's in Washington, but the army never made it. The journey across America proved fraught with difficulties, about which we know a great deal, thanks to one of its participants, a young Jack London. He was right there in the thick of it—jumping trains, singing songs, hustling food, and dodging authorities along with his fellow "hoboes"—before the whole movement fell apart well short of Washington. For his troubles, London got tossed in jail for thirty days on the charge of vagrancy. His written account of the Army of the Unemployed's epic misadventures is quite sympathetic to what ultimately proved to be a lost cause.

In terms of substance, Coxley's 1894 movement was a bust, but it remains important historically because it marked the first time citizens staged a popular protest march on the nation's capital.

It has one other notable legacy as well. Scholars believe L. Frank Baum's *The Wonderful Wizard of Oz*, published in 1900, was inspired by Coxley's Army and is essentially allegorical. By this reading, the Emerald City is Washington and the Wizard of Oz is the president. And the Wicked Witch of the West? Evidently there are a couple of possibilities, but a leading contender is industrialist Mark Hanna.

Now flash forward twenty years. A new Army of the Unemployed was on the march to Washington, and Charles Kelly had reassembled his own West Coast contingent. Joining him to provide moral support were Lulu Wightman, husband John, and daughter Ruth.

Unfortunately, if 1894 had been a failure for the "General," 1914 turned out to be a disaster. There would be no riding the rails this time. No singing around campfires. No sympathetic farmers bringing them food. The Sacramento authorities were determined to stop the Army of the Unemployed in its tracks. "The line of deputies extended three deep for about seven blocks and these unarmed, helpless, ill-fed men were forced by water from a fire hose and by the pick handles of the crowd to run this gauntlet while each deputy took a whack at them," Lulu recalled.

That didn't hold Ruth back, though. She took to the streets, "yelling encouragement to the unemployed," and for her trouble "was beaten across the back with a pick handle" when she attempted to seek refuge in a railroad car, leaving her to lament, "I never believed that men could be so bloodthirsty."

Charles Kelly was quickly thrown in jail, and the protest movement collapsed. For Lulu, the Army of the Unemployed march proved an embarrassing fiasco. Never again would she place her personal reputation on the line and the safety of herself and her daughter at such risk in support of radical direct action.

Public speaking, Lulu realized, was probably the better path for her, and she quickly adopted a new cause: the anti-Prohibition movement. It proved a natural fit, given her strong commitment to individual liberty, but it marked yet another break with her Seventh Day Adventist brethren, who were staunch members of the temperance camp. Even her erstwhile ally Jack London, a notorious drinker, had embraced the movement to outlaw alcohol.

Undaunted, Lulu began traveling with her husband and daughter to different cities along the West Coast where she would give street-corner orations, standing on an apple cart. She drew mostly friendly crowds but was sometimes heckled by "drys" who labeled her "the devil in skirts" and called her "un-American, incorrect and Emma Goldmanish." One group of ministers even brought along a church choir to drown her out. Through it all, Lulu never backed down, but once again she was on the losing side.

That Lulu was the animating force in the Wightman household is all too apparent, but it begs an important question: What was Ruth doing when she wasn't at her mother's side fighting the latest good fight? Did she attend school, and if so, where? Did she have age-mates, and what did they do together? How was her life shaped by her family's financial circumstances, and what exactly were those circumstances? All great questions, but none with ready answers. There are no diaries or letters from the period to let us into that part of their lives.

A newspaper profile of Ruth from a few years later does reveal that she studied "violin for nine years," briefly aspired to become an opera singer and took "voice lessons for two years," and, as she cheekily put it, studied "'litter-ture' and art for three years." How and where all this occurred is not revealed, but it does indicate that she grew up with a healthy exposure to books and music and art.

She was also exposed, it turns out, to risky and dangerous activities.

Take horseback riding, for instance. Where others might have settled for dressage or show jumping, Ruth pursued the more difficult challenge of riding bucking broncos and managed to win a prize at the California State Fair.

Or take flying. Nothing seemed quite as risky and daring and flat-out thrilling as taking an airplane up into the heavens, and from the moment Ruth first saw Lincoln Beachey, "the father of aerobatics," perform an exhibition one afternoon in 1914 at Oak Grove Park in Stockton, California, she was determined to learn how to fly.

On that particular occasion Ruth would have settled simply for a ride, which she unabashedly requested, as a newspaper account later described. Politely Beachey explained to her that his Curtiss biplane, which resembled a tricycle with wings and an engine, had only one seat, so Ruth would remain earthbound that day, watching with rapt attention as Beachey flew upside down, made a vertical dive from a mile up, cut figures in the sky, and looped the loop.

But earthbound Ruth did not wish to remain. Flying and performing stunts were what she was after, but it took a while, because the welcome mat for female flyers was conspicuously not out.

Finally in 1917, a flight school in Riverside, California—the Riverside Aircraft Company—agreed to open up its doors to this ambitious young woman. She rather quickly impressed her instructor, Clarence Oliver "Ollie" Prest, a stunt pilot, who singled her out as "one of his star pupils." By the end of July, Ruth had completed basic flight training, along with eight male classmates, and was able to "make a straight-away, turns and execute a figure 8."

But Ruth wanted more. Performing a figure eight was all well and good, but Ruth wanted to learn showstoppers like the loop the loop. She wanted to become an ace, so she continued training with Prest for several more months, most probably in exchange for help around the school, and she became proficient at stunts, including the scary stuff like the death dive.

Then she hit a glass ceiling that in those days was barely above the ground. Yes, she could take flying lessons. No, she could not turn those skills into a paying gig. Not in 1917. Not without a Y chromosome. Here she had trained to be a pilot and had taken to flying like a sea otter to a kelp bed, but no display of skill or judgment or daring could erase one indisputable fact: there was no professional career path forward for women as pilots. None.

Even Katherine Stinson, America's most famous female flyer of the era, had encountered barriers. Stinson could pack a state fair to watch her loop the loop, but when she offered to help the war effort during World War I, she was told "no women need apply." At another point, an aggrieved outcry from her male coworkers drove Stinson out of a job as an airmail pilot within days of her hiring.

For Ruth the frustration had to have been compounded by the fact that a stream of young men passed through the Riverside flying school as part of a government program to train future military pilots. By the summer of 1917, the nation was on a war footing and was consumed by what was going on overseas. Liberty Bond drives were in full swing. Citizens were encouraged to abstain from eating meat one day a week. And military recruiters were on the prowl for any trained pilots they could find—male, that is. Female pilots, not so much.

However, Ruth was so talented, she couldn't be completely ignored. One government official happened to swing by the Riverside facility in

October 1917 and was so impressed by her that "he recommended her to higher authorities." Not as a pilot, but as a "government inspectress of airplanes," becoming the first woman in the country so appointed. Notably she reported directly to General George Squier, the chief of the Aviation Section, US Signal Corps, the top guy.

So it was that Ruth went to work on behalf of the military at the Wright-Martin factory in Los Angeles, operated by a company grown out of a merger between an entity originally created by Wilbur and Orville Wright and one founded by aviation pioneer Glenn Martin. Ruth's job was to inspect the materials used in the interiors of the Wright-Martin Model V, a "two-seater tractor biplane of 150 horsepower, designed for long range military reconnaissance, with the observer's cockpit well forward of the entering edge of the lower wings."

Clearly this was not what Ruth had in mind when she took up flying, but she put the best face on it, saying that it was "entirely appropriate that the American woman should take her place in active war work." A noble thought, no doubt, but deep down inside she had to have been hoping for more than this.

Fortunately luck or fate or whatever you want to call it just happened to be on her side. It couldn't give her exactly what she wanted, which was flying an airplane, but it could give her many of the same risks, challenges, and thrills.

And it could do something else: it could change her life forever.

CHAPTER TWO

THE FASTEST WOMAN ALIVE

It was a simple decision with profound implications: the long-standing ban on female race car drivers was suspended, effective immediately. Until that precise moment, women weren't allowed to get near a race car in any official capacity. They couldn't own one. They couldn't be passengers in one. They couldn't work at a racetrack. Hold a stopwatch. Wave a flag. Nothing. Then with the blink of an eye, the ban was lifted, thanks to World War I.

Able-bodied men were being shipped off in droves to that bloody mess, and the American Automobile Association, arbiter of all things automotive, formally suspended sanctioned races in November 1917. By their action they effectively suspended the rules that kept women out of auto racing as well, and a group of women who had formed the Southern California Women's Automobile Association recognized the possibilities immediately. They quickly recruited aviatrix Katherine Stinson, who had performed flying stunts at racetracks, to help them organize an auto race for women.

She personally lobbied the track management at Ascot Speedway in Los Angeles with a simple argument: "Motor car driving isn't a question of brute strength, but rather of nerve and skill and daring."

Those were skills, she asserted, that women were fully capable of demonstrating.

The argument worked. The first-ever professional auto racing event for women was planned for Sunday, February 3, 1918, at Ascot Speedway, located a few miles south of downtown Los Angeles. Katherine Stinson herself put up the trophy for the championship race, "the largest silver cup she could find in the city," and declared, "Away with the big hulking brutes of men. Let us girls show you the way to thrill the public, to give Father Time a whipping every time we get on the track."

This was Ruth's moment. She was going to own this. Her dream was to fly, and that would always be her first love. But the skill set and personality profile that made her such a natural for flying were a perfect fit for auto racing as well. Katherine Stinson was the female star of the skies, without dispute. Now there was an opening for a female star in a new sport, and Ruth Wightman was ready to make her claim, asserting, "I intend to stick to this game and become the woman Barney Oldfield of the track." (That would be the living legend Barney Oldfield, America's first great race car driver.)

If she was going to pull this off, however, she needed a serious race car. And in its pursuit, another aspect of the Ruth Wightman skill set came into view. It is not for nothing that the *Los Angeles Times* would soon call her "a gal about town." Her ease and charm in social situations were almost preternatural, and she was uncommonly comfortable in her own skin. Making friends came easily, and she built and navigated social networks with the grace and efficiency of a spider. So, not surprisingly, when Ruth needed something, or as in the case of a powerful race car, really needed something, her success rate was generally quite high.

In this particular instance, Ruth employed every morsel of charm she could muster to persuade wealthy auto enthusiast Addison Brown to temporarily loan her one of the race cars in his collection. She drove away in the Mercer No. 4 that had carried racing legend Eddie Pullen to a world record speed of 87.8 miles per hour at Corona in 1914. With four cylinders, a 293-cubic-inch engine, a four-speed transmission, and a twenty-five-gallon gas tank mounted behind the driver's seat, the low-slung Mercer was all the car Ruth needed to be a serious contender.

Once she had her vehicle situation squared away, Ruth made her first appearance at Ascot to run some practice laps, and her arrival caused an immediate stir with reporters scrambling to grab a word. Before the day was out, the *Los Angeles Times* was proclaiming, "The aviatrix is a 'natural' driver, and nothing in the line of competition is apt to cause her loss of nerve."

Soon the *Times* followed with a short profile, headlined "Ruth Wightman Tells How to Become a Speederette." Here's a key quote from Ruth: "On Friday I saw the Ascot track for the first time in my life. I made the first lap in 58s, but I can do it in 52 when the big test comes on Sunday." A bold claim to be sure, considering the fastest time recorded by a male driver was in the midforties, and speeds in the low fifties were common on the men's racing circuit. This from a woman who was five feet tall, "a mere slip of a thing."

As race day approached, five other women emerged as finalists— Nina Vitagliano, Mrs. C. H. Wolfelt, Mrs. Cecil George, Mrs. P. H. Marmon, and Bertie Priest—but they were not Ruth's biggest problem. Her real challenge came from the organizers. They didn't like her car. It was too powerful. Too much of a guy car. Too much of what a real auto racer would drive. Which, from Ruth's perspective, was precisely the point.

In a bid to keep all participants on equal terms, the organizers introduced a rule excluding professional race cars. Conventional passenger cars were fine, as were race cars that had been stripped of all distinctive race car features. To Ruth that was like driving with training wheels, so she stood her ground. Unfortunately, so did the organizers. Either she accepted their terms or she was out of the championship race. No championship race meant no Katherine Stinson trophy. But Ruth refused to compromise.

She was still allowed to participate in the first event of the day, the cycle car race, in which women drove miniaturized versions of race cars, sometimes referred to as "baby racers." Ruth was also permitted to compete in the final event, the Free-for-All Handicap, on two conditions. First, she had to drive a qualifying lap. Second, she had to delay her start for fifty seconds, which amounted to a one-lap penalty in a five-lap race.

None of this had turned out the way Ruth had envisioned, but she arrived on race day prepared to do what she could with the reduced opportunities remaining for her.

The event itself was a grand spectacle. The one-mile oval track at Ascot had a large, covered grandstand along the straightaway that on this Sunday afternoon was filled with a sea of faces, ten thousand in all, many of them female. For the male sportswriters in attendance, the presence of so many women at an auto race was maybe the most eye-opening surprise of all. "It was as though," one observed, "all the cohorts of 'equal rights' had gathered to lend their moral support to their more zealous and daring sisters."

It's important to remember that women would still have to wait two more years before they would earn the right to vote, but on this day they could enjoy an event in which women played all the major roles. The drivers were all female, of course, but so were the race staffers, including the starter, Mrs. Barney Oldfield, wife of the famous race car driver. Even the security detail was female.

There had never been an auto racing event like this before, and everyone in attendance was dressed in his or her Sunday best. The men wore suits and ties and either a fedora or a flat cap. The women favored long dresses and large, festive hats. And everyone seemed to be in a happy, celebratory mood.

As the opening festivities drew to a close, Katherine Stinson glided down onto the straightaway in a plane she called her "air limousine," signaling that it was time for the racing to begin.

That meant it was time for Ruth to perform, and she made quick work of the baby racer event. Mrs. Barney Oldfield had barely dropped the flag to start the race before Ruth began pulling away. She spent the balance of the five-lap race extending her lead and flew past the checkered flag essentially unchallenged. Nina Vitagliano, driving a vehicle not fully repaired from a practice-run crash, struggled badly in her wake, finishing a distant second.

Ruth then moved to the sidelines, where she could only bite her lip and imagine what might have been as the competitors in the championship race flashed by her. Mrs. C. H. Wolfelt would own the ear-to-ear grin and the Katherine Stinson cup on this day.

Little about the last race of the day, the Free-for-All Handicap, provided much joy, either. Ruth's fifty-second handicap effectively doomed any chance she had of winning. In the end, she had to settle for a third-place finish, coming in behind Nina Vitagliano.

There was one bright moment for Ruth, however, that almost made up for everything else. It came when she performed her qualifying lap. For that little stretch of time, those ten thousand people in the stands were hers and hers alone, and she did not disappoint.

Quietly slipping behind the wheel of the legendary Mercer, Ruth powered up and then raced off in such a fury that she "grazed a guard-rail" as she leaned into the near turn. Moving down the backstretch, Ruth opened up the throttle. She tucked into the far turn, came whipping onto the straightaway, and flew past the grandstands, bringing the crowd to its collective feet.

Her time: fifty-one seconds flat. In less than one minute, Ruth Wightman had entered the history books. Three decades, the Great Depression, and the Second World War would pass before a female driver would surpass that mark.

Looking back over the day, Ruth had reason to feel disappointed. She had missed out on the championship race and on the winner's trophy, the big headlines, and the endorsement deal that would soon follow. Still, the day had not been a complete loss. She had won the opening race handily and had managed to set a women's speed record. Without exception, her disappointments had been a product of rules and restrictions she had no control over. When she had been given the opportunity, she'd performed well, but that had not diminished her desire to win the big races, capture the silver trophies, and get the flattering headlines. Given her stated ambitions, it is easy to imagine that what Ruth wished for more than anything was another chance, one without conditions or handicaps or strings attached.

It was a wish that soon would be granted.

CHAPTER THREE

A TIME FOR TEARS

Twenty thousand eyes had watched Ruth Wightman's every move that day at Ascot, and two of them belonged to Omar Toft, a retired driver turned promoter. The others may have seen a woman of rare talent and courage. What Omar Toft saw was dollar signs.

He wanted to build a whole new event around Ruth. She was marquee material. "Ruth Wightman," he observed, "can handle an automobile as well as any man I ever saw. The way she shoots down the stretches and takes the turns is a caution. I never have seen anything like it before so far as women drivers are concerned."

Rather quickly a vision came into focus. The Ascot event had been staged on a concrete track, so he would promote the first Women's Championship on Dirt. Once he had the concept, all he needed was a track, so off he headed to the Central Valley of California, home to a vast abundance of rich, fertile, agriculture-loving dirt. As it turns out, some of that dirt even found its way onto racetracks. Toft's travels took him to Fresno and Sacramento before he settled on the oval in Stockton, some sixty-three miles east of San Francisco and forty-nine miles south of Sacramento.

For Ruth, all the confidence and conviction and determination her mother had instilled in her were about to pay off. With a second competition in the offing, and with the potential of many more to follow, the idea that she could become "the woman Barney Oldfield of the track" was beginning to seem genuinely plausible. Sensing the possibilities, she seized the moment with relish, throwing down a challenge to her Ascot competitors to come up to Stockton and take her on.

With that bit of business out of the way, Ruth hopped the next train to Stockton, and upon arrival headed straight to the track to look it over. Her presence in town did not go unnoticed: "Miss Ruth Wightman, the aviatrix who has gone in for the auto-racing game and who aspires to the title of woman champion at five miles on a dirt track, arrived here this morning by train from Los Angeles."

Meanwhile, Ruth's fighting words had reached their intended targets. A few expressed some interest, including Bertie Priest and Mrs. Cecil George, but the distance from LA slowed them down. Not Nina Vitagliano, however. Ascot had been a huge disappointment for Nina. Her car had been a dud, and she was embarrassed by how poorly she had performed.

Now, like Ruth, she had a chance for a do-over, and she headed north to Stockton. Soon after her arrival, Nina, "a very pleasant and attractive little woman with dark hair and flashing dark eyes," laid down a challenge of her own. Just her and Ruth. A match race. Head to head. Five miles. And Katie, bar the door. Not surprisingly, Ruth was more than happy to oblige.

There was more good news for the women: all the participants would drive professional race cars, a decision no doubt urged upon Toft by Ruth, his marquee star. It may even have been a condition for her participation, which might explain why Ruth's old patron, Addison Brown, became the source for professional race cars for all the participants with the special stipulation that Ruth and Nina were to receive the two best cars in the bunch: Eddie Pullen's Mercer No. 4 for Ruth and Earl Cooper's Stutz No. 8 for Nina. Four other women, Mrs. E. F. Pepper, Eleanor Bambauer, Nellie Battaglia, and Mrs. F. M. Bowman, rounded out the field.

In yet another bid to differentiate the Stockton event from Ascot, Toft scheduled three distinctive races that would be high on thrills. The big race was the showdown between Ruth and Nina, which would come immediately after time trials, but more excitement would follow.

An Australian pursuit race would start drivers at four different points on the track, and as each car was passed, it was eliminated, until only one driver remained. Finally, there would be a ten-mile free-for-all.

Toft also placed great emphasis on safety. Each participant was to have a professional mechanician riding along with her to perform routine tasks like pumping air into the gas tank to keep the gas pressure up and to serve as a separate set of eyes for the driver, who in those days had no rearview mirror. At Ascot, Ruth had blown off using a mechanician, but this time she quickly agreed and with good reason. Mechanicians were used in male auto races, so their presence in the women's event placed it on a more professional footing. Ruth was assigned Bill Pruett, who had ridden at Eddie Pullen's side when he captured the championship. Nina also got an experienced pro to work with her: Bob Currie.

Finally, there was the safety talk. Six drivers and their mechanicians assembled in the dining room of the Hotel Stockton for this final, all-important briefing. Clearly and carefully, Toft went over each of the rules, but there was one rule in particular that was presented with verbal underlining and exclamation points: under no circumstance should any driver attempt to pass on a turn. It was simply too dangerous. The way the turns were banked made it nigh impossible to control a vehicle at high speed. Bottom line: don't pass on turns.

After much preparation and all the buildup, the first women's championship on dirt was set to begin. Fortunately, Sunday, March 3, 1918, turned out to be a fine day for racing. The weather was clear, and the mercury was pushing into the high fifties. Enthusiastic racing fans started arriving at the track in early afternoon, dressed like their Southern California brethren in their Sunday best. Most notably, many filing into the grandstand were there with one express purpose: to cheer on Nina Vitagliano, Ruth's main rival.

As Ruth and Nina discovered early on, Nina had a built-in fan base in Stockton because of her country of origin. She was Italian, from Genoa, and Stockton had a large, vibrant community of Italian immigrants, many of whom had relocated from the agricultural regions of Northern Italy. The president of the Italian Club, Dr. J. V. Craviotto, was even from Nina's hometown of Genoa and knew people her family knew. And it was the local branch of A. P. Giannini's Bank of Italy, forerunner to the Bank of America, that provided the silver trophy for the winner of the Ruth-Nina showdown.

Ruth certainly had admirers in the crowd as well, but she had nothing to match Nina's crowd-pleasing display of an Italian flag billowing behind her Stutz No. 8 before the race, which pumped up her supporters even more but also placed an extra burden of expectations on her.

The crowd was huge, emotions were running high, and all eyes were on the track as each driver in turn performed her qualifying round. For Nina, it could not have gone better. The Stutz was humming, and Nina was feeling in control as she flew around the track in 58 seconds flat, a fast time on a dirt track. Ruth seemed on her game as well, but she came in just a beat or two slower at 59⅗ seconds.

The women appeared so closely matched, it looked as if the race would go down to the wire. The crowd was stoked.

First, though, the coin toss. Ruth and Nina climbed carefully out of their vehicles and walked over to where Omar Toft awaited them in front of the grandstands. As they came to a stop, all eyes refocused on the shiny object in Toft's hand. The coin spiraled up and then down, the crowd following its path. Many no doubt exhaled in disappointment. Ruth had won the toss and was awarded the pole position. Ever so slightly she now had the advantage.

The two women crossed back over to their awaiting vehicles, fired up their engines, and eased into the warm-up lap. For Nina, things got off to a ragged start, because one of the cylinders was misfiring. She limped down the backstretch until the cylinders got into rhythm. By the time she came back around to the straightaway, the Stutz was purring, and it drew abreast of the Mercer as they reached the starting line.

With a wave of the flag, Omar Toft sent Ruth Wightman and Nina Vitagliano "off in a cloud of dust and belching smoke." The drivers were neck and neck with Ruth on the inside as they raced down to the first turn.

Then Nina "electrified the crowd by going into the turn at a furious pace." It was as though the entire safety talk had been completely forgotten, as "the car swerved and all but went off the track." Nina somehow managed to keep the Stutz under control as she came out of the turn. Entering the straightaway, she had pulled a full car length ahead, bringing the cheering crowd to its feet.

The cheers quickly evaporated as Ruth, who possessed "nerve and skill, admired by all the veteran racing drivers of the male persuasion who were present," quickly drew even and then began pulling away in a "wonderful burst of speed."

Ruth was now winning. Worse for Nina, Ruth seemed destined to keep winning. She was winning the straightaways, and winning the straightaways was winning the race.

This is the moment when the burden of carrying the hopes and dreams of her countrymen might have begun to color Nina's judgment. Rather than resign herself to coming in a close second place, Nina upped the ante with more dangerous driving.

It was as though she had this mantra running through her head that she could not lose the race. That she could not let the Italian colony of Stockton down. That she could not let Italy down.

Don't pass on turns, she had been warned. Don't pass on turns. But the warnings at this point seem to have been completely ignored. Coming off the straightaway and into the far turn, Nina powered past Ruth again. But it did not hold. Ruth roared down the straightaway, and by the time she reached the grandstand, she was a good 150 feet ahead.

A pattern was now set. Nina would attempt to pass on the turns. Ruth would pull away on the straightaways, and Ruth's lead would continue to grow.

Throughout the race, Ruth never altered her style. She was composed and steady, and she never took the bait to try to keep up with Nina in the turns.

Nina's situation, meanwhile, continued to deteriorate. She couldn't compete on the straightaways, and to compound her difficulties, Ruth held the inside track. To pass, Nina had to go to the outside on the dangerously banked turns, and there was a point at which the laws of physics would not tolerate ever faster speeds on the turns. Yet nothing could restrain Nina. All sense of proportion seemed to be slipping away.

Going into the upper turn, Nina jammed the pedal to the floor with all her might, and "suddenly the great white Stutz shot forward like a cannon ball," exceeding any speed she had ever attained on the straightaway—roughly eighty miles an hour, or a full fifteen miles an hour faster than Ruth was traveling at the time.

As the Stutz flew past the Mercer, Nina completely lost control. Her car "was seen to give a mighty leap. It struck one of the pine trees at the upper turn. There it left the front axle and both wheels. Then it bounded over the embankment caused by the banked track, hurdled a ditch, crashed through the fence injuring three spectators and finally turned over, a mass of crumpled steel."

Ruth and her mechanician heard the sound of the crash, and Ruth yelled to Pruett, "What was that?" He couldn't see anything through the cloud of dust the Mercer was kicking up, so he replied, "Nothing. We're all right, go ahead." Soon they spotted Toft waving the yellow flag and rolled to a stop.

An ambulance raced down toward the crash site, but by the time it arrived, members of the crowd had already rushed the injured people off to the hospital in private cars. The news from the hospital when it came was grim: Nina Vitagliano had been pronounced dead on arrival. Her "head was driven down into her chest by the terrific impact, her neck being broken in several places and many of the bones of her chest being fractured. She was completely scalped from the eyebrows back. Death was instantaneous."

Nina's mechanician, Bob Currie, was hospitalized in critical condition with a fractured skull. He never regained consciousness and died the following day. A four-and-a-half-year-old girl, Jacquelin Mazzera, who was among the spectators caught in the path of the careening automobile, later died of her injuries. Two other spectators, Mrs. Gilbette Raffo and Tony Musto, suffered serious cuts and lacerations but were treated and released.

When Ruth finally made it to the pits and climbed out of her car, she was in tears. "Why, oh why did she attempt to pass me on the turn? Mr. Toft warned us repeatedly against attempting to pass each other on the turns. He told us that it was dangerous."

Ruth did not realize it at that moment, but more bad news would soon follow. Once word of Nina's death reached Los Angeles, the reimposition of the ban on women drivers came quickly and irrevocably.

All that was left for Ruth was to grieve. And even that painful process was rudely interrupted. Ruth had to appear as a witness at the coroner's inquest. Thankfully, it did not last long. It was a joyless task for all involved, and everyone wanted it over as quickly as possible. The focus of the questioning was on tires. The tires on Nina's car were retreads. The tires on all the cars were retreads. There was a war going on. Retreads were the only tires race car drivers could get their hands on. So what did Ruth think of the tires? "Well, I would have driven on them," she quietly replied. Then she noted that she had retreads on her car as well. In later testimony, Omar Toft would point out that even racing superstar Barney Oldfield used retreads. With the issue of retreads thoroughly hashed over, there was little else anyone wanted to talk about. In the end, the jury assigned no blame for the crash, and the inquest was quickly adjourned.

Throughout the night and into the day, mourners lined up at the Godeau funeral parlor for an opportunity to view Nina's casket and offer a prayer. For members of the Italian community in Stockton, Nina's death was an incomprehensible tragedy, and many were consumed by tears.

Even those who thought they could weep no more were dabbing at their eyes as Nina's casket slowly moved through the streets of Stockton on its way to the Southern Pacific Depot. The Stockton Verdi Italian Brass Band led the way, playing mournful dirges.

The train for Los Angeles would depart at 6:40 p.m. For Nina, this would be her last train ride. Once her body reached Los Angeles, there would be a funeral, conducted in both Italian and English. Following the service, she would be buried at the Angelus Rosedale Cemetery in Los Angeles.

For Ruth, it would be the longest train ride of her life.

CHAPTER FOUR

REWRITING THE SCRIPT

The demise of women's auto racing had been a cruel blow to Ruth Wightman. In a few heartbreaking seconds, her dream of becoming the female star of auto racing, a national figure, celebrated and admired, was left in a broken, mangled heap. And then to compound the misery, her father, John Wightman, succumbed to tuberculosis only months later. For someone just shy of twenty-one, this was sobering stuff. Life was tenuous, she was reminded, and all the talent and drive and skill in the world were no match for the prevailing mores about what women could and could not do.

It would take Ruth time to regroup and recover as she groped for a way to move forward on society's terms, and in the end it would be her social skills that would prove her most valuable asset. Her brief time in the public eye in Hollywood's backyard had provided "the gal about town" with some important new friends. Friends with connections. Friends whose phone calls were always returned. Friends like Charles Spencer Chaplin.

In Ruth's telling, it was Charlie Chaplin who helped her break into the motion picture industry. As the story goes, Charlie had a writer friend at Goldwyn Pictures who was in a funk over a failed marriage and was drinking too much, and Charlie felt that his friend desperately needed someone to get his office and, by extension, his life in order. That someone, Mr. Chaplin thought, was Miss Wightman.

So it was that Ruth Wightman became a combination personal secretary and aide-de-camp to Gouverneur Morris, a popular and successful writer on contract to Goldwyn Pictures, whose backstory Ruth, no doubt, found quite intriguing.

It begins with his curious first name, which was handed down to him from his great-grandfather, one of the Founding Fathers of the republic. The original Gouverneur Morris was right in the mix with Franklin and Jefferson and Washington and Adams, and his words are among the most famous and hallowed in all of American history. "We the People of the United States, in Order to form a more perfect union . . ." Govie's great-grandfather had written the preamble to the United States Constitution. The elder Morris also served as George Washington's minister plenipotentiary (one notch below ambassador) to France and was witness to the French Revolution. Later he became a member of the United States Senate.

In his home state of New York, Morris served as the founding chair of the Erie Canal Commission, overseeing a waterway that transformed New York into the economic powerhouse it remains to this day. Morris also helped to transform the island of Manhattan as chair of the three-man committee that planned the city's street grid. We have Fifth Avenue and Fifty-Ninth Street today thanks to Morris and his colleagues.

To say the least, those were big brass-buckled shoes for his great-grandson to fill, but the younger Morris's family circumstances afforded him the finest education money could buy. Schooling in France and Switzerland. Prep school in New England. Degree from Yale.

While still at Yale, Govie showed his first promise as a writer, catching the attention of journalist Richard Harding Davis, a friend to Teddy Roosevelt and an honorary Rough Rider. Davis, who is best remembered today for the clean-shaven good looks that persuaded men all over America to give up nineteenth-century-style facial hair, personally took one of Govie's manuscripts to Richard Watson Gilder, editor of the *Century* magazine, and declared, "You mustn't miss this."

The timing for Govie was perfect. At the turn of the century, magazines were a hugely popular source of entertainment. Movies were still in their infancy. Radio and television had not yet appeared on the horizon, so it was into magazines people escaped in search of adventure, suspense, action, and romance. Soon Govie was cranking out short stories on a regular basis, eventually expanding his portfolio to include novels. His style was popular not literary, but he was for a time "the highest-paid writer per word in America."

With his professional career firmly under way, he married socialite Elsie Waterbury in 1905, and soon thereafter the young couple happily greeted the arrival of two daughters, Bay and Patsey. All seemed well with their world.

Then the dogs of war were let loose in Europe, and Govie headed overseas as a correspondent for the Hearst newspapers. When his tour as a reporter was over, Govie extended his stay to drive ambulances for the Red Cross.

All this was good for his career, but lengthy stays overseas work best when you are unmarried. Hemingway, then a bachelor, could get away with it. Govie could not.

When he returned home he discovered that Elsie had abandoned the family home in Westchester, relocated to the upper-crust Upper East Side in Manhattan, and opened a chic salon for the fashionable. Reconciliation was off the table as far as she was concerned, so the marriage quickly flatlined.

Then came an attractive offer: a job in Hollywood. Film mogul Samuel Goldwyn and writer Rex Beach had dreamed up a new approach to motion picture marketing: build your image around well-known writers. Hence, Eminent Authors Inc., a division of Goldwyn Pictures, was born. Rex Beach was president and Samuel Goldwyn was chairman of the board.

Beach initially approached six writers: Gertrude Atherton, Rupert Hughes, Mary Roberts Rinehart, Basil King, Leroy Scott, and Gouverneur Morris. They would become the core upon which Eminent Authors was built. Gertrude Atherton was the great-grandniece of Benjamin Franklin. Rupert Hughes was the uncle of Howard Hughes. Mary Roberts Rinehart was the first writer of a murder mystery to have the butler do it. Basil King was a preacher, and Leroy Scott was a social activist. Later, other writers would be invited to join the fold.

The deal worked this way: Each was offered a contract, typically for three years. The writers agreed to grant the studio all film rights for everything they had previously written and anything created during the life of the contract. In turn the studio promised to pay a $10,000 advance and a percentage of the earnings for any story selected for production. Built into the deal was a flow of continuing income even if nothing was selected for production.

For a writer this was tempting. The money was good, and it was steady. Equally tempting was the promise of creative control. Here's what the initial company announcement said: "The author will have the final power of direction and supervision over his picture."

For Govie this was an opportunity difficult to pass up. He had already sold some stories to Hollywood, so he understood the math. Even the highest-paid writer on a per-word basis stood to make more money writing for film.

Once again, his timing couldn't have been better. Magazines had been the right choice at the turn of the century, but two decades later, motion pictures had become the fifth-largest industry in the country. By 1920 there were eighteen thousand movie theaters in the United States, with new ones popping up all the time, and the average daily attendance was eleven million. That translated into a total box office take at the end of the year of roughly a billion dollars.

Ruth Wightman, of course, was arriving at just the right time as well. Her pay grade, at least in the beginning, would be considerably lower, but she now had her foot inside the door of Samuel Goldwyn's fantasy factory in Culver City.

As she walked through the massive Greek columns that marked the entrance to Goldwyn Pictures, she was entering a world that was "virtually a city in itself, with its parks, libraries, theatres, and long striking highways." There were no movie-musical-ready soundstages in those days—the movies were called silent for a reason—but spread out over the forty-acre site were six production stages with the full array of lighting and camera equipment, two theaters, and multiple outdoor sets, including that old reliable, a western town. It would soon expand to include an adjacent parcel Sam Goldwyn had leased that had a brook running through it. In a few years, the entire site would become the home of fabled Metro-Goldwyn-Mayer.

Ruth's timing was right for another reason as well. As counterintuitive as it may seem, Hollywood in its early days offered opportunities for women that were almost unheard of in other industries. There were female writers, for instance. And even female directors.

It was almost as though Hollywood hadn't gotten the memo that only men had the skill set to do the important jobs, but there was a historical legacy at work here. The motion picture industry grew out of the world of theater, which had a distinctive culture all its own. When show people put on a production, everyone pitched in. Men wrote. Women wrote. Men made costumes. Women directed. As the world of the dramatic stage evolved into the world of lights, camera, action, the theatrical culture carried over, at least into the first half of the 1920s.

Sadly, as the culture of Hollywood evolved from one shaped by theatrical values into one shaped by business values, opportunities for women to write and direct would quickly dry up. Ruth, fortunately, took on her new role before that unhappy ending finally played out.

Before she could think about writing, however, Ruth first had to master her more immediate responsibilities. There was organizing. There was typing. There was deciphering Govie's handwriting, which fell somewhere between a doctor's prescription and the Enigma code. And there was the more subtle task of lifting Govie's spirits and boosting his morale, for which Ruth was particularly well suited.

Govie's office, which became Ruth's new home away from home, was located within a building on the lot set aside for the studio's staff writers in what was known as the scenario department, and for big-name hires like Govie. Grouping all the word people together facilitated easy interaction and consultation. It also meant that when Gertrude Atherton threw on a pot of tea at five in the afternoon, as she typically did, her fellow writers didn't have to go far to gather for after-hours banter.

As it turns out, there was much to talk about. Their new life as Hollywood writers was not going quite as they had expected, mostly because their responsibilities seemed to have little to do with the making of movies or even supervising their own work as it went into production.

Not that they hadn't been treated royally when they arrived in town. Flowers at the train station for the women. Luxury hotels until they got settled. And a respectful nod from the gatekeeper when they arrived at the studio. Everyone at Goldwyn was friendly and deferential, as long as the Eminent Authors didn't get in the way of the actual moviemaking process.

Part of the problem was territorial. Goldwyn Pictures already had a writing staff in place, and the resident staffers resented the newcomers. You might call them the noneminent authors, but they did most of the actual writing for the screen. Or maybe the better word would be *translating*, because they were taking written language and turning it into visual language appropriate to the silent screen, or "picturizing" it.

Think of the scenario department as a machine. You inserted a novel or story at one end. The essence was strained down, producing a basic story outline. Those elements that "didn't work" on-screen were tweaked or completely changed. What remained was turned into a visual presentation with shot selection, camera angles, and basic stage directions. The term of art for this was *continuity*. The last step was the creation of title cards, which were plugged in to provide key clues as to what was going on. Time of day, maybe. Location of setting. Identification of characters. Dialogue. Once the title cards were planned, the final shooting script or scenario would pop out.

The staff writers at Goldwyn Pictures, led by department head Jack Hawks, were journeymen at best, but they understood the film medium well and knew instinctively how to shape a narrative visually, something they doubted the Eminent Authors had a clue about. It was their firm belief that there was a "vast gulf between the picture audience and the reading public," and they didn't think the folks with the big reputations fully understood the difference between writing for the page and writing for the movie stage. What's more, these staffers saw little benefit for themselves if the Eminent Authors acquired those skills. Simple fears about job security motivated the scenario department staffers to cling to their turf.

Thus, Govie and his compatriots were welcome to work on stories in their offices, but whatever they produced was handed off to the scenario department, where it was adapted for the screen. The rest of the time the Eminent Authors served as props for publicity. In the case of Mary Roberts Rinehart, she was made up like a movie starlet "with a thick mask of grease paint, and over that a dusting of yellow powder." She was led onto the set, where she made small talk with the cast and crew. Someone handed her a copy of the scenario. *Pop, pop, pop* went the flashbulbs. Then she was politely led off the set so that the real work could begin. When the publicity folks got finished, a photo went out with the following caption: "Mary Roberts Rinehart, discussing her new picture with the director and the cast."

Rinehart's original story had long since been reworked by a scenario writer, and any similarity between the film and the original story upon which it was based proved purely coincidental. Gertrude Atherton's experience was similar: "I wrote one story—I never attempted to write a 'scenario'—which was made into a picture, beautiful to look at; all that could be said for it."

From her vantage point in Govie's office, Ruth was soaking up everything that was going on and was the sympathetic ear when Govie found himself presented as a brand by the studio without having much to do with the production of his first film, *The Penalty*. Sam Goldwyn had actually told a reporter with a straight face, "Gouverneur Morris, for example, spent nine months on the coast working with us on 'The Penalty.'" What Goldwyn failed to mention was that "working with us" did not include preparing the scenario, interacting with the director, or in any way supervising the way his story was brought to the screen.

A scenario writer, Charles Kenyon, who cut rather a dashing figure around the Goldwyn lot, took over responsibility for adapting Govie's story for film. Cocksure and handsome, Kenyon wore "his clothes better than most leading men" and "found in Mr. Morris' novel a series of powerfully conceived situations and actions merely waiting to be translated into 'script' language." When Kenyon needed help or advice about the script, he did not consult Govie. Instead, he turned to Philip Lonergan, a veteran scenario writer in the department.

In the version he wrote for the screen, Kenyon did preserve essential elements of the original story but made changes as well. Most notably he moved the setting from New York's Lower East Side to San Francisco, and he shifted the focus from the novel's protagonist, a sculptor named Barbara Ferris, to the antagonist, a gangster named Blizzard, who was brought to life on the screen by Lon Chaney.

Briefly, when Blizzard is a young boy, a doctor mistakenly amputates both of his legs. When he grows up, he becomes a diabolical gangster, not unlike a villain in a Batman movie. He thirsts for revenge and masterminds a scheme to take over the city, capture all of its wealth, and fix his disability. Not surprisingly, the doctor who performed the original surgery gets drawn into Blizzard's web, and the doctor's daughter, Barbara Ferris, serves as the bait. The film's climactic scene retains the hokey and unexpected twist that appeared in the novel: simple brain surgery removes a growth that had turned Blizzard evil, transforming him into a model citizen.

Critics raved, one exclaiming, "Hats off to Lon Chaney! As 'Blizzard,' the deformed ruler of the Barbary Coast underground, he gives one of the screen's greatest performances." The ending of the film, critics loved not so much. "A clap-trap movie finish," one called it. On the strength of Lon Chaney's performance alone, however, the film did well at the box office.

For Govie, *The Penalty* was a mixed blessing. He got his name up in lights, above the title, all over America, but he knew in his own mind that he had been little more than a passive observer as the story was brought to the screen.

Fortunately, when he was not posing for publicity photos, he was able to spend his time on the Goldwyn lot working on an original story for the screen called "The Water Lily." A scenario writer would still do the film adaption, but at least he was writing with the screen in mind.

As Govie began working on stories intended for the screen, Ruth was busy learning the second, all-important stage in the preparation of a story for film: writing the scenario. She had been in the unique position to observe how the system worked at the studio and where the power centers were. It probably didn't take her long to figure out that the scenario department was a key power center. Whoever wrote the scenario controlled what got put on film, subject to the final decisions by the director. If one of the Eminent Authors wanted to increase his or her power, the way to do it would be to learn this new skill, but none of them, with the important exception of Rupert Hughes, was willing to try. Hughes was fascinated by the whole process of moviemaking and was eager to learn whatever he could. Ultimately he would become a successful director.

Ruth, of course, was a pilot and race car driver turned secretary. The title of scenario writer would be a move up for her, so she set about learning how it was done. Never mind that she wasn't a professional writer. Never mind that most of the Eminent Authors wouldn't even try to write a scenario. She was already on the studio lot. She had ample opportunities to pick things up. She could lean over shoulders. Sit in on discussions. Read scripts. Watch filming. Ask questions. Seek advice. Most important, studios, including Goldwyn, were open to female writers in the early 1920s. Executives would not begin work on the glass ceiling until later in the decade.

In the meantime, Ruth's principal responsibility was to help Govie deliver a complete and readable manuscript of his latest story, about a subject dear to his heart: Chinese culture. His plot, though, was fairly conventional: two men competing for the same woman with exotic locales thrown in. Love triangles seem to have been a plot device Govie returned to again and again. The irony of that particular fixation would only become apparent much later.

After "The Water Lily" manuscript was turned over to Charles Kenyon, it underwent a name change. The new, presumably more marketable title was *A Tale of Two Worlds*.

In *A Tale of Two Worlds*, a Caucasian girl becomes an orphan in China, following the murder of her parents. She is raised by a Chinese family, and it is not until the family emigrates to America that she discovers she is not ethnically Chinese. An evil man named Ling Jo, played by Wallace Beery, who happens to be the murderer of her parents, wants her hand in marriage, but a young, handsome man named Robert Newcombe tries to prevent the marriage. Throw in the recovery of "the sacred scepter of the Mings," and a steel room with walls that close in and crush a victim, and you have your movie. The steel room, something a James Bond villain might hide in his lair, is the highlight. Like the clever Mr. Bond, Newcombe outsmarts the evil Ling Jo, and it is Ling Jo who ends up in the steel room. As Bond might say, "He had a pressing engagement."

Goldwyn publicist Howard Dietz did his best to sell the picture, claiming it a "triumph for the artists as well as for the director and the author," but the reviews and the box office were mixed. "Yes, the picture is a fine one," said one reviewer. But more typical were these: "There is a forced air about the picture" and "Conscientious but uninspired."

There was no disguising it. Govie was struggling with this new medium, but then most experienced writers would. When you have spent your whole life using words to tell stories, it can be difficult to give up words as your essential storytelling tool.

It's probably no accident that the most effective filmmakers during the silent era were primarily performers first, not writers. Charlie Chaplin and Buster Keaton immediately come to mind. They both understood instinctively how to relate to an audience and how to use actions rather than words to tell stories.

A disagreement Govie once had with Charlie Chaplin speaks volumes about the challenges he faced as a writer for the silent screen. The two men enjoyed each other's company and would get together quite frequently at their respective homes. One night the subject of a film Chaplin was about to release entitled *The Kid* came up. It was for Chaplin an important milestone in his career, his first feature-length film, and he had invested a great deal creatively and emotionally in the project.

Chaplin, who had dropped by the Morris home, carefully described to Govie what he was attempting to achieve by "keying slapstick with sentiment." Govie, whom Chaplin considered "a charming, sympathetic fellow," responded, "It won't work. The form must be pure, either slapstick or drama; you cannot mix them, otherwise, one element of the story will fail."

Chaplin countered, "The transition from slapstick to sentiment was a matter of feeling and discretion in arranging sequences." Adding, "Form happened after one had created it." And continuing, "If the artist thought of a world and sincerely believed in it, no matter what the admixture was, it would be convincing."

Chaplin never backed down that evening from his intuitive belief about what would work on the screen, but his insecurities began to kick in. He started harboring doubts about his judgment, which came to a head the next time he ran into Sam Goldwyn.

"Sam, I wish when you have nothing else to do you'd come over to my studio and look at my new picture. I'd like to get your opinion of it—advice, too, if you have any to offer."

"What do you think of it?"

"Rotten! I'm awfully discouraged over it."

Chaplin at this point needed reassurance, so Goldwyn rounded up Govie, and the two of them headed over to Chaplin's studio for a private screening. While Charlie worried himself silly, Govie and Sam sat back for one hour and eight minutes of motion picture magic. In every way, the film lived up to the line on the opening title card: "A picture with a smile—and perhaps, a tear."

As Goldwyn would recall, "Just as the whole world was afterward to do, Morris and I laughed and cried and gasped as the wonderful story unrolled." For Govie, the film had been a revelation. Almost everything he had said to Chaplin that evening at his home proved to be wrong.

Still needing to be convinced, however, was the filmmaker himself. When the lights came up, Goldwyn said to Chaplin, "Charlie, if you never had done or never should do another picture, your name would go down into history as the creator of *The Kid*."

"You really think it's good then? You're not just saying this to make me feel encouraged?"

Ultimately the public would offer the definitive verdict: *The Kid*, which costarred child actor Jackie Coogan, became the second-highest-grossing film of 1921 and has since been preserved by the National Film Registry as an American classic.

Whether Govie would be able to apply any of the lessons he learned from viewing Chaplin's masterpiece remained to be seen, but he was about to gain an important new collaborator. Ruth had mastered the basics of scenario writing, particularly continuity, and had just earned a new job title. The aviatrix, auto racer, and sometime secretary had become a scenario writer.

CHAPTER FIVE

A NAME IN THE CREDITS

Something was changing in the relationship between secretary and boss. Well, two things, actually. The first and most outwardly visible change was that Ruth and Govie were becoming creative partners. He wrote stories. She wrote scenarios. In effect they could now deliver finished scripts for production without handing anything off to the scenario department. This meant more power. More control.

The second way Ruth and Govie's relationship had changed was much less visible but no less important. They had become a couple. Govie, it seems, had not been immune to the Wightman charm, but then few men ever were. A master at making a man feel good about himself, Ruth could stroke an ego with the deftness of a masseuse, and there was an openness about her, or seeming openness, that men found utterly disarming.

At the same time, Govie was possessed of a wry twinkle and an engaging manner, and Ruth clearly enjoyed his company. A man of above-average height, sturdily but proportionally built, showing the first hints of a widow's peak and invariably sporting large circular-framed glasses, Govie was erudite, worldly, a gifted raconteur, and, of course, an accomplished writer, all qualities Ruth admired, particularly the writer part. A sometime poet and voracious reader, she had a soft spot for writers.

That said, unbridled passion this was not. Whatever wild streak Ruth may have possessed—and there is ample evidence she possessed one—was held in check in her relationship with Govie. Still, Ruth had genuine affection for him, and at this stage in her life that was all that seemed to matter to her.

This change in relationship status did come with complications, however. First, there was the age thing. When Govie graduated from Yale, Ruth was one year old. When Govie married Elsie, Ruth was eight years old. When Govie's older daughter, Bay, was born, Ruth was nine. Then there was his marital status: Govie was not single. In the public's mind there was a Mrs. Gouverneur Morris out there, and it was not Ruth.

For the time being, though, none of this was of much concern, because the public had not a clue what was going on between Ruth and Govie in that office at Goldwyn Pictures anyway. Besides, the Morris-Wightman team had a movie to make.

Govie had written yet another story for the screen, and he hoped this one would reflect the lessons he was attempting to learn about telling a story visually. Then it became Ruth's turn. First, she had to organize the story into a series of scenes. Once she had the scenes worked out, she had to decide on camera angles. Finally, she had to create title cards. While the story was not visually complicated, there were basic aspects of the tale that needed explanation, and some dialogue on cards was essential.

When Ruth was finished, she had crafted the shooting script for *The Ace of Hearts*, which starred Lon Chaney, Leatrice Joy, and John Bowers. As one review put it, "This is a melodrama, pure and simple, and it maintains a high tension throughout by means of tricks that are as unexpected as they are effective."

Here's the gist: A secret band of radicals meets to decide the fate of a local businessman they believe must die. Solemnly they play a game of cards to select the assassin. All is going according to plan until a love triangle emerges between two of the men, Farallone (Lon Chaney) and Forrest (John Bowers), and the lone woman, Lilith (Leatrice Joy), a zealous true believer. Lilith is attracted to Forrest but is less interested in Farallone.

The game reaches a critical moment when Forrest draws the ace of hearts, meaning he has earned the honor of killing the businessman. Unexpectedly, Forrest's selection upsets Lilith. Her passion for the cause seems to dissolve as it is consumed by her passion for Forrest, and her only concern becomes his welfare.

The following day she pleads with Forrest not to carry out the assassination, but he really has no choice. Someone is destined to die, and if it's not the businessman, it will be Forrest. Cue that old scene stealer himself, Lon Chaney. His character, Farallone, steps up to save the day, planting a bomb that kills all the radicals, sacrificing his own life in the process so that the young couple can live happily ever after.

As originally shot, the film ended with the lovers having an extended discussion, all delivered to the viewers via title cards, about the virtue of love over violence as a way to change the world. Noble sentiments, no doubt, but Samuel Goldwyn hated the ending. As he would famously say on another occasion, "If you want to send a message, use Western Union." He promptly ordered a reshoot, and the ending was toned down.

For her debut, Ruth performed as well as could be expected. Her shot selection and ordering of scenes make perfect sense, and the story is coherently told. It's hard to imagine the film looking dramatically different had one of the boys in the scenario department handled the job.

The success of the film ultimately rose or fell on the strength of Govie's underlying story, and the reviews were at best mixed. "The face-card among authors of shivery printed tales, Gouverneur Morris, falls behind, apparently upon writing directly for the screen. At least his 'Ace of Hearts,' showing at the California, is below par." Versus: "There is no denying its suspensive lure and strong dramatic appeal, due to good acting by a talented company."

Unfortunately, this was not the ideal time for mixed reviews and the weak box office that followed, because tremors were rumbling through the studio, and they threatened to undermine its very foundation. No less a figure than Samuel Goldwyn found the ground under him shifting, the unfortunate consequence of bringing in new investors to strengthen the company's capital position.

These were bottom-line guys, not show business romantics, and they were not happy with the return on investment they were getting from Sam Goldwyn's "classy writers." They stripped Goldwyn of his authority to approve film projects, and in true bean-counter fashion handed that authority over to the sales department, leaving him as little more than a figurehead.

Once their power was solidified, the new studio bosses moved to break up the Morris-Wightman creative team. The scenario Ruth had been working on for Govie's next project, *Yellow Men and Gold*, based on one of his early novels, was summarily tossed out, and an officially sanctioned scenario was knocked out by one of the staff writers. Upon release the film would garner tepid reviews and prove weak at the box office.

Meanwhile, Ruth quickly recovered from her demotion, taking her newly honed scenario-writing skills to First National Pictures, where she was hired to turn a story by George Marion called "Peachie" into a movie script. In Ruth's hands it became *The Beautiful Liar*, starring former model Katherine MacDonald, a tireless self-promoter whose publicist had dubbed her the "American Beauty." Handling the directing was Wallace Worsley, who had also worked on *The Penalty* and *The Ace of Hearts*.

The story employs one of those gimmicks that reappear over and over in motion pictures: an average Joe or Josephine happens to be the spitting image of someone famous. Circumstances dictate that the commoner temporarily step into the role of the famous person, and then the unexpected or surprising happens.

In *The Beautiful Liar*, MacDonald plays a secretary who happens to look just like a popular celebrity. Circumstances dictate that she step into the role of the celebrity at a social function. Mr. Right appears while she is pretending to be someone she is not, forcing her to keep up the ruse, lest he discover who she really is. Unsurprisingly he figures out who she is and loves her anyway.

The film is remembered, if it is remembered at all, primarily for its glamorous costumes and fancy sets, for which "no expense or pains were spared in the staging of the big scenes."

The other noteworthy thing about the film is that it's a story about a secretary adapted for the screen by a secretary. That Ruth earned yet another screen credit is no small accomplishment. She had not been a professional writer. She had not been hired as an Eminent Author. Yet, with no prior experience, she became sufficiently proficient at writing scenarios that she was able to deliver two producible scripts. Her credits for the two scenarios are listed to this day in the official directory of the American Film Institute.

Then Ruth did something even more unexpected: she went to work on a novel. Set in Hollywood and featuring a scenario writer as its central character, Ruth seems to have followed the classic dictum that you should write about what you know. Unfortunately, after she had labored sufficiently to put over forty thousand words on paper, she seems to have run out of ideas or out of steam. The debut novel by Ruth Wightman was never completed.

By the fall of 1921, Ruth's and Govie's frustrations with the studio were growing, with Govie complaining that he felt like a cannery worker. Compounding matters, Sam Goldwyn's tenure at the studio that bore his name was only months from ending, and the new powers in charge had expressed little interest in keeping the Eminent Authors around. Gertrude Atherton had long since headed out of town. Mary Roberts Rinehart was thoroughly disenchanted. The others, aside from Rupert Hughes, seemed to simply drift away. And Govie, with his contract coming to an end the following June, had his eye on the exits as well.

This may in part explain why, in the fall of 1921, he was willing to stick his neck out on behalf of Roscoe "Fatty" Arbuckle, who was swept up by Hollywood's first big scandal. Arbuckle, a chubby, round-faced comedian who had parlayed the screen persona of a guileless, clumsy bumpkin into superstardom suddenly found himself playing a very different role: the chum in a media feeding frenzy.

Govie had spoken out before, specifically in opposition to Prohibition and blue laws—both matters of great concern to Ruth's mother, Lulu Wightman, but neither was a terribly daring stand. Prohibition was an easy target, and blue laws were particularly reviled in Hollywood because they kept movie theaters closed on Sundays.

With the Arbuckle case, though, Govie's was a lonelier voice. Hollywood was already under attack for undermining the moral fiber of the country, and almost no one in the industry felt any incentive to defend a guy who it seemed was only dragging Hollywood's image down further. To be sure, the allegations being aired in the Arbuckle case were ugly: that he contributed to the death of a young woman, Virginia Rappe, after a night of drinking in a San Francisco hotel, with rape speculated as the underlying cause.

Worse for Arbuckle, the news media had little interest in a thoughtful examination of the evidence in the case. "Roscoe Arbuckle Sought in Hotel Orgy Death," screamed one headline. "Raper Dances While Victim Dies," shouted another. "Plan to Send Arbuckle to Death on Gallows," shrieked still another. The stories themselves were a veritable character-assassination stew: healthy portions of salacious innuendo delicately seasoned with vile speculation. It might have been a recipe intended to sell newspapers, but it was Roscoe Arbuckle's reputation that was being pureed.

Then there was the prosecutor, District Attorney Matthew Brady. Political ambition oozed from every pore of his body, and he viewed Arbuckle's conviction as his ticket to higher office, whether Roscoe had actually committed a crime or not.

So this was the maelstrom Govie was stepping into when he entered the courtroom in San Francisco as an observer, and he soon came to realize that the prosecution's case was tissue-paper thin. Most telling, DA Brady elected not to put his star witness and Roscoe's chief accuser on the stand, probably because he feared her story would fall apart under cross-examination. In the end all but one juror found Arbuckle not guilty, but that one juror was all that Brady needed to demand a new trial. It was also all Govie needed to take his disgust public.

He dashed off an angry open letter defending Arbuckle and found a home for it at *Screenland* magazine. "It looks to me," he declared, "as if the Prosecution aspired to raise itself from whatever order is theirs, to positions of prominence in California, and believes that a hanged Arbuckle (guilty or not) would be of immense political advantage to them." He added, "I do not know Arbuckle, but, because of the laughs

he has given my kiddies and me, I am his friend until there are better reasons (than now exist) for believing that no man should be his
friend."

It took two more trials before Roscoe was a free man, but when
the not-guilty verdict was finally announced, it was accompanied by
a remarkable statement from the jury. It reads in part, "We feel that a
great injustice has been done to him. We feel also that it was our plain
duty to give him this exoneration under the evidence for there was not
the slightest proof adduced to connect him in any way with the commission of a crime."

Still, even what amounted to a personal apology from the jury was
not enough to convince some movie moguls in Hollywood to resume
distributing his pictures. They concluded he was damaged goods and
frankly wanted to have nothing further to do with Roscoe Arbuckle,
setting off Govie's courageous support for him in sharp relief.

Govie's next move was equally bold: he proposed to Ruth. The occasion was a December party at the home of French actor Max Linder,
celebrating both the release of Linder's latest film *The Three Must-Get-
Theres*, a satire of swashbuckling Douglas Fairbanks films, and Linder's
birthday, which he maintained was his thirty-sixth, rounding down
from his actual age of thirty-eight. There was also a hint of the holidays
with tinsel cascading down the living room walls.

Hailed as a comedic innovator, Linder is widely regarded as an early
influence on Charlie Chaplin, something Chaplin readily acknowledged, so it was only natural that Chaplin would be one of the invited
guests at Linder's intimate gathering.

Equally appropriate was the appearance of John Gilbert, "the Great
Lover," who happened to be Linder's neighbor from around the corner.
He arrived with Leatrice Joy, star of *The Ace of Hearts*, whom he had
only recently married and then promptly unmarried when it became
apparent his divorce from his previous wife was not final. In early 1922,
Gilbert and Joy would remarry, officially this time, though it wouldn't
last long. Leatrice would soon discover that "the Great Lover" did not
necessarily confine his romantic activities to one bed.

Remarkably, on this particular evening there was another young
starlet at the party, Barbara Bedford, who had a history with John

Gilbert. In what sounds like the plot of a B movie, Gilbert had spotted her as an extra on the film set of *The White Circle* and convinced director Maurice Tourneur to give her a role in his next film. Gilbert even came up with the screen name of Barbara Bedford for the young woman formally known as Violet May Rose, and with her new name freshly minted, Bedford appeared with Gilbert in the film *Deep Waters*, launching her career.

Bedford, as it turns out, was not the only ingénue at the party who had, in classic Hollywood fashion, been plucked out of obscurity. Young Juanita Horton, who became Bessie Love at director D. W. Griffith's suggestion, dropped out of Hollywood High after Griffith gave her a small part in the film *Intolerance*, and a series of film roles would soon follow. Less than a decade after the Linder party, Love would be nominated for an Academy Award for Best Actress in *The Broadway Melody*. Then there was Patsy Ruth Miller, who happened to be attending a party in Hollywood when Russian actress Alla Nazimova spotted her, leading to a small role in *Camille*, starring Rudolph Valentino. Two years after Max Linder's party, Patsy Ruth would be cast in the role for which she is best remembered, Esmeralda in *The Hunchback of Notre Dame*, opposite Lon Chaney in the title role, for which he is best remembered. Patsy Ruth Miller would also remain friends with Ruth and Govie.

Rounding out the guest list were two French actors, Gaston Glass and George Gormier, who were great friends of Max Linder.

The mood for the evening was lighthearted, with everyone at one point sporting a silly hat, and a lively jazz band got everyone up on the floor dancing. The highlight, though, had to have been when all the women in attendance were presented with special gift boxes. Each woman opened her box in turn, and four of the boxes contained conventional party favors. The fifth box, addressed to Ruth Wightman, contained something more: a diamond engagement ring set in platinum.

Ruth could only smile, show it to assembled guests, admire its sparkles, and then tuck it away for safekeeping. Govie was still married, something it would take years to undo.

By late January, any question as to whether Govie and Ruth were short timers in Hollywood or not was answered when a column appeared in the *Los Angeles Times*. It was penned by Ruth, who was identified by the editors as "a young woman who has succeeded as a photoplaywright." "In Defense of the Author" is an undisguised assault on studio scenario departments and the power they exerted over the moviemaking process.

The filmgoing public, Ruth wrote, was "wondering why motion pictures resemble nothing quite so much as sausages all freshly ground from the same machine," and she laid the blame at the feet of the scenario writers. "A continuity is the mechanical form in which a story is placed before the camera. The mechanical form should always be subservient to the story and should lose neither the integrity nor individuality of the story."

Ruth continued, "It surely seems that the scenarioists should be the first to welcome capable stories. But they do not." Instead, she suggested, "they spend as much time writing articles damning the author as they spend in writing continuities."

She complimented Sam Goldwyn for leading "very admirably with his 'Eminent Authors,'" but then she went back on the attack: "Kipling, Barrie and Joseph Conrad all look alike on the screen. But that certainly is not the fault of those inimitable stylists—and should only be held against the manglers who are responsible."

Those were fighting words, the kind you express only when you are already heading out the door. As it happened, the escape plan had already been mapped out. The key date was May 9, 1922, and what unfolded clearly and unequivocally foretold what the future held for the writer and the secretary: divorce papers were filed and real estate was acquired.

On that day in a Los Angeles court, Gouverneur Morris filed for divorce from Elsie Waterbury Morris on grounds of abandonment. On the same day in the county recorder's office in Monterey County in Northern California, a grant deed was recorded for a prime piece of land, containing a historic stone building, located in the seacoast community of Monterey. The name on the deed was Ruth J. Wightman, effectively keeping the property out of the pending divorce settlement.

With her original dreams and ambitions firmly buried forever, Ruth wasn't merely turning the page. She was breaking the seal on a whole new book.

CHAPTER SIX

LIVING IN SIN

Ruth Wightman arrived in Monterey a single woman and Govie a married man, which made for decidedly unconventional living arrangements. This was the early 1920s after all. A moral crusade had already driven alcohol underground, and Hollywood and its perceived licentiousness were now in its sights. Under the circumstances, an unmarried woman and a married man choosing to "cohabitate" had the potential to raise eyebrows.

Fortunately the community the couple had chosen as their new home made it easier. With its vibrant art colony in Monterey and bohemian enclave in Carmel, the Monterey Peninsula was a relatively more tolerant and accepting place than most.

Besides, Ruth and Govie were careful to be discreet, and their new home was ideal for fending off prying eyes. Sitting on a bluff overlooking Monterey Bay, the large parcel of land had no homes nearby, and their new mansion, which materialized rather quickly, was at the end of a long driveway.

A local contractor, J. C. Anthony, who specialized in Spanish revival designs, was responsible for the new mansion. Starting with the existing stone structure, which was either the first- or second-oldest residence in California, and building out from there, Anthony managed to create a delightful living space for the couple, complete with inner courtyards and a walled garden.

That Ruth and Govie would be attracted to the Monterey Peninsula, which sits on the coast some 120 miles south of San Francisco, is hardly surprising. It was and continues to be an uncommonly interesting and appealing place, owing in no small measure to a felicitous mix of California history and a beautiful, natural setting.

It was at Monterey, of all places, that the Spanish began their colonization of California in 1770, and it served as the political, economic, and military capital for more than three-quarters of a century. California's mission system got its start there. The Custom House, which controlled trade along the entire coast, was located there. And when the United States took over in the 1840s, California's first state constitution was written there.

Then Monterey was blessed with a miracle: the Gold Rush. As the wild and the greedy flooded California in pursuit of riches, San Francisco became the principal port of entry, which overnight transformed it into California's largest, most influential city, a title it held right into the twentieth century until Los Angeles and its never-ending sprawl seized the crown.

All the while Monterey remained mostly forgotten and relatively untouched, as though the whole region had been placed in a time capsule. In 1875 French painter Jules Tavernier stumbled onto the area and became so captivated by its natural beauty (ghostly cypress trees clinging to craggy rocks amid exploding waves) and all the visible remnants of its Spanish past that he stayed on, planting the first seeds of an art colony that has continued in one form or other to the present day.

In 1880 the railroad barons of California built the Hotel Del Monte, a luxury resort, or "flaunting caravanserai" as Robert Louis Stevenson described it, which placed the peninsula on the map as a destination for well-heeled travelers.

Still, it remained a small community, though no longer completely forgotten, and when Ruth and Govie arrived in 1922, the Monterey Peninsula continued to be, as mythology scholar Joseph Campbell would later describe it, "the Earthly Paradise."

How Ruth and Govie selected Monterey as their new base of operations has everything to do with their prior experiences there.

In Ruth's case, she had traveled to the area on a number of occasions because a cousin, Gertrude Otto, with whom her mother was particularly close, lived in nearby Santa Cruz, and the multiple exposures to the Monterey Bay region left a decidedly positive impression.

For Govie, a visit in 1903 that grew out of his interest in the writer Robert Louis Stevenson was what fostered his affection for the area. Though it may not be generally known, the Scottish writer spent several months in Monterey in the fall of 1879. Govie, for one, did know, and he may even have been familiar with the details. That Stevenson had traveled across an ocean and a continent to seek the hand of the woman he loved, Fanny Osbourne. That he had waited for months in Monterey while Fanny sorted things out with her husband, finally leaving him. That Fanny and Stevenson went off together to San Francisco and got married. That they remained together for the rest of Stevenson's short life.

Govie had also no doubt read one of the stories circulating at the time about a man named Jules Simoneau, who had become Stevenson's friend during his stay in Monterey and with whom the writer continued to correspond up until his death in 1894. That was all Govie needed to know to get him on the train to Monterey.

Once in town, he found his way to Simoneau's cozy little house on Van Buren Street, where the bewhiskered old man greeted him warmly. Delighted by Govie's interest, Simoneau pulled out the many letters Stevenson had sent to him, which he kept stashed in a big porcelain bowl, and allowed Govie to read them. Also among Simoneau's treasures were the copies of Stevenson's books that the author had sent to him, each containing a personal inscription. It was Stevenson's way of thanking Simoneau for the many small kindnesses he had extended to the then-unknown writer, not least of which were the free meals Simoneau had provided at his café downtown. For Govie, the visit with Robert Louis Stevenson's great friend would become a rich memory.

Additional memories were created as well during his visit to Monterey, as he later recalled: "I had been loaned in those old happy dusty days a grey pony named Fiddlesticks who could find his way blindfolded into the heart of the maze at Del Monte and with whom I became intimately acquainted with every square foot of the beautiful land on the peninsula."

It all left an indelible impression: "There is no small geographical unit in all this immense world so variedly, deliciously and peacefully beautiful as the Monterey peninsula. Nor has any other region an air so sweet, so fresh, and so compelling."

Fortunately for Ruth and Govie, many of their famous friends from Hollywood shared their love for the Monterey Peninsula, so once they had relocated permanently, their active social life was in no danger of flagging.

Flash-forward to January 1923. Ruth and Govie were finally settled in. Not "legally married" settled in. But clothes-in-the-closets, pictures-on-the-walls settled in. And they were about to assume the roles of gracious host and hostess, and they didn't even know it.

A certain little fellow, known to the world for his trademark mustache, baggy pants, and bowler hat, was headed their way, but it was a secret trip. As least that had been the plan. Charlie, it seems, was in love, and he was acting like it was serious this time. There had even been a ring and a proposal.

And the object of all this attention? Polish actress Pola Negri, a screen siren with piercing dark eyes. After shooting had wrapped on her latest picture, *Bella Donna*, Charlie came up with a madcap idea: they would sneak out of town by car for a romantic getaway to Pebble Beach, or Del Monte as it was then known. It was a notion Pola quickly embraced, and off they went.

Charlie did the driving. It was just the two of them, cruising through the foothills north of Los Angeles, before dropping down into the flatlands of Ventura County with the Pacific Ocean coming into view. All around was largely unspoiled scenery, and as they approached Santa Barbara they skirted the coastline, waves rumbling up onto the beach, the Channel Islands huddled like ghosts off in the distance, and the vast expanse of the Pacific Ocean spread out to the horizon.

Occasionally, Charlie would play tour guide and enthusiastically point out an interesting sight, but for the most part it was just a peaceful, relaxing drive as the car hummed its way north.

Then the spell was broken. Tension began to repopulate Pola's body as she sensed that she and Charlie were being followed.

"Why? Who are they?"

"Take it easy. It's only a bunch of reporters. Darling, we're public property. It's their job. The only time we really have to worry is when those vultures stop trailing us. That means we're no longer news. We're on the way down."

As they continued on up through San Luis Obispo, Paso Robles, and into the Salinas Valley, the mood had been killed. There was no shaking the newspaper guys now. They were tagging along right behind.

When Charlie and Pola pulled up to the Del Monte Lodge at Pebble Beach and prepared to get out, their car was surrounded by reporters, and the questions started flying like incoming shells.

"What's going on?"

"Give us the lowdown."

"Are you eloping?"

"What's the scoop?"

"Take it easy, boys. Can't you see the lady's tired? Give us a little peace, and I promise we won't do anything without first telling you."

"That's not good enough, Charlie. What's the real story? Are you getting married?"

"As a matter of fact, I'm hoping Miss Negri will marry me very soon."

The reporters quickly raced off to file their stories, and Charlie and Pola headed into the hotel. As they entered the room, Pola had a cold realization: if reporters knew they were staying at the same hotel together, it could be a recipe for scandal. Reluctantly Charlie agreed, "I guess you're right. My friend Gouverneur Morris lives nearby. I'll call him and see if he can put me up."

That evening Charlie Chaplin became the first important guest to stay at their new home. The next morning he drove back the six miles to the Del Monte Lodge to join Pola for breakfast. The place was now swarming with even more reporters, and Pola was trapped in her room. As Charlie entered, she cried, "This cannot go on. We might as well return to Hollywood."

"I'm sorry, dear. I'll tell you what—let's promise we'll give them an interview and some publicity shots on the condition that they leave Del Monte."

That day Charlie and Pola faced the media. Yes, they acknowledged, they were engaged. No, a date had not been set. Speaking of his fiancée, Charlie said, "She is a wonderful girl. The world knows her beauty, but she has that combination that is so rare: beauty, brains, and talent."

Then it was time for the publicity shots. *Pop. Pop. Pop.* Pola swinging a golf club. *Pop. Pop. Pop.* Pola and Charlie leaning over putters. *Pop. Pop. Pop.* Pola and Charlie sitting on a couch. *Pop. Pop. Pop.* Pola and Charlie shaking hands.

There was one other shot the photographers also captured: Pola and Charlie with Govie and Ruth. Amid all the pandemonium, Govie and Ruth had quietly slipped into Pebble Beach to join their friends.

They became the tour guides for the next couple of days, showing off their new hometown to Charlie and Pola, from vantage points as varied as the back of a horse and the deck of a boat.

The horseback experience took place right there in Pebble Beach. Heading out from the stables, located not far from the Lodge, they wound their way through a forest of pine trees and up onto sand dunes, revealing a panoramic view of the rugged, rocky coastline. Celebrated painter Francis McComas, a friend of the Morrises, memorably described it as "the greatest meeting of land and sea in the world."

Another of their excursions took them offshore, providing them with a different perspective of the meeting of land and sea. Sailing from the wharf in Monterey, a boat carried Charlie and Govie and Pola and Ruth out through the mouth of the bay into the open ocean, where they were able to indulge in some deep-sea fishing.

About this time, Charlie began getting the itch to return to Hollywood. He had a film project that needed his attention, *A Woman of Paris*, but there was time for a round of golf. Charlie and Ruth teamed up to play against Govie and Pola. As Govie tells it, the Chaplin-Wightman team prevailed through a combination of "higher mathematics and graceless cheating."

During the visit there had been rumors the Morris mansion might be the site of a Chaplin-Negri wedding. There was even talk that Govie would be the best man. In the end, no wedding took place on the Monterey Peninsula. Not long after the couple returned to Southern California, it became apparent there would be no wedding at all. Charlie wasn't ready to settle down, and Pola wasn't willing to put Charlie ahead of her career.

The glow from the Chaplin-Negri visit had barely dimmed when Ruth and Govie received more good news. It came by telegram. Govie had inherited $250,000 from a relative on his mother's side. A few weeks later another telegram arrived. His aunt Mary, his mother's sister, had died, leaving him another $250,000.

They were now officially rich. Not Vanderbilt or Rockefeller rich, but a half-million dollars was serious money in the 1920s, the equivalent of about five million dollars today. Within a year, Govie would inherit even more with the passing of his mother, so it seemed they would never have to worry about money again.

With their financial future secure, Ruth and Govie focused on entertaining. They had the perfect home for parties, and the Monterey Peninsula was a popular stopping-off place for the rich and famous. There were also many interesting people already living in the area, like the aforementioned Francis McComas, the painter, and his wife, Gene (short for Eugenia), also a painter, who were rather quickly swept into Ruth and Govie's social orbit. Over time it would include writers and boxers and poets and polo players and artists and actors, creating something of a salon.

A well-lubricated salon, gin the lubricant of choice. This was the 1920s, of course, the Prohibition decade, which meant Ruth and Govie had to work around its rules.

Importantly, the Eighteenth Amendment to the Constitution outlawing the sale of alcohol and the Volstead Act, which served as the implementing legislation, did not make it illegal to possess or consume alcohol. The legal sanctions were directed at production, distribution, and sale.

That meant that citizens like Ruth and Govie were free to imbibe, but they were forced to obtain their alcoholic beverages by clandestine means. They weren't breaking the law, but they had to deal with people who were.

As has been well documented, the era of Prohibition fostered a massive underground bootlegging industry, which drove up the cost of liquor and compromised its quality.

For Govie, who quickly got a line on a reliable supplier, the cost issues were more than manageable, so the Morris household always had gin on hand, along with a commensurate amount of ginger ale, which helped to take the edge off quality-compromised gin.

As the Morris parties grew and the gin flowed, the word spread through certain elite grapevines around the country that the Morris home in Monterey was "wet."

What also became well known is that Ruth and Govie were great hosts. They had live-in help, so the service was always impeccable, and they knew how to set the right mood, sometimes with a live band. Most important, they had a style and a manner that seemed to draw people to them. Govie was always ready with a clever quip or an astute observation, and he was as masterful at telling stories as he was at writing them. All this he managed without ever becoming boorish or seeming too full of himself.

Ruth in her own way was even more magnetic. She had a certain sparkle in social situations, never focusing on herself but rather on the people around her. Offering the well-chosen compliment, asking the thoughtful question, and showing the kind of intense interest that meant she was really listening. She could also hold her own in any serious discussion, regardless of the subject matter, and she had a great sense of fun. Her mere presence seemed to elevate the energy and good feeling in the room.

Between parties, Ruth tried to recapture some of her old zest for physical activity with two newfound interests: golf and tennis. Neither offered the risk and danger she relished, but at least they got her outdoors and, in the case of tennis, gave her a good workout. As was typical with Ruth, she threw herself into both activities with a vengeance, hitting the links and the courts several times a week, her old competitive nature in no way diminished.

The other noteworthy change in Ruth was her appearance. With money now awash, Ruth began traveling up to San Francisco, where she had once walked the streets in Chinese clothes, to shop for the latest fashions. Out went her simple, unpretentious outfits—secretary clothes—to be replaced by more expensive fabrics and a looser, trendier look. Her hairstyle changed, too. Like Bernice in the Fitzgerald story, Ruth bobbed her auburn hair.

On a more serious note, Ruth made a forceful decision about the terms of her future life with Govie, and it involved Govie's teenaged daughters, Bay and Patsey, whom Govie adored. It was his fervent desire to fight for custody, but Ruth was adamantly opposed. In later years she was silent on the reason for her opposition, but it's reasonable to suspect that Ruth feared stepmotherhood would significantly cramp her style.

Whether Ruth ever harbored fantasies of having a child of her own is impossible to know. She certainly never expressed any regrets about not having children, though her gushy enthusiasm while doting on the children of friends indicates she did have a soft spot for kids. It's even possible she was not able to have children, though it's not something she ever mentioned.

It's also worth noting that while Ruth had not relished playing the role of stepmom, she would eventually develop close relationships with her stepdaughters, particularly Bay, as they entered adulthood.

On the marriage front, there was some progress. In the summer of 1923, a judge granted an interlocutory decree in Govie's divorce case, putting the final judgment off for a year. What that legalese meant in theory is that there was still time for Govie and Elsie to work out their differences, though what it meant in reality was a year's delay.

When confronted by a reporter as to the implications of the legal ruling on her relationship with Govie, Ruth responded, "There must be some mistake, as Mr. Morris has just been granted a divorce in Los Angeles. It will be a year before the decree is final and Mr. Morris will be free to remarry. And many things can happen in a year."

"Are you going to marry Mr. Morris at the end of that year?"

"If Mr. Morris should happen to ask me to marry him, I might be in a better position to answer. Any statement now would be premature."

The newspaper account went on to note the following: "Miss Wightman was in the handsomely appointed study of the noted writer in his hilltop residence near the San Carlos Mission, when she made the above remarks. She has frequently accompanied the writer to social functions at Del Monte and Carmel, and participated in the entertainment extended by Morris to Charlie Chaplin, Pola Negri and other motion picture stars." The reporter was too polite to mention that Miss Wightman lived at the hilltop residence full-time. That she owned it as well probably would never have occurred to him.

With their relationship now a subject of public speculation, Ruth and Govie decided to go public with their intentions. On one of their frequent trips to San Francisco, they organized a luncheon at the St. Francis hotel, their home away from home in the city, and invited some of their closest friends to join them. As the din of merry chatter rang through the St. Francis dining room, Govie rose from his chair, excused the momentary interruption, and asked for everyone's attention.

"I should like to announce my engagement to the most charming, the most lovable girl in the world. Every day I am more astonished over her wisdom. She has everything I admire in a woman. But, of course, I can't announce our engagement until I have her permission."

"Well, let's admit that we are engaged."

And with those words, it was official, some fifteen months after Govie had given Ruth an engagement ring at Max Linder's party. No doubt the news, though hardly unexpected or even really a surprise, prompted guests to celebrate in a manner contrary to the spirit of the Volstead Act.

While officially they had to wait another year to marry, they secretly slipped down to Ensenada, Mexico, for a marriage ceremony that might have served to symbolically confirm their bond to each other but would later be viewed as not legal by California authorities.

Before 1923 had run its course, Ruth would prove she had not lost her competitive spirit. In a Thanksgiving golf tournament at the nearby Hotel Del Monte Golf Course, Ruth "overcame a five-hole handicap and defeated Mrs. R. B. Carter" for the women's local title.

The following summer Ruth and Govie would, legally this time, become man and wife at a simple ceremony presided over by a judge in a

Spanish-style garden in Salinas, located twenty miles east of Monterey, and Ruth would henceforth be known as Ruth Morris. Ruth's mother, Lulu, was there to witness the wedding of her only child.

Lulu, having long since withdrawn from the public spotlight, had moved up to the Peninsula soon after Ruth to be closer to her daughter. Govie, now feeling Daddy Warbucks rich, had a home built for her on Dennett Street in the nearby town of Pacific Grove. It was a modest but cozy affair, more cottage than mansion, nestled in a whispery, quiet pine forest a short walking distance to the ocean and just down the street from Asilomar, the Craftsman-style conference grounds designed by Hearst Castle creator Julia Morgan. Here Lulu devoted her time to an important new passion: sewing.

One other noteworthy thing happened in 1924. Roscoe Arbuckle and his fiancée, Doris Deane, were guests of the Morrises at their Monterey home in mid-December, and during their stay they would become involved in a seemingly innocuous incident that would in the end lead to a landmark legal ruling.

The setting was a barbecue picnic out at Point Lobos just south of Carmel, a sanctuary of gnarled cypresses arrayed at cliff's edge with the artfulness of a bonsai garden, a place so sublimely beautiful, Eden itself would have been flushed with envy at its sight. Amid these surroundings, Ruth and Govie and local friends watched with delight as Roscoe, adorned in a jaunty chef's cap, tended to the steaks and clowned around in his trademark fashion.

Then the mood was broken. Even the envy of Eden is not off limits to the press, and suddenly the sound of crashing waves and sizzling steaks was drowned out by shouts from the reporters as to whether Roscoe was planning to marry "Doris Keane."

"Maybe I am and maybe I am not. Meantime beat it while the beating is good, and don't try to catch me in that black box or I'll do a movie comedy with this steak." Govie jumped in to back up Roscoe, demanding that the reporters stay away from their private party, a wish that was quickly heeded.

Overlooked by everyone, however, was a glaring blunder by the reporters. Arbuckle's fiancée was Doris Deane, not Doris Keane. They were two different people. Doris Keane was an actress with no connection to Roscoe, and, most critically, she was married. So it was that when the *New York Evening Graphic* ran a story on December 12, 1924, stating that "Doris Keane is, according to rumor, Fatty Arbuckle's latest lady love," Doris Keane Sydney, as she was known privately, took serious offense and sued the publication for libel. She would eventually win, and her case, which is known as *Sydney v. McFadden Newspaper Publishing Corp.*, went on to establish an important legal precedent in the area of libel law that broadens the powers of potential litigants.

For Arbuckle the exchange with the reporters was just one more dose of unneeded aggravation. While he looked forward to better times with his future wife, he was in many ways a broken man. Given what he had already been through, it was little wonder that one of the true kings of Hollywood, once spoken of in the same breath with Charlie Chaplin, had become a shadow of his former self. Roscoe Arbuckle, known to millions by the name he hated, "Fatty," would never again return to his old form. He was too beaten down, and his increasing reliance on alcohol only made matters worse. To the very end, though, he knew he had friends in Ruth and Govie Morris.

As the year came to a close for Ruth Morris, it seemed she now had it all. Married to a sweet, bright, charming man. Living in a place of great natural beauty. Blessed with access to more money than she knew what to do with. And never needing to work again. It was a life most people would kill for.

Still, some things had not changed. Ruth was a woman in her twenties and Govie a man in his forties, a seemingly benign distinction that masked an underlying tension. Ruth was someone who thrived on risk and danger, qualities not normally associated with a happy, contented household.

For the moment neither Ruth's age nor her need for stimulation seemed to trigger any yellow warning signs, because the newlyweds were about to depart for Spain, and that promised to provide Ruth with all the stimulation she needed.

CHAPTER SEVEN

COLLECTING BULLFIGHTERS

As Ruth Morris settled in at the Hotel Ritz in Madrid, Spain, in April 1925, her transformation from working woman of modest means full of purpose, ambition, and drive to that of full-time member of the international leisure class was now complete. Not that she would soon have time to reflect upon any of this, because she found herself at the center of one of the great European cities, offering an array of rich experiences and endless distractions.

The distractions quickly became assured when Ruth and Govie met a master of distraction: United States ambassador Alexander Moore. This gregarious native of Pittsburgh, Pennsylvania, who was once described as "hardboiled and colorful as an Easter egg," would quickly become the Morrises' new best friend and greatly influence how they spent their time.

Govie began hanging out with the ambassador several times a week, going on long strolls around the city with him, and it's easy to see why the two hit it off. Alexander Moore was a former newspaper publisher, giving him a fair amount in common with a writer and former foreign correspondent like Govie. Then there was the show business connection. Govie was fresh out of Hollywood, and Moore had been actress and singer Lillian Russell's fourth husband. Needless to say, they were rarely at a loss for things to talk about.

But if Moore enjoyed his time with Govie, he cherished his moments with Ruth. He simply adored her. As Govie put it: "The ambassador hates to have her out of his sight." And the feeling seems to have been mutual. Ruth was enchanted by what an old-fashioned romantic Moore had been as he wooed Lillian Russell, having heard him describe in tender detail how for years he had sought the hand of the music hall sensation with the elegant gowns and the hourglass figure, only to look on helplessly as she kept exchanging vows with other suitors. Finally, in 1912, his perseverance was rewarded: Moore became her fourth and final husband. They would be together for the last ten years of her life, and Moore would be by her side when she died.

For Ruth and Govie, friendship with the US ambassador came with an important fringe benefit: he provided them with what amounted to an all-access pass to Spanish high society. Moore was about as well connected socially as any nonnative of the region could possibly be, and he rather quickly pulled them into the social swirl of aristocratic Madrid, a world of dukes and marquises and pearls.

Soon Ruth was confiding to a friend, "Everybody is giving parties now before the court goes north next month. We get no sleep at all." And she went on rhapsodizing about "long walks in the moonlight, dancing till daylight on the embassy grounds or on the hotel terrace, and glorious mornings spent in the soft and welcoming shadows in the Prado."

It was all quite wonderful, but Ruth's greatest social triumph during her time in Spain was yet to come: serving as hostess for a formal reception for the king and queen of Spain at the United States Embassy. Normally the hostess responsibilities would have fallen to the ambassador's niece, Mildred Martin, who had come with him to Madrid following the death of her beloved aunt Lillian to assist him with the social side of embassy affairs. In a bit of bad timing, however, Mildred fell ill just days before the big event, and a substitute hostess became a necessity. That was when the ambassador turned to Ruth.

She had already been in a state of high anticipation about the reception with the king and queen, "struggling for a week to get the right dress and headdress," and suddenly she found herself if not the star attraction then at the very least an important featured player.

When the grand night arrived, Ruth was as charming as ever as she greeted King Alphonse XIII, whom she found "smart and handsome and good looking and extremely friendly." But it wasn't the king who made the biggest impression on her. Rather it was his aunt, arguably the most popular member of the royal family. "Isabel de Bourbon is the most thrilling one of the lot. She's immortal!" As Ruth worked the room, Govie could only marvel: "For Prince Colona, the Duke of Tovar and all the way down to the lowly earls and marquises, she has the same spirit and naturalness she has for the traffic cop. Anything in Spain she wants she can have."

For her part, Ruth found Prince Colona, the king's cousin, "very sweet," and she thought Marquis Misciattelli "the most attractive man I have met in Europe." He in turn insisted that she come visit him at Palace Bonaparte in Rome, where he promised to show her his exquisite collection of illuminated manuscripts, the finest in Italy, he claimed.

It was an extraordinary assemblage of the rich and powerful of Spain, including the Duke of Alba, whose importance and influence extended well beyond the Iberian Peninsula. Don Jacobo Fitz-James Stuart y Falco, the seventeenth Duke of Alba de Tormes, was a direct descendent of James II of England, a grandee of Spain, and the most titled man in the world, and he wasn't even the only duke in the room. This, then, was the crowd Ruth was hosting that evening, but all the titles, historic legacies, and piles of money didn't faze her a bit.

At the appropriate time, the assembled guests were ushered into the dining room, and then according to protocol were directed to their appropriate seats. The power spots were at the two ends of the long table. At one end Ambassador Moore was seated with Queen Victoria Eugenie of Battenberg to one side and the Duchess of Alba on the other.

At the opposite end of the room sat the hostess for the evening, Ruth Morris. Next to her on one side was King Alfonso XIII of Spain, and on the other was Prime Minister Miguel Primo de Rivera. Each listened in rapt attention as Ruth, in passable but imperfect Spanish, gaily described the place of her birth and childhood, Upstate New York.

Later in the evening, Ruth took to the dance floor and continued whirling around long after Govie had excused himself and crawled off to bed.

It all sounds like some storybook fantasy: kings and royal balls and handsome princes and dancing until dawn. And there is no doubt that Ruth loved every minute, but there was something else in Spain that made an even bigger impression on her: the corrida. The bullfight. That rocked Ruth's world. The intensity. The artistry. The violence.

At first, it shocked her. As she experienced her first corrida, sitting in one of the private boxes that ringed the upper tier of the stadium, she initially recoiled from the "panorama of carnage and cold brutality" on display. But she couldn't look away. Not for a second. She was transfixed by the spectacle of it all.

In many ways her reaction was not unlike that of Elinor Glyn, a writer in Hollywood during Govie's time, who wrote, "Once one has controlled one's nerves and riveted one's attention solely upon the bull and the matador when, at last, they are alone together, I can only say that it is the most madly exciting exhibition that one could possibly see in this age. You will be very shocked when I tell you that something wild and tigerish and primitive in me rose."

A bullfight is a three-act drama, but it is the third act that Ruth, like Elinor, found so riveting. Here was the torero, alone in the ring, facing a raging, thousand-pound beast with horns that could rip the guts right out of him, as he performed a muscular ballet, highly ritualized and utterly raw. It is truly a life-and-death struggle. The matador has the advantage, but his life is always on the line. For the spectator it is an edge-of-the-seat experience unlike anything else in the world. With one possible exception: auto racing.

That may explain why the corrida so captured Ruth's intense interest. Not since the day she stepped out of the Mercer No. 4 in Stockton, California, had she found anything that so spoke to her desire to confront danger and risk.

Initially Ruth's interest was as a fan, and one up-and-coming torero caught her particular attention: Marcial Lalanda, a handsome twenty-two-year-old. Soon she was talking up his potential to anyone who would listen, and as his star rose, Ruth began boasting, "I almost discovered him."

She became a regular at the corridas, attending at least twice a week, and sought any opportunity to spend time with the toreros. Though she was quite new to the world of bullfighting, she was showing all the classic signs of becoming an aficionada, the female version of aficionado, or lover of the corrida. That was transgressive enough, but then Ruth went a step further: she proposed taking up a cape, stepping into a ring, and facing down a bull.

In Spain that was simply not done. It was against custom. It was against the law. It was against all that was decent and moral. The edict banning women from the bullring during that time period actually says that it is "opposed to our culture and sensitive feelings, and offensive to morality and good customs."

This American woman had some audacity even suggesting such a thing, but then this was the same American woman who had stepped in front of a fire hose when she was fourteen. She was also the American woman of whom Govie had only recently said, "Anything in Spain she wants she can have." In this instance, she wanted help finding a way to circumvent the ban on women, and Ambassador Moore and the Duke of Tovar were quick to oblige.

First, they discovered a loophole in the law. It turned out someone forgot to include private property in the ban. Which meant it didn't apply to the Duke of Tovar's castle and bullfighting facility, located some twenty miles outside of Madrid. For Ruth and Govie, it was an easy commute in Ambassador Moore's chauffeur-driven Rolls-Royce.

With all the hurdles overcome, Ruth's training began. Like other amateurs, Ruth faced young bulls with underdeveloped or padded horns. Like a professional, she always had a second in the ring with her to provide backup, should something go awry. And these were not just any backups. One was Marcial Lalanda, her hero and now her friend and teacher. Another was Niño de la Palma, about whom more will be told later.

The final phase for Ruth was a public performance, or as public as you could get on a private ranch. A select group of friends was invited to attend on the appointed day. Ambassador Moore was there, of course, and the Duke of Tovar. The Duchess of Frias was in the stands as well. The most surprising guest, though, was Isabel de Bourbon, the king's aunt. Her attendance was pregnant with implications. As a member of the royal family, she had traveled twenty miles for the express purpose of watching a woman engage in behavior that was "offensive to morality and good customs."

What could she have been thinking? It's impossible to know, but consider this: she was twice heir apparent to the throne, and both times a male relative ended up with the job. It's easy to imagine that she was thrilled to witness a woman openly defying a law that was written by men to restrict women.

Once the spectators were seated, the stage was set for Ruth's entrance. With her second, or backup, at hand, Ruth made her way into the ring, smartly outfitted in traditional Andalusian bullfighting attire—a heavily embroidered silk jacket, skin-tight, knee-length pants, and stockings—that was, in Ruth's words, "too cunning." She found herself, all five feet tall of her, face-to-face with the bull.

He was a youngster, of course, and his horns were padded. Still, he was strong and fully capable of inflicting damage and pain.

As the small but supportive crowd watched with rapt attention, Ruth strode toward the bull with a confident bearing, always keeping him in her gaze. Coming to a stop, she gracefully raised her bright-red muleta, or cape, and held it in front of her with two hands. She had begun the Veronica, the classic bullfighting move that has come to define the sport. Movement of the muleta provokes the bull to attack, which sets in motion the intricate ballet.

Which was precisely what happened in this instance. The bull came charging toward Ruth with a burst of youthful vigor, and she determinedly held her ground. As he was upon her, she executed a smooth pivot and rotated the muleta in an elegant wave, artfully dodging the attack.

As quick as he had passed, she had to reposition herself and brace for the next attack. It came quickly, but she was ready. Once again she swirled the muleta and pivoted out of harm's way. Ruth was beginning to read the bull's behavior and find her rhythm, as one Veronica flowed into another and then another.

Until, somehow, Ruth misplayed a move just enough to throw off her timing. She got wrong footed, throwing her weight distribution completely off. The laws of physics then took over, and Ruth tumbled most inelegantly toward the ground.

To make matters worse, as she scrambled to get up, she was facing away from the bull, and her derriere presented itself to him as an irresistible target. There would be no graceful pivot this time. Before she could reclaim her footing, the bull plowed right into her, leaving her splayed on the ground.

Govie, who had been glued to the viewfinder of his movie camera, attempting to capture Ruth's exploits in the bullring, quickly lowered the camera and squinted against the sun to make sure she was OK. By all appearances she was, as she got to her feet and grabbed for her muleta.

She was now determined to see it through to the end, to prove she could hold her own against the bull. Planting her feet, she gripped her muleta and resumed the ballet. Repeatedly she incited the bull to charge and then executed effective dodges until she had made her point.

She had also added another little footnote to the history books, becoming the only woman on record, and certainly the only American woman, to step into the ring with a bull in Spain during the many years women were subject to a ban.

To put what she accomplished in perspective, it's useful to consider a famous observation made by sportswriter Kenneth William Purdy many years later: "There are three sports that try a man: bullfighting, motor racing, mountain climbing. All the rest are recreations." Ruth had now successfully proved her mettle at two of the three.

For Ruth, though, her Spanish adventure was not yet over, because Ambassador Moore would soon invite her to travel with him to the little town of Pamplona in the Basque country of northern Spain, and she was about to come into close proximity with an ambitious young writer named Ernest Hemingway.

The occasion was the Fiesta de San Fermin, an annual event in Pamplona marked by bull runs in the morning, corridas in the afternoon, and drinking and dancing all night long. Hemingway and his entourage had already arrived, carrying fond memories of the previous year's fiesta.

Unfortunately for Hemingway, the carefree days of 1924 were over. His marriage to Hadley (Elizabeth Hadley Richardson), his first wife and eight years his senior, was deteriorating, following the birth of their son, and would not survive much longer. And the mix of friends who joined him in 1925 was not providing him with the same easy camaraderie he had enjoyed in the past.

The previous year, Hemingway's buddies had turned it into "a male festival, a glorified college reunion," but now the cast of characters had changed and included an attractive, charming woman named Lady Duff Twysden. Instead of camaraderie, there was now drama as three different men vied for Lady Duff's attention: Pat Guthrie, her nominal boyfriend. Harold Loeb, a writer and magazine editor. And Ernest Hemingway, a married man.

Not long before coming to Pamplona, Loeb and Lady Duff had a brief fling, and when Hemingway found out the couple had traveled in the same sleeping car together, he was livid, continuing to fume even after they reached Pamplona and Lady Duff reunited with Guthrie.

Then came the amateur bullfights, an opportunity for men to prove their manhood in the public arena. The previous year, writer Donald Ogden Stewart had been tossed in the air by a bull, leaving him with broken ribs, a reminder of the risks even a young bull presented. But this year, with the stakes seemingly higher, little thought was given to the risks, and Harold Loeb used the event to show up Hemingway.

Loeb later recalled the moment: "I had no time to think. When the bull lowered his head I dropped the towel, twisted around so that my back was facing him, and sat down hard on his head, grasping the horns for support. The bull lifted me up, carried me across the arena in three long, rolling lopes, and then tossed his head. I went up into the air and landed on my feet, upright." The athletic Loeb had ridden with style and then executed a gymnastic landing with a stick worthy of a 10.

"Hem, not to be outdone, caught one of the animals from the rear, seized his horns, twisted his neck, and threw him to the ground." If that wasn't enough, the two men almost got into a fistfight later that evening. The vibe from 1924 had definitely changed.

Between the episode in the amateur bullring and the ugly confrontation that night, Hemingway sat down with a new pal to review what had happened in the ring that day. The pal was none other than Niño de la Palma, just up from Madrid, where he had been training a certain American woman.

The young torero had become Hemingway's new personal favorite, and after seeing him in action, the author had become convinced he had the makings of a star. Not surprisingly, Hemingway would talk up Niño de la Palma at any opportunity. Sound familiar? To Donald Ogden Stewart, Hemingway said, "What do you think of Niño de la Palma's cape work? Did you notice how he sighted his sword before charging? The spot they got to hit's no bigger than a quarter."

The circle was completed when Ruth Morris rolled into Pamplona with Ambassador Moore and Moore's niece, Mildred, sparking a reaction from Hemingway and his buddies that bristled with contempt. Donald Ogden Stewart said of seeing Ambassador Moore's Rolls-Royce parked in front of the Hotel Perla, "The presence of the American Ambassador didn't add anything to the spirit of peasant gaiety."

So why the hostility? It was a combination of things. First, the Hemingway group resented any other Americans showing up in their town. This was their scene. Their private scene. Making it worse, the interlopers in this instance arrived in a Rolls-Royce and took rooms at the classiest hotel in town. A snake and two snakettes had slithered into their once pure garden.

It was a big enough deal that Hemingway took a shot at Moore, Ruth, and company in the novel he would soon write: *The Sun Also Rises*. While the novel is a work of fiction, it is heavily autobiographical, tracking closely with what actually happened with Hemingway and his friends during the Fiesta de San Fermin. Lady Duff Twysden becomes Lady Brett Ashley. Pat Guthrie becomes Mike Campbell. Harold Loeb becomes Robert Cohn. Donald Ogden Stewart becomes Bill Gorton. Niño de la Palma becomes Pedro Romero.

Here's one more: Ruth Morris becomes an "American woman." It's a one-line reference. No name is ever mentioned, but Hemingway was clearly thinking of Ruth. In the novel Jake Barnes, the narrator of the story and the character most closely resembling Hemingway himself, is in his hotel room. The owner of the hotel, named Montoya, comes to his room with a message. After some small talk, Montoya and Barnes have the following exchange:

> "Look," he said, "Do you know the American ambassador?"
> "Yes," I said. "Everybody knows the American ambassador."
> "He's here in town, now."
> "Yes," I said. "Everybody's seen them."
> "I've seen them, too," Montoya said. He didn't say anything. I went on shaving.

Hemingway isn't being too subtle here. He is referring to a real person who had been in Pamplona at the time. The "them," of course, refers to Moore, Ruth, and Mildred. Hemingway changes the name of their hotel to the Grand Hotel, which sums up what he thought of the Hotel Perla. The dialogue picks up a few lines later:

> "Look," he said, "I've just had a message from them at the Grand Hotel that they want Pedro Romero and Marcial Lalanda to come over for coffee to-night after dinner."

Pedro Romero (Niño de la Palma) and Marcial Lalanda were, of course, the two toreros Ruth had worked with a couple of weeks earlier. We skip a few more lines to this:

> "Don't give Romero the message," I said.
> "You think so?"
> "Absolutely."

A few lines after that we get to the central issue, and Hemingway, through his character Jake Barnes, takes a direct shot at Ruth:

"Look," said Montoya. "People take a boy like that. They don't know what he's worth. They don't know what he means. Any foreigner can flatter him. They start this Grand Hotel business, and in one year they're through."

"'Like Algabeño,'" I said.

"Yes, like Algabeño."

"They're a fine lot." I said. "There's one American woman down here now that collects bull-fighters."

"Collects bull-fighters!" Which begs the question: What precisely had Ruth done that was so different from what Hemingway himself had done? They both developed a passionate interest in the corrida. They both identified rising stars and championed them. They both developed friendships with toreros and became pals. They both had a deep need to court danger and risk, and they both had demonstrated courage by entering a ring with a bull. How were they all that different?

For Ernest Hemingway, 1925 proved to be a pivotal year. Professionally, the novel that emerged following his trip to Spain would become the launching pad for an illustrious career. Personally, a new woman, Pauline Pfeiffer, would capture Hemingway's attention before the year was over and would later become his second wife.

For Ruth Morris, 1925 was her first full year of marriage, revealing to her the future for which she now seemed destined but also reminding her of the life she had left behind. Ruth may not have even grappled with any of this at a conscious level, so consumed had she been by the wild carnival ride of stimulations that seemed to dominate the year. Still, the presence of so many attractive, interesting men at the various social functions, men who happily kept her company long after Govie was snuggled in bed, and the genuine rush she felt when she returned to the field of action, in this case the bullring, would eventually trigger nagging doubts: Had she made the right choices—about everything?

CHAPTER EIGHT

A NOT-SO-CASUAL FLIRTATION

Ruth Morris was a flirt. It was just part of her natural charm. She was friendly and approachable, and men loved that about her. They were drawn to her. They delighted in her company and were tickled to get a turn on the dance floor with her, and at the end of the day it was all quite innocent. Govie, for one, never seemed concerned.

Maybe he should have been. In Spain there had been something manic about her behavior. Between the corridas and the parties and the sightseeing and her time in the bullring, she never seemed to slow down. Sometimes she would eschew sleep altogether and dance until dawn, as though if she just kept dancing, the party would never end.

But parties always end. Someone will eventually turn off the lights and send everyone home. For Ruth, that must have been what it felt like when the nine months in Spain drew to a close. The party was over.

Worse, on the long voyage home in January 1926 aboard the *Lochgoil*, a Royal Mail Steam Packet ship, they were the only two passengers. Everyone else was crew. Few passengers meant few if any diversions. For a voyage of modest length, it might not have mattered that much, but for a trip from Europe to California, you could count on being at sea for several weeks. So Ruth found herself trapped on a ship in the North Atlantic with little to provide her the stimulation she craved.

It is said that nature abhors a vacuum, and the vacuum in Ruth's life was about to get filled in ways that would surprise her and would have shocked Govie had he known. The source of this surprise and potential shock was young and handsome, spelling trouble the moment Ruth encountered him, and he was about to give her marital vows their first real test.

It was just one of those random, unplanned things. One afternoon, in a fit of boredom no doubt, Ruth decided to wander out, get some air, and have a smoke. Except she was out of cigarettes. Somewhat annoyed, she set out to find the ship's steward, who she knew would fix her problem. That was the great thing about ship's stewards. They were at your beck and call, particularly if you were one of only two passengers on the whole ship.

As Ruth moved through an interior corridor of the vessel, she spotted what looked like the ship's steward and called after him. A uniformed man, who happened to be strikingly handsome, turned toward her with a quizzical look. Assuming the casual but assertive air of the entitled, Ruth asked if he would run and fetch her some smokes. What came next was not what she was expecting. Glaring at her with an are-you-serious gaze, he angrily spat out that ship's officers don't run errands for passengers.

A slightly shaken Ruth struggled to make sense of what had just happened, and two things became immediately clear: (1) she needed to make things right with him as quickly as possible, and (2) she needed to get to know him much better.

Not surprisingly, given the passenger-to-crew ratio, it was not too long before Ruth and the ship's officer encountered one another once again, and Ruth quickly went to work trying to make amends. Once she had sufficiently atoned for her embarrassing faux pas, the officer's cool reserve began to melt away, and as he dropped his guard, he became susceptible to what might be called the Ruth Effect, that thing about Ruth that drew men to her. Part of it, of course, was her keen sense of how to make a man feel good about himself, but there was also this:

Ruth had such an intensity about her, almost a wildness, that it added a certain frisson to any encounter she had with a man.

During her so-tell-me-about-yourself conversations with the officer, she learned that his name was Howard Barnes and that he had grown up in Wales. She also learned that he was twenty-two years old, six years her junior, which may have given her pause but did not dampen her interest. Instead, she gave him a nickname: "the Lad."

Now if Ruth had a weakness at all in her relationships with men, it was that she was not entirely immune to their charms, either. In almost all situations, she had the upper hand, but Howard Barnes had managed to throw her a little off balance. Certainly no one had come along since her marriage to Govie who had concentrated her attention quite like the Lad, a young man who was possessed of "such glamour and such a wicked wit" and such a deep, rich voice.

All of a sudden the voyage home didn't seem like it would be boring at all. Of course, it is a tricky business for a married woman to socialize with a man not her husband when her husband happens to be on board. Shipboard romances work best when they involve unattached or unaccompanied parties. Ruth fit neither category, but she did have a husband who was quite preoccupied with other matters.

Govie, it turns out, was trying to catch up on all the writing he had been neglecting. The ostensible reason the Morrises had gone to Spain in the first place was so that Govie could write a novel. That had been the plan, anyway, but there were just too many distractions: corridas, parties, museums, shopping. In striking contrast to Ernest Hemingway, who sat down and banged out a first draft in short order, Govie barely picked up a pen the entire time he was in Spain.

Now he had steeled himself away in the stateroom, trying to produce something to show for his year in Spain, even if it was only short stories. This was a productive use of his time, but it meant he was neglecting his wife. He was also unaware his wife was spending quality time with a handsome ship's officer.

The captain of the *Lochgoil* was aware, however, and he was not pleased with what he observed. He felt compelled to have a chat with Howard Barnes and give him a simple, direct order: stay away from Mrs. Morris.

Unfortunately that did not solve the problem, because there was one other actor in this drama, over whom the captain had no control: Mrs. Morris. She did not want Howard Barnes to stay away from her, and she set out to insure that did not happen.

At the same time, Ruth didn't want the Lad to get into any trouble, so she devised a clandestine communication system. The key was a discreet third party, and Ruth found the perfect third party for the job: the ship's steward—the real one, this time. She would write down a time and a location on a piece of paper and sneak it to the steward. The steward would then find a way to surreptitiously pass it on to Howard Barnes.

Thus began a series of private encounters between Ruth and the ship's officer that most probably did not include the kind of physical intimacy that would be considered adulterous but which might have tiptoed right up to the line, a line Ruth was determined she would never cross.

Still, the relationship that was budding between Ruth and Howard had grown sufficiently romantic that neither party seemed ready to end it as the ship approached Los Angeles, the Morrises' point of debarkation, and a quirk in the ship's itinerary opened up the possibility of at least one more encounter. The *Lochgoil* was scheduled to travel up the coast to Vancouver and then back down, stopping briefly in San Francisco. Ruth promised she would be there when it arrived.

In the meantime, she was returning to Los Angeles, a town where she had many friends and many more memories, and the minute she stepped off the gangplank, she and Govie got the star treatment. The following day the picture of them sitting dockside would appear on the front page of the *Los Angeles Times* along with a story about their return from Spain.

Their travels, though, were not the focus of the piece. The reporter was more interested in Govie's response to a controversy Rupert Hughes, his old colleague at Goldwyn Pictures, had stirred up with a suggestion that George Washington was a "virile, pleasure-loving gentleman," a description some, who preferred tales of cherry trees being chopped down and lies not being told, could not abide.

The whole thing seemed silly to Govie, and he leaped to Rupert's defense, saying of Washington, "He was entirely human and there is no reason why we should not realize that fact, rather than paint him as a saintly creature who never cursed or violated the truth."

So what did Govie think about all the sex in literature those days? "You can't get away from it. Sex is the one big problem in life and it must also be that in literature, as long as that literature is truthful." He concluded, "Frankly, I am in favor of doing away with all this hypocrisy and seeing the people of the world as they really are." Whether Mrs. Morris concurred that "sex is the one big problem in life" is not a matter of record.

Before heading home, the Morrises took advantage of their time in Southern California to catch up with their many Hollywood friends and regale them with stories of bullfighters and aristocrats. Then they caught the Southern Pacific at Union Station for the trip home.

Ruth's return to her comfy mansion on the bluff meant unpacking and readjusting to life in Northern California, all the while keeping an eye on the calendar and counting off the days. She didn't have long to wait. In mid-February 1926, the *Lochgoil* stopped in San Francisco, and Ruth, as promised, was there when it arrived.

That is when things got complicated. Once Howard and Ruth were alone together, the Lad took charge of the conversation. Solemnly, if a bit nervously, he looked into Ruth's eyes and told her he loved her and added that he knew she loved him, too. All quite flattering, no doubt, but it's easy to imagine Ruth becoming increasingly leery as he got to his main point: He wanted her to run away with him. Right then. Right there. Say good-bye to the past. Say hello to a future as Mrs. Howard Barnes.

That was a bit more than Ruth had expected. Or even wanted. And yet. And yet. It's easy to imagine that for just the briefest of moments, just a few beats of her pounding heart, she was tempted. The sheer audacity, the utter craziness of it, was wildly romantic. Were Ruth's head ruled by her heart, she might even have gone for it. But her head was never completely out of control.

To be sure, she'd had her issues with Govie: he drank too much and seemed moodier of late, and his propensity for early bedtimes was just one of the many reminders that he was old enough to be her father.

Still, she was terribly fond of Govie and grateful for all he had done for her, and she genuinely did not want to hurt him. Also, she was not ready to walk away from the financial security he provided and the luxurious style of life to which she had grown accustomed.

Besides, how would it ever have worked? Howard Barnes sailed around the world for a living. Where was Ruth going to live? On the ship? What was she going to do? Running off with the Lad might have sounded romantic, but upon sober reflection, she realized it was completely nuts.

The challenge then became how to tactfully say no to Howard without it coming across as a rejection. They should take it a little slower, she suggested. They should correspond by mail to stay in touch. Yes, she cared for him, but this was too much too soon.

Howard would not hear it, however. He wanted Ruth, and he was absolutely positive that she wanted him, and that was that. Ruth's no now became firmer, and she insisted it was not negotiable.

OK then, Howard decided, he would take matters into his own hands. He stormed off. It would be several minutes before Ruth discovered what he was up to, but in those critical minutes, the Lad had rented an automobile and was on his way to Monterey with the intent of confronting Govie with the brutal truth. Howard loved Ruth. Ruth loved Howard. They wanted to be together. It was time for Govie to let go.

When Ruth finally figured out what Howard was up to, alarm morphed into panic. Quickly she took off after him, heading south along the road that was only months away from being designated Highway 101.

It really wasn't a fair chase. Eight years had passed since Ascot and Stockton, but Ruth still knew how to handle an automobile like few people alive. As the two cars raced down the peninsula south of San Francisco, along what had once been El Camino Real, Ruth just kept closing. With each mile, the gap narrowed, until there was no gap at all. Right around San Mateo she pulled even and then forced him off the road.

Now completely outplayed by Ruth, Howard agreed not to go any further and reluctantly turned around and headed back to San Francisco. Ruth pulled in behind him and followed. Once they were both back at the pier, the shipboard lovers had a final, emotional good-bye. Then as the Lad boarded his ship, Ruth drove off and found a point high up in the city where she had an unobstructed view of the Golden Gate—before there was a bridge—and beyond.

She remained there waiting until the *Lochgoil* pulled away from the dock, and tracked its movement as it worked its way out into the open sea. Then quietly she turned around and prepared to go home.

CHAPTER NINE

STANDING UP VALENTINO

For Ruth Morris, disaster had been averted. She had left Howard Barnes reconciled to the fact that they could be pen pals and nothing more. Ruth even rented a secret post office box in nearby Pacific Grove to fulfill that promise, but she was sticking with Govie—about that she was quite clear.

The quick trip to San Francisco had required one unfortunate sacrifice, however: she had to skip dinner with America's number one heartthrob, Rudolph Valentino. No small deal, that. Valentino, the face that had launched thousands of daydream fantasies, thanks to his dark, simmering good looks and his starring roles in films like *The Sheik* and *Blood and Sand*, was the very epitome of the great lover. As one lovestruck fan described him, Valentino was "triumphantly seductive" and put "the love-making of the average man into discard as tame, flat and unimpassioned." This, Ruth missed out on, and a bit more.

As the evening began there were no hints of the surprising behavior that would emerge later on. Dinner itself at the Del Monte Lodge in Pebble Beach was a fairly conventional affair, as Govie; Francis McComas and his wife, Gene; author Sinclair Lewis; and Peggy Neville, wife of the creator of the Pebble Beach Golf Links, Jack Neville, gathered around a table with the guests of honor, Rudolph Valentino and the newest woman in his life, Pola Negri.

Peggy Neville provided the most interesting contribution to the dinnertime schmoozing with an anecdote she had come determined to share. As the movie idol locked his trademark gaze on Neville, she began recalling a time when she was younger and maybe a bit more foolish. Still single and living in New York, she was invited one evening to go out dancing with a man she had never met, a blind date if you will, and chose to decline. It was only years later that she realized that the man she had blown off without a second thought had become the screen legend who was at that moment sitting across from her at dinner.

Valentino's eyes twinkled, and a broad grin broke out over his face. As Peggy Neville would later recall, "He thought the whole thing was hilarious." With that, the evening seemed to be getting off to a great start, but the evening was young.

As dinner grew to a close, Govie invited everyone to come over to his place in Monterey for a nightcap, and with that the entire dinner party, save Peggy Neville, migrated over to the Morris mansion.

That's when the Morris cache of gin and ginger ale made an appearance, and one guest in particular seemed to keep coming back for seconds. History will record that Sinclair Lewis, a writer destined to win the Nobel Prize in Literature a few years later, had a buzz on during his entire stay on the Monterey Peninsula in 1926.

This particular evening Lewis's lack of sobriety seemed to encourage or permit a level of social forwardness that was astonishing in its audacity, and the target of his attention was the screen siren Pola Negri. Almost from the moment he set eyes on her at the Del Monte Lodge, Lewis was beguiled by Pola, by her eyes, by her complexion, by the color and drape of her clothes. He was like a lovesick teenager harboring unrealistic fantasies about his chances with the homecoming queen.

By the time the party had reached Ruth and Govie's place, Lewis had decided to make his move. Once he had Pola alone on a couch, he tried to act cool and debonair, giving her a knowing look and talking to her in German. Leaning in close, he showered her with flattery. She was, he purred, a cross between Cleopatra and Helen of Troy. Slowly he slipped his hand into hers, looked into her eyes, and asked, with alcohol-fueled assurance, if he could have her phone number. While it seems extremely doubtful that Pola was taking Lewis seriously, she chose to indulge him by sharing her private phone number, a number he would later wisely choose never to call.

Watching from across the room as this little drama unfolded, Rudolph Valentino could not conceal his annoyance, which delighted Sinclair Lewis. Annoyance to Lewis meant something else entirely: it meant Valentino was jealous. As Lewis would wistfully later recall: "So the most improbable thing one could have imagined has happened. I have lived to make Rudolph Valentino jealous. I now have but to knock out Jack Dempsey and beat [Bill] Tilden at tennis . . . and then wake up."

The following day, Lewis met his friend, the poet George Sterling, at the train station down by the wharf and quickly recounted the tale of his greatest romantic triumph. Sterling would later gossip to writer H. L. Mencken: "He was lit up all the time when at Pebble Beach, and at a dinner at Gouverneur Morris' tried to vamp Pola Negri! She was nice to him, and he joshed Valentino so intimately that now he (L.) thinks that he made Valentino jealous! I'll say that's going some for alcoholic imagination."

By the time Ruth rolled back into town, Valentino and Pola Negri had already departed, so she missed them entirely. She did return in time to meet Sinclair Lewis, to whom she would later turn for writing advice, and to visit with longtime pal George Sterling, the acknowledged ringleader of the original bohemian enclave in Carmel some two decades earlier that numbered among its members Jack London, Mary Austin, Jimmy Hopper, and Sinclair Lewis. She had first met the poet when she was roaming the streets of San Francisco as a young teenager attired in Chinese clothing and he was palling around with his buddy Jack London, a friend of Ruth's mom. Sadly, her brief visit with Sterling in February 1926 would be her last. He would not survive to the end of the year.

Even more shocking, Rudolph Valentino would be dead in six months at age thirty-one. The very picture of youthful vitality and a veritable god of the silver screen, Valentino suffered the fate of a mere mortal. Appendicitis and gastric ulcers were the first to take him down, and then complications from those ailments delivered the final blow.

On August 15, 1926, coincidently Ruth's twenty-ninth birthday, emergency surgery was performed on Valentino at Polyclinic Hospital in New York City. Initially he seemed to be enjoying a normal recovery. Condolences poured in from politicians, movie stars, and athletes from all over the country, and Valentino began planning how he would spend his time after he left the hospital.

Unbeknownst to the doctors who were issuing upbeat daily reports, however, infection was quietly taking hold in his body and beginning to spread. Before long, the infection made its presence known. Severe pains pierced through Valentino's chest and abdomen, his temperature spiked, and doctors detected pneumonia.

At 8:00 a.m. on August 23, 1926, Rudolph Valentino lapsed into a coma. He stopped breathing at 12:10 p.m. The great screen idol was pronounced dead.

When word reached Pola Negri in California, she became hysterical, and doctors were summoned to calm her down. One of Pola's close friends, Charles Eyton, described the scene: "Throughout the morning Miss Negri spoke again and again with heartbroken sobs of the tragic shattering of their romance." Eyton quoted Pola as saying, "I have lost not only my dearest friend, but the one real love of my life." Later Pola would insist upon visiting Valentino's home, where she walked the halls, repeatedly calling out his name. Eventually she would take the train to New York for his funeral.

Tens of thousands of people lined the streets of New York as Valentino's body was borne to St. Malachy's Catholic Church on West Forty-Ninth Street. Inside Pola Negri seemed to take center stage, as the *Los Angeles Times* reported: "Miss Negri knelt at the bier and prayed. She wept and collapsed and gave to the public all of the spectacle of grief that the greatest of the dramatic writers had pictured in song, story and opera from the beginning of things theatrical."

Ruth and Govie were no doubt as shocked as anyone was at the news of Valentino's death, but the passing of George Sterling, a good and dear friend of long standing, was more difficult to bear. They learned about it on November 17, 1926, while they were staying at the

St. Francis hotel in San Francisco, preparing to depart on a voyage to New Zealand for a fishing expedition.

When word reached them, Govie raced right over to the Bohemian Club, Sterling's long-time residence, with writer and friend H. L. Mencken, to learn what had happened, and the news proved sobering. The body of their beloved friend had been discovered midday after a room valet received no response when he knocked on the door. The room valet immediately chased down the club manager, John E. Maddocks, who used a passkey to gain access to the room. Once inside they confirmed what they had feared: George Sterling was dead. Maddocks summoned the police and the coroner, and they rather quickly determined that Sterling had consumed a fatal dose of cyanide.

Speaking to reporters afterward, Govie somberly explained, "Sterling often said that suicide is the way out for poets. Sterling used to discuss suicide. He used to tell how his wife had committed suicide—and in the same manner chosen by himself—but I don't remember his ever threatening the same thing. His was purely an artist's reaction to the thought of suicide." He added, "The world has lost a fine spirit. Freedom and directness of thought and expression has lost a champion."

Losing their dear, sweet friend George deeply saddened both Ruth and Govie, and it cast a dark pall over their trip. Still, they had to press on, heading first up the coast to Vancouver before setting off by ship to the South Seas and beyond.

Their time in New Zealand, a mix of deep-sea fishing and sightseeing, was quickly overshadowed by what was to come next, which on the face of it was just a routine twenty-hour stopover on the way home to California.

Nothing, however is routine about Papeete, Tahiti, capital of the South Sea islands group known as the Society Islands, which includes Moorea and Bora Bora and is at the heart of the larger collection of 118 islands that composes French Polynesia. Robert Louis Stevenson once wrote that "no part of the world exerts the same attractive power upon the visitor. . . . The first experience can never be repeated. The first love, the first sunrise, the first South Sea island, are memories apart and touched a virginity of sense."

For Ruth and Govie, everything about Tahiti touched them. The tranquil lagoons that glimmered like elegant turquoise jewels, set against thin bands of white sand. The stalwart palm trees standing lonely sentinel along the shore. The riot of color in the central market-place: flowers freshly cut, fish freshly caught, fruit freshly picked. The gentle caresses of the balmy tropical breezes. And the sweet, alluring scent of the tiare, the delicate white gardenia.

They were beguiled by Tahiti, but time was their enemy. With the clock ticking down, they reluctantly trudged back up the gangplank and boarded the RMS *Makura* for the final leg to California, vowing to return before the year was out.

All the while they never noticed that a new passenger was boarding at Papeete, a passenger who was about to enter their lives in ways they could never have imagined.

He was British and a writer, and his name was Alec Waugh.

CHAPTER TEN

THE OTHER MAN

Howard Barnes may have been Ruth Morris's first serious temptation, but Alec Waugh would prove to be her greatest temptation of all. Her marriage had managed to survive the Lad, but it was placed in a good deal more jeopardy with the arrival of Alec Waugh.

Born in London on July 8, 1898, eleven months after Ruth, Alexander Raban Waugh, modest of height and fair of complexion, entered the literary Waugh family as its eldest son. Arthur, his father, managed Chapman & Hall, the publishing house Charles Dickens had once called home, and Evelyn, his brother, wrote *Decline and Fall*, *A Handful of Dust*, and *Brideshead Revisited*, among other titles, and earned the epithet "the greatest novelist of my generation" from Graham Greene.

Alec was by all accounts their father's favorite, making for a complicated and at times strained relationship with his brother. At the same time, Evelyn would become the more successful writer, though Alec would enjoy his moments in the spotlight as well.

His debut novel, *The Loom of Youth*, which channeled his experiences at an independent school for boys, met with immediate success. The *Times* of London saw it as "a most promising first book." H. G. Wells praised Alec for writing "easily and unaffectedly," and Arnold Bennett called the novel "a staggering performance."

Sales were brisk, and its bestseller status was quickly assured. Then a backlash hit. A minority of the critics began focusing on one element of the book they found disturbing. Alec had revealed the never publicly acknowledged secret that some boys in English schools sexually experimented with each other. "Pernicious stuff," one critic called it. "Uniformly dull, occasionally unpleasant, and in my judgement at least, almost wholly untrue," a former headmaster from Eton declared. And Sherborne, Alec's former school, all but disowned him, forcing younger brother Evelyn to attend another school, much to his chagrin.

Despite the controversy, or maybe because of it, Alec's writing career was off to a promising start. Unfortunately, he was mostly otherwise engaged. It was 1917, and World War I had reared its bloody, gas-mask-bedecked head. The good news for Alec was that he spent most of the war training rather than fighting. The bad news? He was captured by the Germans and had to wait out the eleventh hour of the eleventh day of the eleventh month in the grim confines of a POW camp, itching interminably from lice and living on "a daily ration of three slices of bread, five bowls of water soup, and six potatoes."

Not much fun, to be sure, but there was an upside: his time in captivity was grist for a second novel. After the war it would come out under the title *The Prisoners of Mainz*.

With the end of the war, Alec went to work for his father's publishing house and picked up where he had left off with his childhood sweetheart, a young woman named Barbara Jacobs, and out of a sense of obligation or because it is what you do at a certain stage in life, they got married.

What followed could best be described as a disaster. And not for the usual reasons. Money wasn't an issue. Or meddling in-laws. Or even a clash of personalities. The problem can be summed up in one word: sex. They couldn't figure out how to do it. As Alec later recalled, "I had imagined that a few casual encounters in the red-light districts of Mainz and Nancy would be sufficient training for me. Actually I should have been better off without it. It made me think that the whole thing was simple and straightforward." For eighteen-year-old Barbara, it was all a confusing mystery, so she was no more help to him than he was to her. For his part, Alec lamented, "I was too ashamed of myself to consult a doctor. By the time we did, in the following summer, it was too late. Mental inhibitions had been created." Eventually they just gave up, and the marriage was never consummated.

The sad part is that they were two decent people who got on well otherwise, but problems in the bedroom eventually soured everything. Alec filed for divorce and was granted an annulment.

That was when Alec met Phyllis. After Barbara, Phyllis was something else again. "A wild, attractive lady," she was several years older and "the first woman of the world" he had ever met. She was, in the rather inelegant language of the day, a "kept woman," but she had no particular qualms about taking on lovers behind her much older benefactor's back.

So for several months, Alec Waugh became Phyllis's extracurricular activity, which was a playful diversion for her but a priceless education for him, meaning in practical terms that she took him in hand and introduced him to the art of making love. And she taught him "the kinds of attention that a woman expects from a man," like how to talk to waiters and handle cab drivers, all to insure that his female companion feels "taken care of" and that her only concern is her "own enjoyment."

Alec's time with Phyllis was strictly no strings, and it was never meant to be more than that. The couple eventually disengaged on the most cordial of terms, and Alec emerged a new man.

He also emerged with fresh writing material and a somewhat better understanding of the opposite sex, all of which was welcome news for Alec because his most recent book, the autobiographical *Myself When Young*, had generated disappointing sales, and he needed something provocative and engaging to recapture the public's interest.

What resulted was a novel called *Kept* about a beautiful young widow in postwar London who relies on the financial support of an older married man while becoming romantically entangled with other men. There is an assurance in Alec's handling of this material that would not have been possible before he came to know Phyllis, and the character in the novel modeled after her, Marjorie Fairfield, is portrayed quite sympathetically.

Someone else who is the beneficiary of warm feelings is Alec's brother, for whom the book has the following dedication: "To my Brother Evelyn With Much Affection." *Kept* was published in 1925, and it sold respectably.

By this time, however, even an uptick in sales was not enough to boost Alec's spirits about his career, because he found stories about British people and British culture simply too limiting. He wanted to shake things up but struggled with the question of how to do it until the answer was revealed in a surprising place: a short story by Somerset Maugham called "The Fall of Edward Barnard."

Here's the plot that lit the fire: Edward, a young man from Chicago, travels to Tahiti for temporary work in hopes of earning enough money so that he can return home and marry his fiancée, Isabel. Little does he realize that French Polynesia, as Robert Louis Stevenson once warned, can cast a spell over the unsuspecting, and Edward falls hard for its charms. "It came upon me little by little," he explains to a friend. "I came to like the life here, with its ease and its leisure, and the people with their good-nature and their happy smiling faces. I began to think. I had never had time to do that before. . . . And gradually all the life that had seemed so important to me began to seem rather trivial and vulgar. . . . I think of Chicago now and I see a dark, grey city, all stone— it is a prison. . . . And when I am old, what have I to look forward to?"

In the end, it is Edward's friend who marries Isabel, and Edward remains in Tahiti, where he marries a native woman and settles down to a simple life without much money but free of cares.

The tug of French Polynesia now became irresistible to Alec, and he was soon on a ship headed to Papeete, Tahiti, with Gauguin-like visions of paradise in his head.

The original plan had been to stay for only five days, but a certain "warm and sensual" Polynesian woman named Tania, whom he had met quite by chance on the day of his arrival, proved strong encouragement to linger. "It was," for Alec, "the greatest fun making love to her," for reasons he rather suggestively explained: "Polynesians, as hula dancers, acquire an astonishing mobility between the knees and navel. In that respect I have had no comparable experience." His wildest fantasies about the South Pacific had rather quickly blossomed into something real, "spontaneously, without planning, unpremeditated," but Alec was not destined to follow in Edward Barnard's footsteps. He would eventually have to take his leave of Eden.

Exactly how was left to chance. Alec had already missed his original departure. Then a vessel that had been due in soon developed engine trouble, leaving only one remaining choice: a ship arriving from New Zealand on its way to San Francisco, which would depart the following Tuesday morning.

With little fanfare, Alec Waugh had climbed aboard the RMS *Makura* and settled in for a ten-day cruise to San Francisco. His mood was one of resignation as he slumped into a canvas deck chair and reflected upon a painful truth: his South Seas fantasy escape was now over, and he was returning to an utterly respectable and thoroughly boring British life.

Or so he thought. Little did he know that there was a five-foot woman with auburn hair somewhere on the same vessel who was about to insure that his life would be anything but boring. That Ruth and Alec were destined to now meet had come about by an odd quirk of fate, and yet each seemed primed for what was about to happen.

In Alec's case he was unmarried, and his highly charged but casual relationships with Phyllis and Tania seem to have been preparing him for this moment.

As for Ruth, she was married and seemingly unavailable, but her relationship with Howard Barnes hints at why her wedding ring might not have meant everything it seemed to suggest. There was, it would appear, a growing sense on Ruth's part that the reality of her marriage had not entirely lived up to her fantasies and expectations. Not working anymore and not having any goals or aspirations beyond the next party or the next voyage seems to have left her feeling a little empty inside.

Worse, her loss of power and her growing dependency, which were a product of her marriage to a man who had the money and the fame in the household, was an apparent source of frustration.

Hence, the fling with the Lad. Sure, there was the personal appeal and the sexual attraction, but what is striking is how the relationship played out. Ruth essentially seduced Howard and inflamed his passions, all the while controlling just how far the whole thing would go, finally putting up the stop sign when she thought she'd had enough.

The relationship offered the risk and the excitement she craved but also the power and control she had lost in her marriage. There's something potentially addictive about that, and it's easy to imagine that once she'd gotten a taste, she would soon hunger for more.

When Alec Waugh sat down across from Ruth Morris that night at the bridge table on the RMS *Makura*, causing Ruth to become nervous and distracted, it wasn't because she was uncomfortable about meeting someone new. That never happened with Ruth. It was because she realized that Alec might be able to provide her with those feelings of power and control and excitement once again. And that realization had to have both thrilled and terrified her.

Ruth, of course, was a risk taker—a part of her thrived on risk—but this was bigger than a fire hose or a fighting bull. It took time, reflection, and intense arguments with herself before she had finally made up her mind. Not only would she continue her seduction of Alec Waugh, but she would ask Alec to rendezvous with her secretly on the island of Tahiti in six months.

And he agreed.

With that request and that agreement, Ruth had now committed herself to doing the riskiest thing she had ever done in her life.

CHAPTER ELEVEN

SIX LONG MONTHS

Ruth Morris had made her choice. She was now effectively treating her marriage like a stack of chips at a gaming table, and in six months' time, in far-off Tahiti, she would learn just how this particular dice roll was going to turn out.

Back in Monterey she had much to think about, but what was most immediately on her mind were memories of the two days she had just spent with Alec Waugh in San Francisco.

Memories of their stroll through Chinatown before taking Alec to her favorite Chinese restaurant for a quiet dinner.

Of their trip to a nearby bookstore, Newmegen's, where Ruth made a show of buying *Myself When Young*, an autobiographical treatment of Alec's early life, published in 1923.

Of their visit to Gump's, the celebrated Asian art store, where she introduced Alec to Marcella Gump, the daughter of the owner and a great pal, after which they carefully studied the jade collection.

Of their pilgrimage to the Robert Louis Stevenson monument, in front of which Ruth read the inscription aloud: "To be honest, to be kind—to earn a little, to spend a little less—to make upon the whole a family happier for his presence—to renounce when that shall be necessary, and not be embittered—to keep a few friends, but these without capitulation—above all on the same grim condition to keep friends with himself—here is a task for all that a man has of fortitude and delicacy." This prompted Ruth to add, "That's my motto. That's how I'd like to live my life."

Of their escape to the coffee shop downstairs in the St. Francis hotel for a leisurely afternoon tea, as they drifted "from one subject to another, exchanging intimacies, building up the basis for whatever life might have to offer," drawing themselves ever closer.

And of their final parting, on separate trains, going in widely disparate directions: one south to Monterey and the other east to New York and an awaiting ocean liner, the RMS *Aquitania*.

Within days Ruth and Alec would be thousands of miles apart. The only thin, tenuous connection they would have left was through words on paper. Many words on many pieces of paper would travel back and forth between them over the coming months, and the first batch from Ruth was posted the day after she returned home:

> *My Dear,*
> *Do forgive the pencil. But I'm in bed, and I couldn't find the one fountain pen that our affluent household possesses.*
>
> *I'm dressed up in a long sleeved high necked cotton-flannel nightie, which my mother thinks the only proper resistance against the California cold. Because it is my first night at home I must give in and capitulate and please—it is such a flagrantly youthful garment that almost I like it. I am so tired—it has been a long and heart breaking day. Perhaps worries and griefs are simpler and easier to bear if one can give in to them. But if one has to put up even an ounce of bravado, and giggle and preen as a form of disguise it isn't very easy.*
>
> *How you did misjudge me those days on the ship. Your error is an acute concern to me tonight. You might easily have thought me noisy, bad mannered, common, ignorant, or any number of such like things, but how even a stranger could consider me a promiscuous*

*purveyor of affection to any young man is beyond me!
Truly, is that the way everyone judges me? I <u>am</u> upset.*

*My bedroom has a lovely old Spanish Colonial fire-
place, as simple and serene as could be, as simple and
serene as it can be (so is the rest of the room—with the
exception of your small amorata—she may be simple
but she is <u>not</u> serene) and there is a roaring, welcoming
fire. Mickey, the wild cat is luxuriously roasting herself
before the fire, and curled up beside me is 'the wild cat's
kitten' (I told you what idiotic names we had for our
cats.) He is purring in a most unctuous manner. Oh, I
do love them.*

*I didn't read any of your book on the train. I want
to be alone for that, for very probably I shall not only
read even the cricket chapter, but kiss every word you've
written about the Beastly game. And that is devotion.
Of course, I shan't be a fair judge of any book you've
ever written or will write because I'm most dreadfully
biased in your favor.*

*Life is a curious thing. How <u>can</u> one hate parting
from someone so very much, and just drive away in a
cab with a most casual wave of the hand. It is unbe-
lievable that the break that the heart gives shouldn't be
heard, isn't it? Or didn't you feel badly, too? I thought I'd
never live to get to the station and all the way here every
time the train whistled (and there is something so thrilling and so melancholy about the cry of an American
train) I kept saying to myself, everything is over, he's on
another train tonight, a beastly train going the wrong
way with the same melancholy yap that this train has,
and he's going thousands of miles away, and I'll never
see him again, never never again. It was so lovely, and
so tortuous, and now it's over. But surely, dear, surely it
can't be over forever. Six months is not eternity—quite.*

*It is such an utterly asinine position to be left here
like this, with no possible hold over you except the*

problematic—'what <u>would</u> it be like in Tahiti?' Good
Lord, that isn't even a promise. It's merely a question
that neither one of us can answer. I have however the
shameful suspicion that in the last analysis I am more
human than honorable. Perhaps not. It is so far in my
life a question that has not been raised.

Please don't feel that you are in any way demanded
to write to me when you are not so inclined. But all I'm
simply praying is that the inclination will be strong
and often. And that the cold English beauty who is to
lure you into a frigid northern climate will not appear
immediately. Even if all this is an illusion, it gives me an
unrest, a contentment, a pain and a pleasure that my
life has not contained before. And I would hate to lose
these mixed emotions quickly.

This is a stupid and disconnected letter, dearest,
and written only with the intention of warning you that
it will be a very long time before you get a cable which
will contain even a word that sounds like finished in it.
Good night, my very dear,
Ruth

As Alec's train labored up and over the Rockies and down into the Great Plains on its way to the East Coast, he began composing a letter to Ruth. His "heart desolate with loss," Alec poured out his feelings in small, neat script about their painful parting, and he "reflected ruefully on the disadvantages of being 'the one who goes away.'" As the distance between them quickly grew, he feared that her letters would not keep up with his fast-moving pace.

Alec needn't have worried. Ruth had sent her first letter via airmail, allowing it to outrace the train, which took four days. Ruth's letter arrived in three.

When Alec boarded the RMS *Aquitania* in New York, Ruth's letter was sitting there waiting for him, and it was a blissful surprise. As he read it over and over, "the spell" Ruth had cast over him only strengthened its grip. Years later Alec still remembered that first letter: "I have no idea how many times I read it. Phrases in it still ring through my mind. My eyes can see it on the page. Six months might be a long time. A great deal could happen in six months, but with that letter to re-read, nothing that would not seem trivial."

In a separate envelope, Alec found the following telegram:

This is to wish you a safe voyage and a most rapid return to this part of the world. I have written to the ship but you seem very far away and England looms up as a hopeless distance and Tahiti sounds like a fiction of a place that never existed nor will ever exist. I am however sending you the most affectionate remembrances of a pleasant interlude.
Ruth Morris

These were complicated times for Ruth. She had committed to a secret rendezvous with Alec Waugh on the island of Tahiti, which carried with it the implied promise of significant intimacy, and that alone was anxiety-producing enough. Worse, though, with each passing day the anticipation and the dread seemed to mount, and Ruth began casting around for some manner of relief.

Sometimes the solutions she chose were quite constructive, as when she began exploring ways to restore more purpose to her life and thought of a focus on writing. She was, after all, a fluid and at times eloquent writer and was surrounded by other writers who could serve as mentors, and she would later tell Alec: "I'm not going to waste one more moment of life than is necessary. And I do want to make something out of that life. Writing seems to be my best bet for the moment." She had even done some writing once before with her Hollywood novel about the scenario writer, but once she lost the thread on that effort her writing had been limited to letters and telegrams. Now she was ready to do something more substantive, once she had found the right focus.

Unfortunately, all too often Ruth turned to a less constructive way to alleviate her anxiety: a bottle of gin. What had begun as social drinking had evolved over time into self-medication, a development that had to have surprised all who knew her well. After all, Charlie Chaplin had first introduced Ruth to Govie in hopes she would moderate his drinking behavior, and she had succeeded to a degree. The problem now was that she wasn't always able to control her own behavior.

There was some good news for Ruth on the writing front, however. During a weeklong visit to Southern California, William Randolph Hearst had suggested an idea. Govie had long known W. R., thanks to his many years as a star writer for Hearst magazines, so the welcome mat was out for Ruth and Govie at the Hearst beach house in Santa Monica. Less well known than Hearst's famous castle in San Simeon, the Georgian-style beach house, designed by Hearst's long-time architect Julia Morgan, was smaller in scale than the San Simeon property but still exquisitely decorated on the inside and included "ten guest rooms and a living room with each." Immediately in front of the mansion was an ornately tiled, Olympic-sized swimming pool, and a few yards beyond lay the Pacific Ocean. Built expressly by Hearst for his beloved, the actress Marion Davies, the Santa Monica location was easily accessible to movie-industry people working across town and visiting out-of-towners like the Morrises.

After they had settled in, Ruth and Govie had an opportunity to socialize with W. R. and Marion, and somewhere in the conversation, Govie managed to slip in an oh-by-the-way comment about Ruth's new interest in writing. Intrigued, the old newspaperman shifted into idea-generation mode, and soon he had what he thought was the perfect topic for Ruth: Prohibition. She should write, he believed, the book that hadn't been written yet, the story of Prohibition. The origins. The politics. The real-world implications.

That the illustrious publisher offered Ruth such a story idea was flattering, to be sure. But it was also fairly nerve-racking for her. This was a bigger plunge than she had been thinking about. Ruth's self-confidence, so often on display, grew out of her sense of mastery of whatever she was undertaking. In the case of writing, however, she was still relatively inexperienced, and fiction had always been her focus. She saw such a nonfiction piece as "a ponderous subject and a big enemy for one small and illiterate woman to attack." Hearst, though, was insistent, and Ruth would leave Southern California committed to giving it her best effort, though she privately fretted it might end up "a flop."

What prompted Hearst to suggest this particular topic is hard to say, given his complicated history with the subject. He personally opposed Prohibition as public policy, but he enforced a sort of private prohibition in his own household, going to great lengths to keep booze out of Marion's hands. Invited guests were another matter, of course, and were afforded gracious hospitality where alcoholic beverages were concerned, but the rest of the time liquor was locked up to keep it away from his mistress Marion.

As one might expect, his strategy was a miserable failure. Marion Davies simply hid the stuff around the house, and she could hide it better than W. R. could find it. Besides, she had willing accomplices, including some of her guests. Ruth and Govie, among others, were invited to join her for private imbibing. This conjures images of Ruth and Marion knocking back gin and gossiping about heaven knows what. It's hard to imagine a more delicious fly-on-the-wall moment.

Another potential fly-on-the-wall moment during the Morrises' visit to Southern California might have been when Ruth briefly encountered the author of *The Great Gatsby*, "young F. Scott Fitzgerald, a handsome little drunkard," as Ruth described him. The occasion was a party thrown by Govie's old boss Sam Goldwyn, to which Scott and Zelda were not invited but which they crashed. Spectacularly. The Fitzgeralds showed up at Goldwyn's front door in a state of advanced inebriation and proceeded to get down on all fours and bark like dogs. In a bid to end the ruckus, Goldwyn invited them in, allowing them to mingle with the guests and meet Ruth.

Why Fitzgerald was in Hollywood at all in the spring of 1927 had everything to do with wanting to make a quick buck. Like Govie before him, Fitzgerald had succumbed to the lure of a rich Hollywood payday, but this time it was a producer at United Artists, John Considine, who had dangled the bait. In return for a fat fee, Fitzgerald was to write a scenario for a film called *Lipstick*, which was intended as a star vehicle for actress Constance Talmage.

Scott and Zelda had taken up residence at the Ambassador Hotel on Wilshire Boulevard, where he was, in his words, "working like a dog"— an unfortunate language choice, given the episode at the Goldwyn party. The reception Fitzgerald's script for *Lipstick* ultimately received was about as warm as the response generated by his barking-dog act. John Considine rejected it and withheld the remaining money still due to Fitzgerald at script completion, proof once again that the silent era was not kind to writers who came to Hollywood armed with words.

There is one interesting side note about the intended star of *Lipstick*, Constance Talmadge. Right about the time Govie filed for divorce back in 1922, Talmadge also filed for divorce. Coincidence, you say? Not in the minds of some gossip columnists. Soon after, the following item found its way into print: "It has been rumored by the newspapers that Gouverneur Morris—also getting divorced about the same time—and Miss Constance Talmadge may become engaged." It gets better: "They are reported to have been seen together frequently in the past few months in and about Hollywood." While Constance Talmadge never became Mrs. Gouverneur Morris, nor was that ever more than the figment of some gossip columnist's imagination, she did begin the tradition, along with Mary Pickford, Douglas Fairbanks, and her sister, Norma Talmadge, of placing footprints in front of Grauman's Chinese Theatre.

Ruth and Govie had one other noteworthy encounter during their swing through the Southland. They met prizefighter Gene Tunney, whom Ruth found to be "beautiful to the eye and a personable lad," while never letting on for a second that she and Govie were die-hard supporters of Tunney's biggest professional rival, Jack Dempsey, a pal of theirs. Despite her personal loyalties, Ruth was her usual charming self as she chatted up the boxer.

She would not be smiling so warmly later in the year, however, when Gene Tunney beat Jack Dempsey to retain the heavyweight boxing title in a fight that is long remembered for the controversial "long count" in the seventh round. As Ruth could no doubt recount in detail, Dempsey caught Tunney with a punch that put him out on the canvas, but the referee delayed counting his time down because Dempsey had not moved to a neutral corner. After Tunney was down for ten seconds, the fight should have been over, but he was allowed to get up after thirteen seconds and continue, hence the "long count."

Veteran observers believe that overall Tunney outperformed Dempsey in the ring that night and despite the long count deserved the win. That was not an argument that sat well in the Morris household, however. Gene Tunney may have been a "personable lad," but as far as the Morrises were concerned, Jack Dempsey was robbed.

From Los Angeles, Ruth and Govie traveled to San Francisco on Southern Pacific's Coast Daylight, stopping over briefly in the city before returning home. The stopover gave Ruth just enough time to fire off a telegram:

San Francisco is desolate without you.

Ruth's plaintive message greeted Alec when he arrived home in London, and he promptly replied in kind:

Arrived in a London that might as well be empty.

Upon returning to Monterey and stepping into the foyer, Ruth's eyes were immediately drawn to a lovely bouquet of yellow roses, clearly a gift from a gentleman admirer. And who should that gentleman admirer turn out to be? The heavyweight champion of the world, Gene Tunney.

Quickly, though, Ruth's attention shifted to a letter and a telegram sitting alongside the flowers. It was the letter Alec had written during his transcontinental train trip to New York, and the telegram was the one he had sent from London. She hurried to her room so that she could carefully read them both. Miraculously her sense of desolation seemed to vanish, and she promptly penned a response on March 7, 1927:

> *Oh I am in such an ecstatic state, I'll <u>never</u> recover. When we reached home last night your train letter (my very first from you) was here, and the lonely cable from London. I feel so comforted by you. You seemed so far away, such a hopeless distance, and there a cable and flash, just like that. A sorcerer's trick surely brings you close. A heavenly consolation. I went to bed, cried a little, not much, and read Ecclesiastes (Why does love incline*

pagans toward religion?) and "Myself When Young," then
the Songs of Solomon, and some more "Myself When
Young," and I finished up with the dire and prophetic
Revelations, and went straight away to sleep.

Her language has all the earmarks of unconditional love. Except there turns out to be a condition Ruth slips in about halfway through:

If I'd married any other man in the world, except the
one that I did marry, why five minutes from now I'd
be sending you a cable asking you if you really want
me and if you answered favorably, I'd be off for London
tonight. It isn't that I don't love you. It will never be
that. But of one thing I am sure, and that is that you
understand the entire situation quite as well as I do.
There is some solace in that knowledge. But little. For I
want to be with you.

For Alec in London, the yellow caution light did not go unnoticed, but there was something about the many green lights in the letter that for the moment seemed to overshadow the yellow. He wasn't quite ready to heed its warning. Far from it, actually.

During the long journey across America and the Atlantic Ocean, much had been on Alec's mind, and one thing had become clear: he simply could not continue at his father's company, Chapman & Hall, any longer. It would be soul destroying and all but guarantee there would be no future with the redoubtable Mrs. Morris.

Telling his father that, however, was no easy task. Arthur Waugh adored his son and made no attempt to disguise the fact that Alec was his favorite, stoking Evelyn's resentment. Still, Alec felt he had to act, so he decided to come right out with it over dinner.

After father and son were seated, Alec began looking for the right opening to broach the subject, but before he could even get a word out, Arthur spoke up: "My dear boy, I can't tell you how glad I am to have you back. At the board meeting today, I was wondering how I could go on. It will be all so different now."

Alec let out a slow breath as he struggled to find the words he needed to say. After a moment he turned to his father, and he haltingly explained that he had decided to resign his directorship and leave the company. He paused and tried to read his father's reaction.

"But my dear boy, you can't. Leaving me all alone."

The *alone* part was the killer. Alec knew what he meant. Three important members of the firm had departed the previous year, and at the time Arthur had said, "It will make all the difference now that you are here."

This wasn't getting any easier for Alec, but he pressed on. He explained that it was not about the firm. None of this was work related. Then the whole story came out. Ruth. The rendezvous. Tahiti. That he had fallen in love.

Bemusement seemed to temper his father's disappointment as he responded, "It can't come to anything. How can it? She's married. She's an American. She won't want to be transplanted, nor will you."

Alec listened silently as his father continued, "You tell me her husband's a fine fellow. He's rich, he's prominent. She won't want to break up. In a year's time you'll have realized that, both of you!"

Arthur encouraged Alec to reserve any final action for a year or two and assured him that a leave of absence could be arranged. It was a fair and reasonable compromise, but as Alec later said, "There are times when one has to burn one's boats; and this was one of them." There would be no second thoughts. No leave of absence. No unburned boat.

With the issue settled, Alec sat down and wrote to Ruth. It was a complicated letter, not unlike some of Ruth's. Amid the expressions of love, there were some concerns and doubts. Arthur's message had seeped in.

At the close of her letter in response, Ruth spoke to Alec's concerns without really addressing them:

> *Five months is a long time. And I do wish you'd stop foretelling all the difficulties which will confront us when we are together on a small island. Do let me have my illusion to bolster me up for the next few months. My illusion does not permit of difficulties, and is entirely made*

*up of a lovely adventure. The realization will possibly
or probably be wretched enough, so why look forward
to that?*

*I've just read your letter again. It's a marvelous let-
ter. Oh, I'm grateful, and in love, and everything. I'm
unhappy too, because you are so far away.*
Love, Ruth

Aside from his letters, Ruth made a point of reading with care and
attention everything that Alec wrote, and her interest in his writing
and the insightful comments she would make about it played a significant role in winning Alec's heart. Their mutual love of literature built
an intimate bond between them, and for Ruth, Alec's writing was also
a window into his thoughts and feelings, some of which were a revelation to her. After reading *Kept* she would tell Alec, "I can't bear it that
you should write of women so (oh I don't know what I am trying to say)
with so much intimate knowledge."

The Morrises traveled down to La Quinta, near Palm Springs, for a
week that allowed Ruth to renew her love affair with horseback riding
and to commune with nature. She would, as she would later share in
a letter, go galloping "merrily for miles and miles across the desert" or
"roam around the desert on foot (with a sharp eye out for rattlesnakes)
picking up bright colored pebbles." On these little expeditions, she was
"accompanied by two yapping dogs, Jim and Napoleon," who couldn't
resist chasing "jack rabbits and kangaroo rats."

Her time in the desert, dressed in "chapereros and spurs, fancy
shirt and gay handkerchief," seemed to mellow her out, and not once
did she reach for a glass of gin.

When Ray Long, William Randolph Hearst's right-hand man,
learned the Morrises were in the desert, he and W. R. traveled down
to meet with them, and Ruth was able to report that she had made
progress on her Prohibition book but that she had a good ways to go.

At about the same time in London, Alec was wrapping up one final
piece of business for Chapman & Hall. His sojourn in the South Pacific
had not been devoted solely to leisure and love. He had made an interesting discovery: a promising author. It had been totally random, out of

the blue. As he was wandering around the island of Tahiti one day, he happened upon a gentleman running an errand on his bicycle. The two exchanged greetings and ended up having a pleasant chat. When Alec discovered that the man was a writer, he pursued the issue further, and before Alec departed, he had obtained the British rights to his stories. That turns out to have been a smart move on Alec's part. Prescient, even. The man on the bicycle turned out to be James Norman Hall, the future coauthor with Charles Nordhoff of the classic *Mutiny on the Bounty*.

Back in Monterey, the Morrises had embarked on a spring remodeling of their mansion, adding new rooms to display oil paintings from Spain by Roberto Domingo, the artist whose work is featured on the first-edition cover of Hemingway's *Death in the Afternoon*, and Ignacio Zuloaga, an important early influence on Diego Rivera, and charcoal drawings from the Morrises' personal friend Francis McComas, about whom Govie would say, "Neither among the etchings of Rembrandt nor Whistler nor the note books of Hokusai is there anything more beautiful than the McComas charcoals." Everywhere Ruth turned there seemed to be "carpenters, plumbers, painters and electricians" disrupting her life, and doing so loudly.

Amid the clatter, she pressed on with her Prohibition book, which she was now intending to call *Dry Circus*, thanks to the suggestion of writer H. L. Mencken, who kept writing Ruth with suggestions. Sinclair Lewis weighed in with his own advice as well, and of course Govie joined in with the chorus.

In May, Francis McComas confirmed that he would join Ruth and Govie on their trip to Tahiti, news Ruth quickly relayed to Alec. From Ruth's perspective, it was all good. Francis would be devoting his time to painting watercolors, and Govie would devote his time to watching Francis paint. With Govie otherwise engaged, Ruth would be free to see Alec without fear of discovery.

However, there was one moment of panic for Ruth late in May when Govie received a cable from Max Blake, the American consul general in Tangier, Morocco, inviting the Morrises to be his guests for the summer, effectively knocking Tahiti off their itinerary, but Govie wanted to do it. With her romantic rendezvous in jeopardy, Ruth quickly went into full damage-control mode and successfully sold him off of the idea.

Meanwhile in London, Alec Waugh was planning a mid-June departure from Marseilles, France, on the French cargo ship *Louqsor* for a six-week journey to Tahiti that would take him, ironically, right past Tangier, Morocco, so close to shore he would be able to see "on the left, high on the cliff, the white and blue houses of Tangier," a memory he would not forget.

When Ruth realized that Alec would be essentially unreachable for several weeks, she sent him one last cable on June 8, 1927:

Don't be depressed be glad that time is flying.
Ruth

Time didn't exactly fly over the next two months, but finally, in August, the moment of departure was close at hand.

On the night before they left for San Francisco, Ruth, Govie, and Francis were special guests at a party at the Lodge in Pebble Beach that also honored writer Anita Loos and her husband, John Emerson, which would have made for an interesting evening. Anita Loos, who stood not quite five feet tall, was something of a human dynamo. She was bursting with story ideas, seemed to know everyone in Hollywood, and by all accounts was a kick to be around.

By 1927 she was probably best known for writing *Gentlemen Prefer Blondes*, which became a Broadway show and a motion picture multiple times, including a version starring Marilyn Monroe and Jane Russell.

Something else that might have intrigued the Morrises was that the Dorothy Shaw character from the book and movie—think Jane Russell—was based on a composite of Anita Loos herself and her close friend Constance Talmadge. That would be the same Constance Talmadge who had once been romantically linked to Govie in a gossip column.

Suffice to say there would have been lots to talk about that evening, but Ruth might have been preoccupied. At that moment she had other things on her mind.

The following day, August 10, 1927, Ruth, Govie, and Francis boarded the RMS *Tahiti* for the week-and-a-half voyage to French Polynesia. On the fifth day out to sea, Ruth would celebrate her thirtieth birthday, complete with a cake, decorations, and some warm champagne. It was a temporary distraction for Ruth from her mounting worries.

Was this all a mistake? A huge mistake?

The time for such worries was long past over, however. The ship had already sailed. In more ways than one.

CHAPTER TWELVE

NINE PERFECT DAYS

Ruth Morris now had exactly what she wanted. Or what she thought she wanted. Alec Waugh had uprooted his life in London and traveled halfway round the world to be with her. In a place that was about as close to paradise as you could find on Planet Earth in the year 1927. And Ruth was losing her nerve. She had sparked a wildfire, and now she wasn't sure how to control it. She had wanted a controlled burn, but that works better with natural vegetation than human emotions.

For his part Alec had already arrived on the island of Tahiti and settled into a beach cabana at a hotel along the coast, roughly halfway between Papeete and a private residence located eighteen miles south of the capital, where Ruth and Govie were to stay with friends. Strategically it was a spot well chosen. Even more so because one of Ruth's friends from San Francisco, Lorraine Haskevitch, just happened to be staying at the same hotel, giving Ruth a built-in excuse to visit any old time, a coincidence that sounds suspiciously like something right out of the Ruth Morris playbook.

The arrangement offered something else right out of the playbook: a third-party go-between. The ship's steward had served that role on the *Lochgoil*, and now Lorraine seemed poised to pick up where the ship's steward had left off.

Once Ruth had arrived at the property of Eastham and Caroline Guild (rhymes with *wild*) and unpacked, she sat down and penned a note to Alec:

> *Friday morning—ah Alec—it's centuries since I've seen you. My nerves now are completely on edge. If twenty-four hours away from you can do this to me, whatever will happen during the months we have to face alone. If only we never met, never, it would have been so much better.*
>
>   *What <u>can</u> we do? I love you—love you.*
> *R*

They had met, of course. Now they were both on the same small island in the middle of the South Pacific, less than ten miles apart. Their reunion was inevitable and imminent. And it would be charged.

After all the waiting and the worry and the tension and the fear, Ruth Morris and Alec Waugh finally found themselves together on a settee outside the Mariposa Café in the port city of Papeete, and any hope of maintaining a proper, respectable social distance between them rather quickly dissolved into a long, slow, passionate kiss. Yes, they had talked, too. But all that quickly receded into the background as Ruth closed her eyes and surrendered to Alec's lips.

During the eighteen-mile drive back to the Guilds', those moments played in her head like a Technicolor movie trailer, and later she poured out her feelings in a letter to Alec:

> *Darlingest,*
> *It's been a big day and I'm tired. But I cannot rest until you know this. I've never loved before. Only guessed at what the real thing could be. Now I know and I'm miserable, and blissfully happy. There's no use at all in thinking about the future. We have the present. Furtive and uncertain, but glorious.*
>
>   *I don't know why you love me. But if you do, and you have said that you do, it's because of whatever*

slight character the years have created. It would destroy
that character if I were to leave Govie, he's been stead-
fastly generous and kind. But at this precise and exact
moment I should cut and run and go away with you
forever.

I love kissing you. You've a young mouth. Younger
than the stately twenty-nine years. And you <u>are</u> young,
darling, exquisitely so. And shouldn't an elderly lady
say such things to a young man.

Lorraine is leaving this moment. I'll see you in the
morning.
All of my love,
Ruth

Ruth was trying to get the burn back under control, but she also intended to keep seeing Alec when she could. The trick was going to be integrating her visits with Alec into the natural flow of her other activities. She did have obligations. To Govie, of course, but also to her hosts, the Guilds, who were both gracious and full of interesting tales.

Just the story of their house, Te Anuanua, was fascinating. It started with a plot of land along the south coast overlooking a placid lagoon that was covered with dense tropical vegetation, including coconut trees and thousands of colorful acacias. *Unbuildable,* the locals cried, as they shook their collective heads at the folly of these silly Americans. Undaunted, the Guilds pressed on, and with the help of native laborers, they were able to hack through the greenery to carve out a building site. But that was just step one.

Step two was to construct by hand their dream house. It took time and even more toil, as the Guilds attempted to work with a building crew unfamiliar with the principle that you measure twice and cut once, a crew that had the unsettling habit of splitting off into angry factions and not speaking to one another for periods of time. There was a crisis over water and a legal wrangle that followed, and it just seemed to be one damned thing after another.

Still, by some miracle the house was finally standing, was livable, and had a source of water, and the Guilds could celebrate. They had just one final important step left: to give their dream home the perfect name. Simply asking for ideas did not do the trick, but offering rum as an incentive brought ideas flying in from all over the island. Ultimately, though, it was an old man, originally from Corsica, who found just the right name: *Te Anuanua*, or "the rainbow with a pot of golden happiness at the end."

Once settled, the Guilds found new ways to keep life interesting. Eastham Guild—or Ham, as everyone called him—decided that French Polynesia needed more birds. Lots more birds. The answer to him was simple: import them. What followed was the creation of a huge import operation that brought in new bird species from around the world and either added a lively new element to the islands or screwed up the ecosystem, depending upon your perspective.

Caroline Guild had a decidedly different interest: deep-sea fishing. While her husband was filling up the islands with little creatures, Caroline was busy reeling in some big ones at sea.

Maybe their most noteworthy achievement was one for which they shared responsibility: giving the mai tai, the popular and lethal cocktail, its name. The source for this bit of trivia is none other than legendary restaurateur Victor "Trader Vic" Bergeron.

No doubt Ruth enjoyed her time with the Guilds, but she was a bit preoccupied. Still, she had to keep up appearances, not only as a gracious guest but also as a loving wife, obliging her to avoid deviating from her normal patterns of behavior, lest she trigger Govie's suspicions. When invitations arrived for social engagements from around the island, and many did, she would dutifully play the role of the attentive spouse.

The odd man out in all of this was Alec. He almost never knew in advance when Ruth was coming, so he found himself just hanging around the hotel waiting, feeling like "an Edwardian mistress, tucked away in a small house on Acacia Road to be visited when a busy man could find the time for her." Only the sound of Ruth toot-tooting her horn as she pulled up at the hotel unannounced would lift his spirits.

Alec did get out and about at times, even attending social gatherings where Govie was present, occasions that were as awkward as might be imagined, with Alec always careful to act like a friend around Ruth and nothing more.

Govie's reactions to these circumstances were surprisingly tempered. Yes, he was probably curious or mildly suspicious about Alec's presence on the island, but he was a fairly self-confident man. He normally didn't feel threatened by the solicitous behavior of other men toward his wife. Govie's typical response was to lather on the charm, leaving the man in question disarmed, intimidated, or both.

Which is not to say Govie did not have his limits. Ruth did manage to overplay her hand a bit on one occasion, earning Govie's ire, as she relayed in a letter to Alec:

> *Dear,*
>
> *I have made a first class idiot out of myself a great many times. Last night was the "apek." Instead of waiting to discuss calmly the subject of going home, I drank much too much and became offensive. Francis accused me of over-fondness for you. I not only admitted it. I boasted. And Govie was furious.*
>
> *When I woke up this morning everybody had gone to town. Even the Guilds. So I am sitting here alone not knowing what is happening, and caring very little. I'm sorry I was drunk last night. Very sorry that I used vile language. Otherwise I am more or less serene in mind and soul. I hope that if Govie chucks me out he will allow it to be decently managed. That I can go home quickly and quietly, and there separate and uproot the mutual ties with the least possible damage.*
>
> *Oh my dearest, <u>Will</u> you be good to me? <u>Always,</u>*
> *Ruth*

Govie wasn't going to chuck Ruth out. That just wasn't going to happen. He was much too fond of her to do anything that rash, and besides, he fundamentally trusted her. Everyone did. She had this quality of utter guilelessness about her that led people to trust her implicitly. She could tell them anything, and they would believe it. For Govie, the idea that she would ever be unfaithful was probably inconceivable to him. Flirtatious? Sure. Overfriendly? Sometimes. But anything more than that he could not have imagined.

Besides, he was at that very moment in the process of strengthening the bonds that tied him to Ruth: he was shopping for the perfect island-paradise second home. In an area known as Paea near the Guild property, he found just what he was looking for: a thirty-acre plantation, featuring a two-story house surrounded by coconut palms.

The only potential stumbling block was cost, which might seem surprising given the fortune Govie had inherited. The problem was the Morrises' burn rate. Money was flowing out faster than it was flowing in, and their current spending habits were becoming increasingly unsustainable.

This was 1927, however. Babe Ruth was on his way to sixty home runs. Charles Lindbergh had just flown solo over the Atlantic. And investments in the stock market were piling up like a high-stakes baccarat game in Monte Carlo. Everyone from cab drivers to bank presidents wanted to get his or her bet down, as the belief continued to grow that the old rules no longer applied. Call it irrational exuberance or what you will, the Morrises were not immune to this go-go fever that was sweeping the land, and Govie made an offer on the property.

Meanwhile, Ruth's resistance to Alec's entreaties began to melt away. As she settled into the languid rhythms of Polynesia, her desires seemed to drive out her doubts. The writer with the "young mouth" was becoming more temptation than she could resist, and finally she signaled complete surrender.

> *Dearest, I <u>was</u> drunk last night. I'm sorry. It's the first time in years that my legs have been wobbly. It won't happen often.*
>
> *We are, as I said before, exactly like lovers in Russian novels. Talk . . . Talk . . . Talk . . . Talk, and never any action. We never get anywhere. You are frightened of the responsibility. In fact you have a most inflated idea about the state of luxury to which I am accustomed. Govie isn't rich, and we live quite simply*

at home with two servants and an excellent gardener. You feel however that the sheer happiness of being with you would not compensate me for the abandoning of whatever I now have. My own fear, worry and reticence is based on much more logical and humane facts. A great many years ago Govie and myself decided to cast our lot together. We had no home, no ties, and very little except mutual trust in each other to go on. Govie has made one home for me, is now in the act of making another. He has given me a splendid chance to meet the amusing people in this world. He has, in America and Europe, taken me, a small person with no dignity whatever, and given me a dignified position. In America, it is of no consequence whether I'm drunk or sober, or how much I chase around at night. I still have the title of 'the virtuous wife' that pleases me. And it pleases Govie even more.

Until now Govie has had the most perfect confidence in me. It would probably hurt him most terribly if anything shook that confidence. And I'm determined not to hurt him. He hasn't earned that. I do love you. Love you almost beyond being. But no happiness could come from our love if we'd hurt something fine and decent.

I love you so much that I must have you. But because of Govie I must have you furtively and with a sense of quiet and shame. A sorry business. I cannot however see any other solution. Can you?

I don't want anyone in the world to know that I would be unfaithful to my husband. Not even Lorraine. Not ever. If we wait until my family goes to another island I know no one will ever know. But you aren't making the wait easy. If casually and naturally I can spend an evening in town alone, it will be splendid. But I will not face such an evening over Govie's objections.

God knows I feel sufficiently like a filthy, plotting cur as
it is.
Do you love me? Truly?
Ruth

With exquisite good timing, Francis McComas decided to travel over to Moorea, just twelve miles across the channel, to paint. As Ruth had predicted some months earlier, Govie went with him so that he could sit and watch and generally hang out with his buddy Frank. They would be gone for nine days.

Nine days. That was all Ruth and Alec had. Nine days. But after waiting six months, those nine days proved glorious. Hollywood at its most inventive could not have conceived a setting more magical. Here they were in French Polynesia at Alec's cabana on the beach, with the hauntingly beautiful silhouette of Moorea's otherworldly contour as a backdrop across the channel.

Now, at last, they could make love. Urgently. Deliriously. Unabashedly. They swam in the warm, aqua blue waters. They quietly and intently read each other poetry. They lazily hunted for shells on the beach. They talked and talked and talked. Secret thoughts. Intimate desires. Nagging fears.

Alone in their own private kingdom, they found a purple crab alone in his own little coral kingdom, and he became their pal. Then they went off by themselves for a picnic. And they talked some more.

Alec would later say of his time with Ruth on the beach, "I felt that I had been vouchsafed a vision, a revelation of the wonder and mystery of life, and of the ultimate purpose that lay behind all living. Life was not, after all, the pouring of so much water through a sieve. There was a meaning to existence; a goal unperceived but apprehended; not knowledge but intuition; a basic certainty of soul."

Ruth and Alec talked of running off together. Vanishing. Never to be heard from again. Alec recalled the beautiful sights he had recently seen in Morocco, and they vowed they would make a new life for themselves in a "white house in Tangier." It was a lovely illusion, but there were no ships coming anytime soon. And even if there were, Ruth had no passport of her own but rather relied on Govie's. The truth was that they were on an island far off in the South Pacific with no realistic means of escape.

Instead they fantasized of a future rendezvous. Ruth shared the story of Alexander Moore, her friend the United States ambassador in Spain. For twenty years, Moore waited to marry his great love Lillian Russell. Twice she had married other people. Still he waited. Finally, Moore became her fourth and final husband. They had a few good years together before she died, and for Ruth, their story was the proof that anything was possible.

Slowly, however, the rude reminders of reality began to creep in. Their time was running out. Govie and Francis were due back. It had been a blessed moment in time that neither would ever forget. Then it was over, and Ruth was consumed with guilt.

Alec dear—the rain is pouring down. It has a cumulative effect of melancholy. And I am depressed beyond all measure. I couldn't sleep last night, and not even for a little while. And I spent all of the rain beaten hours in a morbid and scathing orgy of self analysis, which ended up in a suicidal mood. I think, Alec, that in this entire affair, I've become melancholy, and without honor. When I married I was not a child, and knew perfectly well what I was letting myself in for. Knew perfectly well what I was promising. And to give myself some small credit, at the time I probably believed in the very depths of my small black heart that I was going to excel as a virtuous and model wife. There seems no atonement that I can make to Govie for what I have done. No atonement to you. And I cannot acquit myself in my own eyes. Even with you, Alec, I've not dealt honorably. I'm patient about a place in the country, a flat in town, a pleasant life together. Knowing all of the time that I would not, could not, leave Govie. Knowing that the long companionship with him has taken deep roots, and that the uprooting would tear from me every solitary chance for happiness. And in the last month I've risked that companionship, that complete understanding and tolerance, risked the loss of it recklessly, as if it meant nothing to me at all. And oh Alec, it does. I'm bad to Govie so often, needlessly cruel, and then afterwards I am so contrite of heart, and would love to crawl on my hands and knees and beg for forgiveness, beg for punishment, and some sacrifice that could balance the whole hopelessly uneven score. But I never do. I just get more defiant, and less approachable.

Of course I'll go on risking everything, because I love you. Loving you is the one thing that I'm not sorry for. I can't help that. It isn't my fault and I'll go on loving you, happily and unhappily. That is beyond my power to control. Perhaps even for a little space of time. But while that love endures, it is steadfast and sincere. If only I could be free! I will be, some day, but by that time I might be so old that you wouldn't want me.

It's a dreadful complication isn't it? When I'm with you I forget all that, and am blissfully content. When I'm home, where I belong, with Govie then I'm miserable and want to wear sackcloth and ashes, and be stoned to death like a first class biblical adulteress (Not a pretty word that).

I'll be driving down this afternoon, to get my make-up. I may not have a chance to talk to you, but I'll give this letter to Lorraine to deliver. Please don't feel badly about this. I'm feeling badly enough to suffice for both of us. Govie's kindness, continual and unselfish, is heaping plenty of the proverbial coals of fire on my small head. And oh beloved, it isn't easy to go from the lover's arms to the husband's arms, without a contrition of heart and soul that is an acute pain.

I cannot see ahead. I'm not even trying to. But I am trying to be fair to both of you, and it just isn't possible. One can't cheat at games and perhaps one can't cheat

at life. But isn't it life after all, dear dear love, life that
does the monstrous cheating.
I do love you so
Ruth

Ruth had entered a strange limbo. She seems to have allowed things to go further than she had intended, and though those nine days had been delicious, she remained as confused about how to sort out her life as ever. She continued to see Alec when she could, but it all felt so tentative and uncertain.

In one of her letters to Alec during this period, she revealed how lost she felt, as she talked about her younger self, in the third person:

> *That was the Ruth you deserved, and should have had.*
> *She was a person as apart from me as Chaplin is from*
> *his screen character. He knew her, and he'll bear me out*
> *in the story. I viewed her inevitable departure with a*
> *twinge of melancholy. She didn't last long . . .*
>
> *You would have loved the other Ruth more, but this*
> *is the one you've got. And you must love her always . . .*

As Ruth continued to struggle with her feelings, a glass of gin became an ever more frequent companion, and one night, possibly under the influence of "liquid courage," Ruth had what she called "the talk" with Govie. It did not go well. From the moment she first raised the subject of a trial separation, the idea was doomed. She was playing a weak hand going in, and Govie called her bluff rather forcefully. She was, he said, "selfish" and a "spoiled brat." There were to be no more scenes, he asserted, no more drama. Ruth would either start behaving like a proper wife or "there would be the devil to pay."

Ruth, who could be brave in so many ways, wilted under the assault. Any thought she might have had of leaving Govie for Alec quickly flickered out.

All that was left now of the rendezvous in Tahiti was the moment of departure. The next ship bound for San Francisco was scheduled to leave soon, and Francis McComas planned to be on it. He had a wife,

Gene, waiting patiently for him back on the Monterey Peninsula, and he wished to hurry home.

Alec Waugh planned to be on the same ship. It was time, he concluded, to return to England. Ruth and Govie meanwhile would remain for an additional month on Tahiti, finalizing the paperwork for the purchase of their new plantation in Paea.

With the day of his departure fast approaching, Ruth sent Alec one final message:

> My darling Alec,
> Some day, sooner (I hope) or later our two lives will no
> longer be two lives, but one and in the dark raid that
> must be endured (decently I hope also), there will be no
> thought in all my mind's vast hall except about you.
> This is a bad day, Alec,
> I love you

Those last moments when the ship pulled away from the dock in Papeete left a vivid impression on Alec: "I was tortured now by the slow drawn agony of the good-bye. . . . I saw Ruth rise from her table on the balcony. She came down on the quay; she waved, then stood there, watching the ship move slowly to the gap. Her features were distinct no longer. She turned away, trailing a white parasol."

As the RMS *Makura* sailed off for its journey to San Francisco, Ruth was now feeling quite alone. Her dream of a grand romantic rendezvous with Alec on the island of Tahiti had all come true. But like all dreams, it did not last.

Finally, in late November, Ruth and Govie boarded the ship to San Francisco. Having closed the deal on the coconut plantation, they had made Tahiti something of a second home, and they would end up returning a number of times, producing many memories. But for Ruth, there was one memory that belonged in a category all by itself: nine days. Nine perfect days.

Alone on the beach. With Alec Waugh.

CHAPTER THIRTEEN

THE JUGGLING ACT

One thing became clear as Ruth Morris's rendezvous in French Polynesia drew to its somber end: Ruth was not Anna Karenina. She was not prepared to risk everything to be with Alec Waugh. She wanted Alec but not at the expense of her marriage.

That's not saying it hadn't been a close call in Tahiti. Those nine days on the beach pushed Ruth about as close as she would ever come to running off with her Count Vronsky, but when Alec's ship sailed out of Papeete Harbor with Ruth remaining back on the quay, any doubt was then removed.

As Ruth arrived back in San Francisco a month later, she was still very much Mrs. Gouverneur Morris, but one thing had changed: Ruth had added two years to her age. When she passed through customs, she listed her age as thirty-two. The previous February, she had written her correct age at the time, which was twenty-nine. She had celebrated her thirtieth birthday in August, but somehow as she crossed the international date line, she became two years older.

But why? Did she wish to narrow the age gap between herself and Govie? Was she trying to justify her claims that she was so much older than Alec? Her motives remain a mystery, but her birth records in Falconer, New York, are quite clear that she was born in 1897. That would put her correct age in the fall of 1927 at thirty. What's more, she never relinquished those two bonus years. Right up to the end of her life, even her husband thought she was two years older than she actually was.

The fudge in her age came at a time when Ruth began fudging a few other things as well. Particularly when she shared stories about her younger, braver self, she would exaggerate a bit. Like the fish that grows bigger with each retelling, the age at which she learned to fly seemed to get younger and younger, and then there was the tale of the bullring in Spain, which would now end with her killing the bull, a nonsensical claim. It's sad and regrettable, because the real stories are impressive enough, but with each passing year Ruth became more haunted by disappointment and regret.

Meanwhile, her balancing act remained unchanged: Govie was her husband, and Alec was her lover. Then things got more complicated. Personal letters awaited her at the St. Francis hotel that she had not been expecting. Letters that threatened to turn her love triangle into three-dimensional chess. The sender? Howard Barnes, aka the Lad. He was giving her a heads-up that he would be in San Francisco soon and expressed a desire to see her.

This Ruth really didn't need, and her first instinct was avoidance. She would return to Monterey, lay low until Howard had come and gone, and just pray that he didn't come down to Monterey looking for her and make a scene.

While Ruth was trying to figure out how to juggle the men in her life, Govie was busy expounding on the current state of marriage in America to a local reporter. It was "breaking down," he asserted. It had become just too easy to get a divorce, the previously divorced author declared, and the essential morality associated with marriage, he argued, "seems to have little significance to Americans at large." But Govie offered assurance that this growing attitude about marriage had not found its way into the Morris household: "Mrs. Morris and I are very happy. We always have been happy."

It's hard not to imagine that Ruth's recent talk of separation prompted this particular line of commentary and that the intended audience was at least in part Mrs. Morris. Whether Ruth read it that way, she certainly sensed the irony in his comments, prompting her to cut the article out of the newspaper when it appeared and send it to Alec without comment.

Once she had some time alone, Ruth dashed off her first letter to Alec, following what had been "a ghastly voyage," and filled it mostly with gossip about the trip.

Later that same night she took pen to paper once again because she felt the need to "write a little more." The "little more" can be summed up in one line from the letter: "It's about the lad." She went on to explain how Howard Barnes had reappeared in her life. How shocked and surprised she had been about the whole thing. How she had no obligation to tell Alec any of this but felt she should. And then she closed with the kind of mixed message that was becoming her trademark: "He had a glamour. And it's over. So it doesn't matter. Nothing is of any importance except that I love you, and cannot be with you. My love forever, Ruth."

If that didn't leave Alec confused enough, once Ruth was back in Monterey, she got it into her head that she wanted to see him again. As soon as possible. He was in London. She was in Monterey. It would require ships and trains traveling halfway around the world to satisfy this whim, but that did not faze her. A letter quickly went out, and here are some excerpts:

> Dear Alec,
> Home again to the sweetest, most intimate and friendly little house in all America. Mickey gave a great exhibition. He enthused for a great while like a dog, then flung himself into my arms, and hugged me for three minutes. Huge clumsy bear.
>
> Three letters and a wire from you. The letter from the boat, dear, I loved. The other two were depressing. You frighten me. For if you really feel so despairing and unhappy you'll be sure to find some diversion for yourself, and I can't bear the thought. . . .
>
> Gene dined with us last night. She liked you, but was damnably inquisitive. She told me she thought you'd come over for the polo tournament if you were

properly coaxed. Would you? I think it will be sometime in the later part of February—it will last all throughout March. It will be splendid, for every worthwhile player in the world will be there. . . .

Dearest, the moment the date is firmly set for the tournament, I'll cable you. Then you might let me know what you really intend to do. You could get back to England in time for your silly croquet games couldn't you? Or is it ping-pong that you daren't miss. If you do come out, it will be only three months. Three centuries . . .
I love you
Ruth

Ruth's invitation created a quandary for Alec. He "lived for her letters and her cables," but he also knew nothing had changed. Ruth was still married to Govie, and if she wouldn't leave him in Tahiti, why would it be any different now? And there was that other little complication: the Lad, with his insufferable "glamour." The mere mention of the guy's name provoked pangs of jealousy in Alec.

The wise, sensible course of action, he knew, was to stay home and begin the long, painful process of getting over her. When it came to Ruth, however, wise and sensible never seemed to rule the day. Alec was deeply in love, in both the best and the worst senses of the word, and he simply was not ready to or even capable of making rational decisions about anything pertaining to Ruth.

Still, he was determined to shift the balance of power in the relationship. That was the plan, anyway. He decided he needed to be more assertive. He needed to draw lines and take stands. No longer would he jump whenever she snapped her fingers. This would be the new Alec.

Yes, he would come to California as she requested, but that was where he drew the line. Ruth had to meet him in San Francisco. He insisted upon it. Then he would ask her to run off with him to Hawaii, as delusory as that clearly was.

The real test for Alec, though, would be whether she showed up in San Francisco. If she didn't, that would tell him everything he needed to know, and he would sail on to Hawaii alone. It was all or nothing for him at this point.

Meanwhile in California, Ruth was still trying to figure out how to deal with Howard Barnes. Should she ignore him? Should she talk to him? Or should she let one of her friends do her dirty work for her? At one point, it appeared she had a volunteer. Her friend Mrs. Brownell was fully prepared to meet Howard when his ship arrived in San Francisco and deliver the news to his face that the affair with Ruth was over.

Then second thoughts crept in. Mrs. Brownell, it turns out, had a soft spot for Howard and his situation. She was an incurable romantic and could not bring herself to deliver the bad news.

All this, of course, begs the question: Wasn't the affair with Ruth already over, done, finito? The answer is yes and no. For all practical purposes it was over. Ruth had not run off with Howard. They had not seen each other in almost two years, and their only real contact was by mail. Still, Ruth had continued to maintain a relationship with him simply by corresponding with him. But then it was entirely on her terms, and she no doubt enjoyed the attention of having a handsome young man continue to express interest in her. She could have stopped answering his letters or forcefully stated that it was truly over. But she never did.

Now, though, he was close at hand, and she finally decided she had to face him once more in person. So it was that with a mixture of curiosity and dread Ruth headed back up to San Francisco to meet the Lad.

The Howard Barnes she encountered was two years older, as handsome as ever, and angrier than she had ever seen him. Who was this Alec Waugh? he wanted to know. And what was this about him being with her in Tahiti?

Ruth tried to answer, but he cut her off.

"You broke my heart."

She still couldn't get a word in.

"I went away believing that you would be a real wife to Govie, in loyalty to me, to us, and then I hear that you are playing fast and loose again."

Ruth quietly heard him out, and when he had finished venting, she responded. It was true. She and Alec had been in Tahiti together, and yes, they did have a relationship. With that admission, the disarming of Howard had begun. Ruth didn't get defensive but instead smothered him with candor.

All the while, Ruth found herself being reminded of the qualities that had attracted her to Howard in the first place. There were the looks, of course, and the voice, and the razor-sharp wit. It would have taken very little for her to throw caution to the wind right then and there with the Lad, but she was already trying to dial things back with Alec. She didn't need any more complications.

She reaffirmed that she still cared for him and wanted him to be a part of her life, to keep writing to her, to keep checking in. At the same time, she reiterated that Alec was important to her as well, but the most important thing he had to understand was that she was still "a real wife to Govie." Neither he nor Alec was going to change that. Howard seemed mollified, and Ruth had gotten essentially what she wanted. A gentleman admirer would continue giving her attention, and little would be required in return.

For the moment, at least, her juggling act had gotten a little less complicated.

CHAPTER FOURTEEN

CONTROLLING
THE BURN

With the Howard Barnes situation sorted out, Ruth Morris turned her attention to Alec Waugh's impending arrival. Why had she invited him? What was she thinking? To be sure, Ruth had genuine feelings for Alec, but to summon him to California, after reaffirming her commitment to Govie, seems almost cruel. The guy was utterly besotted with her, and she seems to have been just leading him on.

Making matters worse, she intended to handle Alec roughly the same way she had handled the Lad, recalibrating their relationship back to a pre-nine-days-on-the-beach state: less than lovers but more than friends. Why she thought Alec would be remotely satisfied with that arrangement is hard to imagine.

Equally hard to imagine is why Alec seriously thought Ruth would run off with him to Hawaii. As it was, whatever romantic fantasies he might have been harboring were rather quickly dashed when he arrived at the St. Francis hotel and inquired after Ruth. "No, there was no message." Had she been there recently? "She had not been in town for several days." Unstated, of course, was that her last visit had been to see the Lad.

Alec now faced the moment of truth. Did he sail off alone to Hawaii like some stoic character from the movies? Or did he pick up the phone and complete the surrender? He picked up the phone.

When he reached Ruth in Monterey, she politely informed him that Marcella Gump, the woman he had met at the Asian art store during his first visit to San Francisco, would be bringing him down on the afternoon train. The daughter of a prominent San Francisco family, Marcella was a popular socialite and frequent presence in the local newspapers. When heartbreak struck, as it often did, it was Ruth Morris's shoulder she would cry on, so when Ruth needed a favor, as with Alec, Marcella was the first one she would call.

She soon arrived at the St. Francis, where she found a rather glum Alec Waugh waiting for her patiently. She was, to his eyes, "a little plump, white-skinned, with long-lashed lustrous eyes, and an amusing birdlike way of putting her head on to one side and looking up and smiling."

"Are you going to give me a drink?"

"How do I do that here?"

"Call this number."

Ten minutes later a bottle of Prohibition-grade gin was delivered to Alec in a brown paper bag for which he paid ten bucks cash.

"Where do we drink it?

"I'll show you."

Marcella then took him behind a curtain that discretely separated part of the hotel coffee shop, and there they enjoyed their gin in peace.

Later that afternoon they caught the Del Monte Express for the ride down to Monterey. From the Southern Pacific station located down by the beach, it was only a short drive to the Spanish-style mansion that Ruth had described to him in letters and conversations but that he was now experiencing in person for the first time.

There would be no long, slow, passionate kiss upon meeting Ruth this time. Instead everything was polite and cordial, just the tone you would expect when friends meet, but then Ruth did not greet Alec at the door alone. Mr. Morris was by her side, and he would join Ruth, Alec, and Marcella for the initial drinks and conversation in the living room with its black-and-white rug, floor-to-ceiling bookcase, and open fireplace. What Govie thought about the young British author appearing once again is anybody's guess, but he seems to have sized up Alec and deemed him not a threat.

On paper, the Monterey Peninsula would seem an ideal location for a romantic reunion. It was and still is a delightful little community with a natural beauty and historic heritage that has inspired artists and writers for generations. And the Peninsula had proved the perfect spot for Robert Louis Stevenson to win the hand in marriage of his future wife, Fanny.

However, a romantic reunion did not appear to be Ruth's objective. In fact, it's not clear exactly what her objective was for luring Alec to California. She did not plan to sleep with him, "young mouth" or no, and she certainly wasn't going to run off with him at this point. Yet she still thrilled at being the object of so much adoration, and she thrived on the intimacy of their correspondence and the romantic fantasy it seemed to perpetuate.

Having Alec with her now in California, however, seemed to make things more complicated, because he had arrived with a certain set of expectations, and she kept trying to dampen them. Almost the first words to come out of her mouth when they were finally alone were "the Lad," which had the predictable effect of killing the moment and stoking a point of contention that simmered for almost his entire stay.

There was also the issue that the schedule Ruth had contrived for his visit seemed to insure they would have little or no time together alone, despite the fact that he was staying in the guesthouse on the Morris property. One minute they were off to Pebble Beach for the polo tournament. Then it was over to Cypress Point to watch golf. And there was one cocktail party after another.

Everything was in groups. The cast might vary, but there was always a crowd. It was lively. It was social. It was about as different from being on a private beach in Tahiti as you could get. And Ruth was completely in her element. Just as she was at ease in the presence of kings and dukes, she was equally skilled at navigating the social world of the local elite. Often Alec was left on the sidelines, where he could only marvel at her performance: "She was the centre of every party, yet she never dominated the scene. Other women liked her. She was interested in everyone, wanted to know what each new acquaintance was about."

Her public persona, however, masked a growing problem: her drinking, which was becoming excessive. It in no way diminished her skills in the social arena, but in private, particularly with Alec, the alcohol made things more difficult. When they had disagreements, her contrariness seemed to increase as her blood alcohol level rose, and there was one issue that seemed to be at the root of the tension. Ruth summed it up for Alec this way: "I love Govie. I'm in love with you. I'm fascinated by 'the lad.'" What had been an impossible situation remained so, and nothing that happened in Monterey seemed to change the dynamic.

Despite it all, however, as Alec's stay drew to a close, Ruth and Alec softened toward each other. Or as Alec put it: "The gold came back into her voice." They ended up in each other's arms, and their embrace dissolved once again into a long, slow, passionate kiss.

Still, as he left, Alec's inner voice whispered to him, "I adore her utterly; but never again . . . never, never again."

Meanwhile, Ruth and Govie were off to Southern California to spend a week with Mr. Hearst and Marion at their beach house. Over the course of the week, they got a daily dose of Charlie Chaplin, who would drop by to hang out and was, in Ruth's words, "the usual whimsical clown." There was much talk about Tahiti, and Charlie seemed quite enamored of the idea of going along with Ruth and Govie on their next trip to Tahiti. However, they politely demurred. An extended stay at their plantation with Charlie Chaplin may have been more "whimsical clown" than they were up for.

Meanwhile the flow of letters back and forth across the Atlantic between Ruth and Alec never slackened, though Alec was having an increasingly hard time coping with their closer-than-friends-but-not-quite-lovers relationship. Still, Ruth was a haunting and perpetual presence in his mind, and that presence became the drive and inspiration for his next writing project: a book written for her. The novel that emerged, *Nor Many Waters*, would feature a female character named Marion Eagar, who was quite small and slim and had reddish-brown hair, and late in the story her lover would suggest to her a place where they might be together: Tangier, Morocco. The novel would bear the following dedication: "For Ruth Morris A Birthday Present August 15, 1928."

This time it would be the novel, not Alec, that traveled halfway around the world for a rendezvous with Ruth in French Polynesia, and it would arrive in time for her birthday. Sitting alone at the plantation in Paea, with the tropical ocean waves not far off, Ruth peeled open the package and turned to the dedication page. As she slowly read the words that begin "For Ruth Morris," she was enveloped by the same rich floral fragrances that had been so omnipresent as Alec had embraced her during those magical nine days the year before, and had she closed her eyes, she might have forgotten the passage of time. But she was alone now, and something more than just vast expanses of ocean separated Ruth and Alec and seemingly always would. Quietly Ruth composed a thank-you letter that captured all her confused emotions:

> *Dear,*
> *It's a lovely birthday present and I do love it so. Every line of it, and most of all I love the thoughtfulness of it. It made me feel very close to you, as if all this great distance between us was imaginary, if only that could be true.*
>
> *I don't suppose I'll ever stop loving you, Alec, but I'll never be happy loving you under the existing circumstances. So that's that. It's been lovely here the last few days, cool and sweet. With all the flowers exploding. The Argentine training frigate is here, with lovely tangos, and charming young creatures, a fairyland kind of boat. Otherwise nothing is happening. Nothing can happen to me in my present mood. I'm drifting with the inevitable current, and scarily wondering why. Last year's agony cannot be lived over again. And nothing is worth that price. It's self defense now, Alec, but I do love you.*
> *Ruth*

Despite her crazy-making contradictions, Alec continued to cling to the thinnest threads of hope that something might in the end come of his relationship with Ruth. To Alec, Ruth could "make you feel as though you were living in an enchanted country, where the air was softer, the scent of the flowers richer, the plumage of the birds more bright." He was almost clinically incapable of letting go.

At the same time, Ruth didn't seem ready to let go, either. A passage from a letter she wrote that year hints at what kept her in the game:

> *Oh Alec, my darling, do love me. Please love me, no matter what I do. For I love you enough to atone for anything, everything. I'll be a good wife to you, someday. A glorious fact! Love me, Alec. And for gods sake make me feel that you do love me, that you want me more than anything or anybody in this world.*

Ruth's steely confidence was starting to show cracks, and there were practical, real-world reasons why. The seemingly bottomless pool of financial resources that had been the underpinning of the Morris lifestyle was quickly running dry. For too long Ruth and Govie had lived as though they were using a credit card with no spending limit and seemingly no due date. In Spain alone, they burned through money like a prairie fire in Kansas, and they pushed ahead with the purchase of the plantation in Tahiti despite a price tag that they could not comfortably afford. Quite simply, they were committing the worst sin imaginable from an old-money perspective: they were spending their capital rather than relying on the income it produced.

At the same time, Govie was writing less and selling fewer stories, and Ruth's book project on Prohibition seemed to be stalling out. It was simply the wrong focus for her energies. Ruth loved to write and was actually quite good at it, but the subject of Prohibition was so ponderous and frankly so boring that she lost interest. For the household, that meant one less source of potential income.

Govie started casting around for new ways to make a quick buck, and when some local businessmen offered him a chance to invest in a bank, he grabbed it. A seat on the board came with the deal, and Govie was able to brag that he was now more than just a writer. He was a banker. Never mind that he was mostly celebrity window dressing or that he knew next to nothing about banking. This was 1928. The stock market was on fire. Almost any investment you touched would turn to gold, and you couldn't miss with a bank. Certainly not in 1928. Easy Street was just around the corner. In 1929.

With their personal bank account now much less flush, Ruth and Govie began cutting back. They didn't stop traveling, but they traveled less. The impulsive shopping trips to the city were curtailed, and in general they became more cautious with their money. Still, they had appearances to keep up, so they continued to spend more than was prudent.

One thing they could not give up was their annual trip to Tahiti. Europe was now out, but they couldn't stay away from Tahiti. For Ruth, each trip back stirred up old memories, and she would inevitably write to Alec Waugh as she did in the summer of 1929.

> *Alec,*
> *It's so very strange, this being here again. It's like reaching a mirage and finding it isn't a mirage at all, but a remembered and concrete thing of beauty. The familiar and oft travelled only road . . . and the forgotten splendid colour. It's such a green island, Alec, and lovely.*
>
> *It's been a long time my dear since the "Tahiti" steamed through the pass and brought me back to you. A long time and much has happened in the century between. I realized that with a little bitterness when reading the three letters that met me here. We are almost like two strangers, aren't we, and after all that is best, isn't it? . . . Or is it? Frankly I don't know. But I am wondering what it would be like if you were here now. Could it ever again be like that tormented glorious summer? I wonder.*
>
> *Ventura is no more. The beach houses are gone. And there's only the lagoon, the surf and the noisy sea. Beyond that are left to me. For you too are gone.*

It seems that time conspires successfully to efface all things utterly. But do you remember that last day, that very last day?

I can't give your love to the small purple crab. I'm sure he's a big purple crab now and has outgrown completely the house in which he lived when we knew him. And anyway I've forgotten where he did live. Oh, I've forgotten much, my dear, but not enough. Not yet.

"For the ages of ages"

R.

Ruth did have one bit of company later in the fall. Gene McComas, Francis's wife, traveled out on the RMS *Tahiti* to join the Morrises, and they once again dipped into their quickly depleting bank account to lay on the hospitality.

The highlight of Gene's visit was a cruise around the Polynesian islands on a luxury yacht, a yacht with a backstory. It had originally belonged to the Morrises' old pal John Gilbert, "the Great Lover," and it had been built expressly for his beloved at the time, Greta Garbo. As an extraromantic flourish he even named the vessel after one of Garbo's films, *The Temptress*. Unfortunately, Garbo sailed on *The Temptress* only once, promptly getting seasick, and never set foot on the thing again. Gilbert decided to get rid of it.

Early in 1929, Samuel F. B. Morse, head of Del Monte Properties and creator of Pebble Beach, had purchased *The Temptress*, and now in the fall of 1929, as the most calamitous financial crash in American history was taking place back home, Govie was using *The Temptress* to take Gene, Ruth, and other friends out for a relaxing cruise around the Society Islands.

When the Morrises sailed into San Francisco on November 22, 1929, less than a month after Black Tuesday, they were confronted by what had happened in their absence. Frantic waves of mindless speculation had driven the stock market to levels that were completely unsustainable, and the market had collapsed under its own weight.

The Morrises' financial situation was now in peril, not simply because they had consumed so much of their savings but also because

Govie's trust fund income was vulnerable to the fall in the market. For the time being, however, they convinced themselves that things would all work out in the end, and they betrayed no signs of panic.

Of more immediate concern was Ruth's health, which took a turn during the holidays. A fibroid tumor was discovered, and on the day after Christmas, 1929, Govie drove her to the hospital, where she underwent three hours of surgery for a hysterectomy. Pneumonia soon followed, and she found herself confined to a bed as she greeted the new year.

Fortunately she was well on her way to full recovery in time to greet the new neighbors who had just moved in up the street: Sinclair Lewis and his new wife, Dorothy Thompson. Instantly, the per capita population of published authors in Monterey's Mesa neighborhood had tripled as Mr. and Mrs. Lewis settled into a charming old adobe that came complete with a garden full of flowers surrounded by a wall of stone. These weren't just any authors, either. Not only was Sinclair Lewis, known to friends as "Red," considered at the time one of the two most important writers of the 1920s, along with Theodore Dreiser, but Dorothy Thompson had established herself as a first-rate journalist while working overseas, and she had even earned the supreme compliment when Dreiser was forced to acknowledge that some of Thompson's words had ended up verbatim in a book he had written about Russia. That these two literary powerhouses had joined forces in holy matrimony made for a formidable team.

It was a team, however, that did not always see eye to eye, and the first example of that was the decision to come to California and take up temporary residence. It was Red's idea, and Dorothy agreed only with great reluctance. She was pregnant at age thirty-six, worried that she was too old to be carrying a child, and her preference had been to stay in New York close to her doctor. Red, though, was determined to write a book about the labor movement, and he needed to do research in California. His wishes carried the day.

Under the circumstances, Monterey was a sensible choice for their pied-à-terre because Lewis knew the area well, and its close proximity to San Francisco allowed easy research trips up and back. There was also the practical matter that two of his potential sources—Lincoln

Steffens, the muckraking journalist, and Ella Winter, his activist wife—lived just minutes away in Carmel. And, of course, he had good friends living in the area, starting with Ruth and Govie, but also including Gene McComas, whom he had known since he was a young man trying to scrape together a living in San Francisco.

Govie, of course, was delighted to have his good friend Red living so close, and Ruth shared his delight with one important caveat. With his research on the labor movement, he was once again veering dangerously close to parts of her past she preferred not to revisit. An earlier novel by Lewis, *Elmer Gantry*, which treats evangelists and tent shows satirically, was an uncomfortable reminder of her years traveling from tent show to tent show as the daughter of evangelists.

His next novel, *Dodsworth*, may have unsettled her for different reasons. Yet another satire, it takes particular aim at the values of a married woman who becomes caught up in the social life of Europe of the 1920s as she and her husband travel the continent. Ultimately she has an affair, and the marriage crumbles. While there is much to distinguish the female character in the novel from Ruth, aspects of the story may have struck a little too close to home for someone who spent almost a year living at the Ritz.

For his latest book, Lewis traveled up to San Quentin to interview labor leader Tom Mooney, a radical activist who had once been a Wobblie (a member of the International Workers of the World) and later a socialist leader in San Francisco during the period the Wightman family temporally resided in the city. Once again this was dredging up old memories for Ruth. Writing to H. L. Mencken after the Lewises arrived in Monterey, she admitted, "Red is mad at me because much as I love him I can't read his books," and it's doubtful she ever fully explained why.

For an insatiable consumer of books like Ruth, who at that moment was reading *Look Homeward, Angel* by Thomas Wolfe and *The Magic Mountain* by Thomas Mann, it's unusual that she would avoid one author so assiduously, particularly one for whom she had such warm feelings, but clearly she had her reasons.

With Red and Dorothy in town, the Morrises naturally wrapped them into their social circle, inviting them to their parties and introducing them to their friends, which pleased Red but not his wife. There were a couple of issues going on here. First, Dorothy had come to realize the extent of her husband's drinking problem, and social events involving bootleg liquor generally led to his inebriation. Second, Sinclair Lewis's reputation was much bigger than hers. The practical effect was that everywhere the couple went, newspaper reporters immediately focused on him, and when they attended parties, his gravitational pull seemed to draw all the guests into his orbit. She was left feeling that her status at these gatherings was as the "wife of."

While Dorothy took great pleasure in her time with Ruth and Govie, she had no use for the social events or the people who attended them on the Monterey Peninsula. Even when the two couples got to meet America's most celebrated and admired hero, Charles Lindbergh, at a party in Pebble Beach, Dorothy Thompson showed little enthusiasm.

For Ruth and Govie, as for most Americans, Charles Lindbergh's solo flight across the Atlantic in 1927 was an event of singular importance in the 1920s. When word reached America that Lindbergh had landed successfully at Le Bourget in France after a flight of thirty-three hours and thirty minutes, it was widely understood that a new frontier had been conquered, a new era had begun, and nothing as far-reaching or profound would happen again until the *Eagle* landed at Tranquility Base on the moon in the summer of 1969.

It seems as well that the man who had made this brave solo journey was every bit the match for the moment. Blessed with leading-man looks, a quiet reserve, and a set of core values that came right out of the *Boy Scout Handbook*, the six-foot-three Charles August Lindbergh became America's most celebrated Jazz Age hero, and his life and the nation's would never be quite the same again.

For Lindbergh, his elevated stature gave him a platform to promote his vision for the future: transcontinental air travel. And arguably as important, he used his considerable influence to insure funding for Robert Goddard's rocket research in hopes of achieving his longer-term vision: sending a man to the moon. It is not overstating it to say that without Charles Lindbergh's unwavering support, Neil Armstrong and Buzz Aldrin would not have made their historic journey.

By the time Lindbergh arrived in Monterey in 1930, the first steps leading to transcontinental air travel were well under way, and he had already secured the first wave of funding from the Guggenheim family to keep Goddard's research afloat. What brought him to Monterey was something new: flying gliders. During his stay, he would perform multiple test flights in different locations, and huge crowds followed him wherever he went.

It must be noted, however, that Lindbergh did not come to Monterey alone. Anne Morrow Lindbergh, his lovely bride of nine months, was traveling with him, and about her there was much fascination. Petite with radiant dark eyes, Anne Morrow Lindbergh was a bright, warm, thoughtful, and attractive woman. She was a graduate of Smith College, and her primary interest was in literature and writing, but she had no fears about climbing into a cockpit and became the first woman in America licensed to fly a glider.

Like Dorothy Thompson, Anne Lindbergh was pregnant when she arrived in Monterey, a source of joy to the Lindberghs at the time, though it would lead in two years to the most profound tragedy of their lives: the kidnapping and murder of their baby.

On the night of the party, however, Charles and Anne were all smiles, as Charles played a practical joke on guests by sneaking Listerine into their glasses of burgundy, a rather carefree and lighthearted gesture by the shy, reserved pilot, and all save Dorothy Thompson seemed amused by his antics. So appalled was she, however, that anyone would tamper with Prohibition-era beverages that she formed a negative opinion of Lindbergh she would carry with her for the rest of her life.

For Govie the highlight of the evening was not when he met America's hero but when he got to meet the hero's wife. Ruth explained, "Govie has so lost his heart to Anne that I suspect any moment he'll hop off for a non-stop trans-Pacific flight in an effort to rival the Colonel."

As for the former aviatrix herself, she seemed pleased to meet both of them and was no doubt among the throngs who gathered out in Carmel Valley to watch Lindbergh's test flights. Many years had passed since Ruth watched Lincoln Beachey take off in Stockton, but her awe for those who soared up into the sky was in no way diminished.

Soon after the Lindberghs departed, so did the Lewises, and as she prepared to leave, Dorothy Thompson would write, "This country is full of cypresses, polo ponies, and morons. We shake its dust from our feet in a few days."

Once he had Dorothy settled in Los Angeles, Red returned for an additional short visit, and one evening found him with Ruth and Govie as they took turns reading aloud from Evelyn Waugh's new book, *Vile Bodies*, a biting and quite funny satire of the excesses and foibles of the "Bright Young Things," a group of affluent and social young people in 1920s Britain. It was, Lewis said, "a joyous super-Saki book," and Ruth and Govie heartily agreed.

Sinclair Lewis would soon rejoin his wife, and nine months later he would become the first American to win the Nobel Prize for Literature.

For the Morrises, their focus now shifted to their home. Despite the ringing wake-up call that Wall Street had sent the previous fall, Govie was determined to embark on a costly addition to the mansion, extending the living room and adding a full second story with additional bedrooms. This would be Govie's project, though. For Ruth, Tahiti was once again beckoning, and she told H. L. Mencken, "I'm frightfully homesick for the place. There isn't any more genuine serenity anywhere in America—or in Europe." Her plan was to take Govie's two now fully grown daughters, Bay and Patsey, with her for the summer.

Then Ruth had another thought, seemingly inspired by her recent reading of *Vile Bodies*: Why not invite Alec to come with them as well? The two had never been out of touch, exchanging letters on a regular basis and always proclaiming their love for each other, but they had remained physically apart. Now Ruth wished to see him again. The Lad was finally out of the picture, Ruth having lost all interest, so in April 1930, she wrote Alec the following letter:

> *Dear Alec,*
> *I'm up here with Jeanie MacPherson. We saw Bay off for N.Y. last night. She is returning here by the 10th of May, and she wants to see you the moment you arrive in New York. I think she wants to persuade you to come to Tahiti, and to bring some agreeable lad along with*

you. I hope she succeeds. Her address is 136 East 64th.
I believe the telephone is listed in her mother's name,
Mrs. Waterbury Morris. So you will get in touch with
her right away won't you dear.

Govie was wishing you would bring Evelyn along
with you. He is quite sold on "Vile Bodies." I think it's
a splendid book. Would it have been written if he had
never read Saki?

But of loyalty to you, because loyalty must include
one's friend, mustn't it. I last night bought Berta Ruck's
"The Kissed Bride" [The Unkissed Bride]. Furthermore
I'm reading it. What more can I do to prove that I still
love you? I think I really do, Alec, but we've been so very
long away from each other that I've lost perspective
about us. I know it will be marvelous to see you, but I'm
frightened too. You may not like me. I've changed a lot
in these two years. And since I've been ill I look centu-
ries older. Even Bay can tell you that.

Patsey will get here today. Also, she is coming out on
the Columbia, via the canal. She's an awfully good egg,
and truly beautiful.

I haven't seen or heard from Lorraine since I got
back from Tahiti, but she this moment rang me up and
asked herself to lunch. She sounded cheerful, and rather
prosperous. It is quite exciting to know you will be in
New York soon. After all, Alec, haven't we been away
from each other quite long enough?
Ruth

Much had changed in Alec Waugh's life. His career seemed to
be taking off with the publication of his latest book, *Hot Countries*, a
memoir of his travels in the South Pacific and the Caribbean islands,
and his social circle had widened. Most importantly, the spell Ruth had
cast over him had weakened considerably, though it had not entirely
gone away. Were Govie no longer part of the equation, the old pangs

might have returned with a vengeance, but the equation was still "Ruth plus Govie equals nothing happening."

The tug was still strong enough, however, or at least his curiosity, that Alec, who had vowed "never again . . . never, never again," set out once more for California. This time he traveled partly by plane but mostly by train across the United States. To Monterey. To Ruth.

Looking "fresh and vivid," she was waiting for him as his train pulled into the station, and their initial encounter went surprisingly well. Gone were the old jealousies. Gone, too, were the tension and the arguments that had so soured his previous visit. As Alec gazed upon his once-upon-a-time lover after so much time had passed, she "had still the same glamour, the same appeal." Ruth "was unique," he realized, and he "was enchanted by her still."

Over the days that followed, Ruth and Alec would rediscover their "old harmony with one another" and would once more "exchange confidences." Whatever had drawn the two of them together in the first place was still alive after the long separation. Alec's stay turned out to be "an enchanted period."

But some things had changed. Ruth had become insistent that Alec come with her to Tahiti, to their special place, just one more time, but Alec was resisting. This was new. He had never resisted Ruth before.

The Alec Waugh of 1930 was not the Alec Waugh of 1927 or 1928 or even 1929. He was a different man now. He had obligations. A career. A hit book. Most important, he didn't need Ruth quite as much. As his need diminished, his power grew. What was more, he fully understood that nothing would come of it even if he did go with her to Tahiti. Those nine perfect days would not have a sequel.

"You are coming down, aren't you?"

"No, no, I can't."

Undaunted, Ruth kept pushing, persuading, pleading to the very end, hoping he would change his mind. But he never did. Well, not completely. Alec did agree to one compromise: he would try to come out to Tahiti in the fall for a one-month visit. Upon that thin thread hung Ruth's last hopes.

On their final day together, Ruth gave Alec a small box, along with a note that read:

*This is a very old Ming dynasty box, which has probably held
hundreds of Chinese love letters. Do you think it would possibly
learn to read in the language you write so well? R.*

What Ruth and Alec had no way of knowing was that this was their
final day together. What Alec could sense was that it was "even more
intense than our other partings" and that they "had never been closer
to one another."

Adding one final note of poignancy, Alec recalled, "On the last
evening we sat up very late, after Govie and the girls had gone to bed.
Once again we were Russian lovers, watching our pipe-dreams form."

The following day, Ruth departed. As her ship sailed out through
the Golden Gate and off to sea, Alec waved to her for the last time.
Then he boarded a train that would follow the same path across the
United States he had taken the first time he had parted from Ruth back
in 1927.

The second night out aboard the RMS *Makura*, Ruth, after indulg-
ing in the now all-too-familiar self-medication, sat down and wrote a
letter to Alec in which she chided him for not joining her on the voyage but still looked forward to his visit in the fall. With that out of the
way, she set right to work on a second letter, more "bread and butter,"
this one to Govie. Then she rather casually placed the two letters into
envelopes, not for a second noticing that the letters were going into the
wrong envelopes.

It was the slightest of blunders, but the consequences were huge.
In the blink of an eye, Ruth Morris foreclosed any chance she would
ever see Alec Waugh again.

CHAPTER FIFTEEN

BAD RUN OF LUCK

Two letters quietly arrived in early July at locations half a world apart: Monterey, California, and London, England. Two seemingly ordinary letters, nestled in with other mail. It wasn't until they were opened that their explosive nature was revealed.

As Alec Waugh unfolded the letter addressed to him in London and began to read, he quickly cycled through a series of emotions. Confusion. Surprise. Recognition. Sadness. Resignation.

The letter, which began "Dearest," was rather plain vanilla, containing an odd reference to a mislabeled suitcase. The surprise came when it dawned on Alec that the letter had not been intended for him, and it didn't take long for him to figure out what had happened and recognize the implications. Hence the sadness and resignation.

Gouverneur Morris experienced a different sequence of emotions as he read through the letter he received in California: Confusion. Surprise. Recognition. Anger. Fury.

Of the many letters Ruth had written to Alec, the one Govie opened was not among her most passionate or revealing, but it was just over-familiar enough to set off alarm bells.

> *Dearest,*
> *Such nice boat letters and I whimpered a little over the*

wire. But after all it was very easy for me to whimper yesterday. It was dreadful to leave you, and equally dreadful to leave Govie. That is difficult to explain, and perhaps should not be said but you know, you <u>do</u> know don't you, that I love you both.

We had very rough weather last night. It prostrated both Patsey and Bay, and even I, Trojan sailor that I am, gave up and went to bed at eight thirty. The mischief kitten woke me up at three, and most charmingly tempted and beguiled me into playing with it for two solid hours. . . .

Bay and myself had a long talk last night, mainly concerning you. I suspect that she knows a great deal about us, although I volunteered no information and she asked no questions. She's enormously fond of you. I think a little puzzled about the outcome, and yet I think she would stake her life on a wager that I will not materially affect the present Morris household. Bay is a big person I think, and has all the necessary tolerance.

September is a long way off, and Tahiti is a great many miles, too many, but if miles can be conquered, then restless spirits can be assuaged, and time perhaps can bring to us a pleasant commingling of all the worthwhile emotions.

I do love you, but you are god damned stupid or I'd be telling you this instead of writing it.
Hurry!
Ruth

By the time Govie had finished reading the letter for the second time, his simmering anger had reached critical mass, and he had identified exactly who deserved the brunt of it: Alec Waugh. No longer was Alec the charming, polite, well-spoken young writer. Now he was an unprincipled manipulator who had appeared unexpectedly in Tahiti and visited Monterey multiple times for the intended purpose of taking advantage of his wife. Somewhat irrationally Govie convinced himself that Ruth had become vulnerable to Alec Waugh's seductive ways because of hormonal changes following her hysterectomy.

It is striking how little Govie truly understood about his wife and the degree to which he seemed willing to absolve her of any responsibility.

Instead, he chose to direct his ire at the man he held responsible. He fired off a letter to Alec in London that is direct and brutal and unmistakable in its message: Stay away from Ruth. And that goes for Bay, too. For good measure, Govie also advised Alec not to set foot in Monterey or on the island of Tahiti ever again. He adds a warning to Alec that he not breathe a word to Ruth about the misdirected letters so as not to upset her, and he demands that Alec respond with an unequivocal acknowledgment that he had gotten the message. A key passage captures the tone of the letter:

> *Many years ago I gave Ruth something very precious. Women with vast diamonds and swollen pearls envied her jewel, because their men could not match it. That was a perfect belief and trust in her truthfulness and loyalty. Well you have taken that away from her and destroyed it. But I shall do what I may to make her think that she still wears it. That will be the hardest thing of all to do.*

Alec's reply was simple and direct:

> *Have Just Received Your Letter It Shall Be As You Wish. Alec Waugh.*

Alec, true to his nature, never breathed a word to Ruth about the letter mix-up, but the fallout it generated had been a shock. This break with Ruth had come swiftly, without warning, and seemed irrevocable.

Almost as difficult had been the harsh rebuke from Govie, a man for whom Alec had enormous respect. Ultimately, Alec's affair with Ruth would become the inspiration for a novel called *So Lovers Dream*, which unfortunately would end up a dull, muddled mess, because he went to such strides to mask the depths of his own true feelings and to disguise the identities of the people like Ruth and himself who had inspired the characters.

As for Govie, soon after Alec's telegram had arrived, he revised his thinking about the whole matter and began to suspect that maybe Ruth was at least the tiniest bit complicitous after all. Sure smooth-talking seducer Alec Waugh was still principally to blame, strongly assisted by those volatile hormones, but Govie came to believe that for this tango to ever have happened, it would have required two willing partners. Soon a letter was on its way to Ruth that explicitly revealed the letter mix-up and demanded an explanation.

For Ruth, the misdirected letters had been time-delayed bomb-shells. The tenuous connections one had with the outside world in 1930 while sequestered in the South Seas were both a virtue and a curse. With mail ships coming and going only once a month, news whether good or bad was significantly delayed. So for a good two months, Ruth was blithely unaware of the damage she had done.

Still she had other sources of worry. Health concerns. Financial concerns. Relationship concerns. Her once unshakeable confidence was being sorely tested, but at least in French Polynesia in the company of her stepdaughters, Bay and Patsey, to whom she had become quite close, there was a chance for rest and renewal. There was also the opportunity to meet some unusually gifted artists who just happened to be in the neighborhood that year: Henri Matisse, the Postimpressionist master and pillar of twentieth-century art, and Friedrich Wilhelm ("F. W.") Murnau, the award-winning German filmmaker, best known for the silent classic *Nosferatu*.

The sixty-year-old Matisse had come from France for an extended visit. While he was there, he was constantly out and about sketching whatever caught his fancy: flowers, landscapes, ships, birds, women. But mostly he was just soaking up the Polynesian experience. The marketplace. The fishermen. The simple dailiness of life. All of which he found calming, rejuvenating, and inspiring. Remarkably, Matisse painted only one picture during his stay in French Polynesia, but that was only because he had become so immersed in the culture that he didn't want to do anything that would break the spell.

He did take time out from his revels, however, to visit the set of another artistic master, F. W. Murnau, who was deeply involved in the filming of a motion picture called *Tabu*, shooting primarily on Bora Bora and Tahiti.

Ruth visited the Murnau set as well, and in many ways it may have made an even bigger impression on her than it did on Matisse. Just consider that two years later she would embark on two film projects of her own in French Polynesia, and it is impossible not to conclude that she was inspired by Murnau and that her time on the set was a learning experience.

And what learning that would have been. The making of *Tabu* has become the stuff of film legend. Academic papers have been written about it. Film students still study it. For Ruth, this was film school on the fly. Every frame was shot on location, and Murnau used an all-native cast and virtually an all-native crew. There were only three pros involved: Murnau; his coproducer, Robert Flaherty, the director of the classic documentary *Nanook of the North*; and his cinematographer, Floyd Crosby, father of rock musician David Crosby.

The filmmaker had so little money to work with that he had to shoot entirely in black and white and without a sound track, choices that would have doomed a lesser film. Murnau and Crosby, though, were veterans of the silent era in Hollywood, acclaimed veterans at that. So by playing to their strengths, they were able to create a stylish and visually arresting film, and Murnau's reliance on native actors gives the film an air of authenticity as he weaves his tale of a young man who violates one taboo by falling in love with a woman considered a sacred maiden, then violates another when he dives for pearls in forbidden, shark-infested waters.

It was a bold and brave experiment, but Murnau would be vindicated when it was released in 1931, earning an Academy Award for best cinematography and garnering overwhelmingly positive reviews. *Tabu* would arouse some controversy as well, stemming from the brief appearance of bare female breasts, but the film's reputation for artistic excellence has survived long after the controversy of the moment faded away.

There is a tragic postscript to the Murnau story, and it has a direct connection to Ruth, but it must wait. Because everything in Ruth's life was put on hold, at least temporarily, when Govie's letter arrived.

Here she had been so careful for so many years. In Pacific Grove, the town immediately adjacent to Monterey, she had set up a special post office box to receive mail first from Howard "the Lad" Barnes and later from Alec Waugh, and she had even taken after the Lad in a high-speed car chase to prevent him from blowing up her marriage. Now one careless moment had screwed everything up. It was an unforced error and entirely her fault. There was only one course of action left in her mind: damage control. Her first move was to deny everything. Completely. Totally. Categorically. Here is a key section from her response to Govie:

> *Must all this year continue to vex one and to be filled with tribulation? This cannot be a letter of explanation, because I've no more idea of what I wrote to Alec in some probably drunken or sympathetic and idiotic moment than a jack rabbit. You know better than anybody else that whatever else I am I'm not a liar. In every possible serious fact of life I have not failed you so much as once. I may have flirted. I always do. It's such fun, but except in front of people I have not even so much as kissed Alec since the time you and Francis were in Moorea. Then I was angry and wanted to punish you. But in all these turbulent years, my one dear, I've never been unfaithful, not even in the sacrament which is thought. In a very definite way I love you much more than my wretched miserable unhappy and useless life. So with all these long and unnecessary miles between us it is hard to tell you how great the hurt of this is. All my small black heart is strewn in gratitude for every kindness and tenderness you've ever shown to me. I've tried to pay it back, but I've no coin of your realm. I've only got a nervous energy which sometimes amuses you,*

*and a loyalty which if I were our very own beloved Jack
Dempsey I could manage to prove.*

Ruth might not have been Jack Dempsey, but at this particular
moment she felt as though she had taken a hard blow to the body. She
had been so effective her whole life at managing situations, always staying one step ahead of the game, accurately assessing risk, and always
figuring a way out. Now, though, her confidence was a bit staggered.

The loss of her last link with Alec had to have left her feeling even
more isolated, because she had enjoyed a level of intimacy with him
that she had enjoyed with few other men. In some ways she might have
been more open with Alec about certain things than she had been with
her own husband, and that suggests they had a real bond. Was she ever
as deeply in love with Alec as she sometimes claimed? It's impossible
to know, but he would certainly always hold a place in her heart.

Of more immediate concern to her, however, had to have been her
marriage, but she had one thing going for her: the tendency for people, including her husband, to believe her when she stated something
emphatically. Her denial of an affair with Alec was so unequivocal and
expressed with such emotion that Govie would have believed her. He
might not have been happy with just how cozy she had gotten with the
young author, but there is every reason to believe that Govie would
go to his grave without ever knowing that his wife had been sexually
intimate with another man. That fact alone made her marriage much
more salvageable.

Finding a way to restore his trust and return to his good graces had
become a priority, and she rather quickly took one important step that
had the potential of helping. Ruth seems to have played an important role in helping Govie win a writing contract with F. W. Murnau to
create a written version of *Tabu* for national syndication, essentially a
novelization. Her presence right there in French Polynesia most probably made all the difference. It was a writing deal that would lead to a
tragic outcome, however, just one week before the premiere of the film.

Flash forward to March 11, 1931. Murnau set out from Los Angeles
with his chauffeur and his valet for a trip to Monterey, where he was to
hammer out with Govie the final details of the contract for a written

version of *Tabu*. They were also to discuss his next film project, also to be shot in the South Seas, which would be based on a cross-cultural love story written by Govie called "Was It for This?" But none of it would ever happen.

Just north of Santa Barbara, as late afternoon approached, Murnau's chauffeur, John Freeland, pulled over to gas up the rented Packard, and for reasons that defy easy explanation, Murnau's valet, Garcia Stevenson, climbed into the driver's seat to replace him. Why? He wasn't authorized to drive the rented vehicle, and he was a much less experienced driver than Freeland. Why make the change? "The old man told me to," Stevenson claimed. But why?

It would prove to be a fateful decision. Within minutes Freeland was warning, "You'd better slow down," but it was too late. An oncoming truck caused Stevenson to panic. He swerved and went into a skid right over an embankment, throwing all the occupants out of the car.

The forty-two-year-old Murnau was left groaning in pain. His head had suffered a hard blow, fracturing his skull, and he would die at a hospital a few hours later.

Back in French Polynesia, it is said, they sensed Murnau's death even before they were informed of it, and for some there was a ready explanation: a curse. In their telling, Murnau had built a home in an area that was sacred to the Polynesians, so what he had done was . . . taboo.

And, they added, the taboo lived on. Douglas Fairbanks Sr. rented the house for three days and became so spooked by the place, he moved out. Later a member of a prominent San Francisco family rented the former Murnau home for three weeks and then committed suicide. Finally, in 1935, the end came when Lord Beauchamp, the inspiration for the character Lord Marchmain in Evelyn Waugh's novel *Brideshead Revisited*, rented the place with friends, and after three weeks, it burned to the ground, leaving only its state-of-the-art plumbing as relics in the smoldering ruins.

Whether one wishes to believe there were curses at work in the Society Islands, there can be little doubt that the year 1930 produced more than its fair share of bad luck.

Take the sinking of the RMS *Tahiti* on August 17, 1930, which occurred the same month Ruth received the bombshell letter from Govie and seems eerily symbolic: it was the ship that had carried Ruth to her rendezvous with Alec in 1927. Somehow a propeller shaft broke through the wall of the stern. As the ship began taking on water, distress calls went out.

Rescuers raced to the wounded vessel and successfully retrieved all the passengers and crew members, but there was no saving the ship itself, stranding some people in the Society Islands for a month, including Bay and Patsey, before they could find passage home.

Another kind of bad luck struck one of Ruth and Govie's good friends, Lord Hastings, which involved of all things an unruly cat. But before learning about the cat, it is useful to know more about Lord Hastings.

Francis John Clarence Westenra Plantagenet Hastings, or Jack to his friends, was the only son of the Fifteenth Earl of Huntingdon, making him a viscount, or heir, to the title. An earlier Earl of Huntingdon was alleged to have been the man who inspired the legend of Robin Hood, so Jack was a product of a long and noble lineage. Unfortunately, he had been all but disowned by his father, who had taken strong exception to Jack's choice of a wife, Cristina Casati, the daughter of Marquis Casati Stampa di Soncino. Her Italian heritage was a problem for the earl. Her Catholic faith was a deal breaker.

No longer welcome at home, Jack and Cristina escaped first to Australia before seeking refuge in French Polynesia. Once situated on Moorea, Jack devoted his time to writing and painting.

Which brings us to the cat, whose name was Zupatina. She was wild and ornery, and she did the unthinkable: she bit the hand that fed her. And this was no ordinary cat bite, merely causing momentary discomfort. Jack became quite ill, life-threateningly so.

To make matters worse, the closest doctor was in Papeete, some twelve miles across the channel from Moorea, and the channel that day was rocking and rolling, so much so that no sensible sailor dared venture out in a boat. A bribe of rum finally did the trick, and soon Jack was in the capable hands of a French doctor in Papeete, who was able to stabilize his health. For full recovery, however, the doctor advised Jack to leave French Polynesia as quickly as possible.

That was it. The Hastings' time on Moorea had abruptly come to an end, all because of a cat. When Ruth set sail for California, Jack and Cristina traveled with her, and in late October 1930, the party of three arrived in San Francisco and then continued on to Monterey.

Here's where that bad luck of getting bitten by Zupatina would finally lead. Jack Hastings would meet Diego Rivera, the Mexican artist famous for his bold, dramatic murals, and end up working for him.

By some stroke of serendipity, Jack Hastings had an art opening on November 15, 1930, at Gump's in San Francisco, thanks to the close friendship between the Gump and Morris families, just days before Diego Rivera had an art opening at the Palace of the Legion of Honor in the same city. Sensing an opportunity, Jack set out to meet Diego Rivera personally, and he played it just right.

On the face of it, Jack Hastings and Diego Rivera might have seemed an odd pairing. One was a product of the British aristocracy, heir to the title of earl, and the other a member for a time of the Mexican Communist Party. Yet they instantly hit it off, an outcome no doubt greatly facilitated by the fact that both Hastings and Rivera, who did not speak English, were fluent in French.

At the time Diego Rivera was about to begin work on two mural projects in San Francisco, one at the Pacific Stock Exchange and the other at the California School of Fine Art, known today as the San Francisco Art Institute, and by the end of their conversation, Jack had persuaded Diego to use him as an assistant on the two projects, providing him the opportunity to learn from the master.

So it was that Lord and Lady Hastings took up residence at the Gaylord Hotel in San Francisco, as Jack took on a new role in life: assistant to Diego Rivera. While the Hastings continued to maintain their close friendship with the Morrises, who were just a short train ride away, new people became a part of their social circle. Not the least of whom was Frida Kahlo, Diego Rivera's wife. Frida and Cristina would become great friends, with Frida developing feelings for Cristina that went beyond friendship, though those feelings would remain unrequited. For her part, Frida Kahlo would draw a portrait of Cristina in pencil, which continues to appear in books and exhibitions to the present day.

The Hastings also came to know Diego Rivera's principal assistant, Clifford Wight, a British sculptor and painter, and his wife, Jean. From these initial encounters, a lifelong friendship would develop between Jack and Clifford.

Meanwhile back in Monterey, Ruth and Govie continued to work on the healing process amid the splendor of their newly expanded home. There was now a second story that contained within it a private residential suite. At one end was a bedroom with an adjacent bathroom, finished in black tile, art deco style, and off the bathroom a sitting room. This was Ruth's end of the building. At the other end was another bedroom with a smaller bathroom, noteworthy for its bright blue-checked tile treatment.

There is one curious thing that happened during this period, however, that still defies easy explanation. Someone, either Ruth or Govie, took the misdirected letter, Ruth's response, a copy of Govie's letter to Alec, and Alec's telegram, placed them in a small safe, and sealed the safe inside a wall, not to be seen again for more than sixty years. But why? For evidence at a divorce proceeding? As a memorial to a great love now lost? It's impossible to know.

As the year 1930 drew to a close, the Morris home had now become a mansion fit for a wealthy, famous, successful writer. The only thing missing was the wealthy part. The successful part was feeling increasingly retrospective as well. Which left the Morrises struggling with one overriding question as they sat back and enjoyed all the elegantly appointed square footage: How in heaven's name would they pay for it?

CHAPTER SIXTEEN

LIVING ON
BORROWED TIME

As the year 1931 rolled around, the financial trend lines in the Morris household were becoming as disturbing as those across the country. For Ruth and Govie, it was the growing stack of unpaid bills, which showed no signs of abating. For the country as a whole, it was rising unemployment: from 3.2 percent in 1929 to 8.7 percent in 1930 and continuing up. Nothing else about the new year seemed to be going all that great for the Morrises, either.

Consider, for instance, what happened just a few days into the new year. Ruth and Govie were on their way back from a weekend getaway to the snow, possibly to do some maintenance on their marriage, and somewhere in the Sierra foothills, not far from Sonora, they developed car trouble.

Govie pulled over and climbed out, a cigarette dangling from his lip Jean-Paul Belmondo style, to investigate what was going on. As he fiddled with this and fussed with that, he happened to open up the gas tank, bringing a dangling cigarette in uncomfortably close proximity to an open gas tank.

A glowing ash shook loose and performed a graceful free fall down into the tank. An explosion of flames quickly followed, blasting into

Govie's face, leaving him severely singed. After several days in the hospital, Govie would be sent home for an extended period of convalescence, with Ruth transformed into the role of nursemaid.

Fast-forward to March 2. Govie remained confined to his bed. The phone rang. It was for Ruth. The Monterey Hospital was calling on behalf of a patient named Carole Hope from Los Angeles, who claimed to know Ruth and was requesting that she come to the hospital. The first thing that went through Ruth's mind was, Carole who? Ruth had never heard of her. Didn't have a clue. Still, intrigued by the mystery of it all, if nothing else, Ruth agreed to come to the hospital.

There was one slight complication: Roscoe Arbuckle was staying at the house for the weekend, and Govie was in no condition to act as a host. Ruth didn't want to leave Roscoe alone, because he had not been doing at all well. His marriage to Doris Deane had fallen apart, and alcohol had become a growing fixture in his life. With no other obvious options available, Ruth invited him to tag along.

Once she reached the hospital, Ruth recognized the woman immediately: it was Edna May Cooper, a former actress whom Ruth had run into at the Famous Players–Lasky studio in Hollywood. Her identity was the easy part. But what was she was doing in Monterey, and why was she calling herself Carole Hope?

As best as anyone could piece the story together, Edna May had set out on a routine shopping errand in Santa Monica, in Southern California, jumping on a streetcar and heading off. Somehow she ended up at the Southern Pacific Railroad station in Monterey and had become Carole Hope. From the train station she took a cab to the San Carlos Hotel, roughly four blocks away, checked in, and stayed.

After about a week the staff at the hotel became concerned about their mysterious guest, not only because she seemed to be acting a bit odd but also because she was complaining about a headache. At this point, George R. Tremblay, the hotel manager, put in a call to a prominent local physician, Dr. Hugh Dormody.

It didn't take long for Dr. Dormody to uncover the reason for the headache. She was suffering from a cerebral concussion, the result of a blow to the back of the head, along with bruises on her leg, prompting Dormody to recommend immediate hospitalization.

Only later, after she had entered Monterey Hospital, would Dormody begin unraveling some of the mystery. The big break came during a routine examination when he mentioned in passing that he would swing back by to look in on her later in the day after he had been out to watch the polo game.

"What polo game?"

"The one at Del Monte."

"Del Monte? But how can you get to Del Monte and back in a day? Aren't we in Santa Monica?"

She was in Monterey, Dr. Dormody explained. In Northern California. Once she had digested this information, a new thought popped into her head. If she was in Monterey, then there was someone she knew who lived in Monterey: Ruth Morris.

At the hospital Ruth learned that the bruises and abrasions were, in Dr. Dormody's opinion, about a week old and that Edna May had been hit by a car, resulting in memory loss. Evidently she had traveled hundreds of miles by train, not knowing who she was or where she was going.

There's one additional twist to this story. Only two months earlier, Edna May Cooper had teamed up with aviatrix Bobbi Trout to set the world's endurance record for women. Trout, who was a contemporary of Amelia Earhart, had assembled the team, recruiting Edna May to join her in hopes that her celebrity as an actress would generate publicity for their feat.

Taking off on January 4, 1931, Trout and Cooper successfully flew nonstop, using in-air refueling, for 122 hours and 50 minutes. A quick bit of grade school math, dividing 122 by 24, reveals that the two women were airborne for more than five days, finally touching down on January 9. They covered 7,367 miles and used up 1,138 gallons of fuel. It proved a landmark in women's aviation history and helped pave the way for Earhart's legendary flight.

Then two months later, Edna May Cooper got hit by a car and lost her memory. Once Edna May was released from the hospital, she came to stay at the Morris residence while she rested and recovered.

As she began to feel like her old self again, she finally provided her version of what had happened: "These things don't really happen outside the covers of books like Gouverneur Morris writes, who is upstairs, but here I am. When I left home I was troubled about something professionally. I remembered hoping I could get away and forget. That is what happened. If you really want to know how I got here—I believe a guardian angel took my hand and led me to Monterey. I found a wonderful doctor, a beautiful home and understanding nurses who care for me tenderly. My treatment is baths, massage, light diet and quiet and rest. I passed some sort of crisis today—my nerves are better and I shall soon be well."

It had already been an eventful year, but there was still more to come. Only days after the Edna May Cooper incident, the Morrises would learn of F. W. Murnau's death in the car accident near Santa Barbara. Before the spring was over, the contractors who built the addition to the mansion, S. H. Hooke and W. E. Hooke, would file a lawsuit in the amount of $16,000, the unpaid portion of the original $40,000 construction contract.

While the bad news continued to pile up for the Morrises, Jack Hastings was busy in San Francisco assisting Diego Rivera on projects that harked back to an earlier time and a much different place: Renaissance Italy. Rivera's murals were frescoes, which employed a technique that had long been out of style until Rivera resurrected it.

During a decade living and studying in Europe, Rivera spent hours studying the frescoes of Italy, the Sistine Chapel being the most famous example. Michelangelo painted the ceiling of the Sistine Chapel by applying wet plaster to its surface and then painting with pigments while the surface was wet, which embedded the images permanently into the ceiling.

When Rivera returned to Mexico in the early 1920s, following the revolution, he brought his newfound knowledge with him and began applying the fresco technique to large public buildings. Instead of religious imagery, Rivera employed cultural, historical, and political imagery, setting off the great mural movement of the 1920s in Mexico.

As his reputation grew, Diego Rivera was invited to the United States to apply his talents, first in San Francisco and later in Detroit, and Jack Hastings found himself as a key part of the support team. The nature of the projects reveals why assistants are so important. Rivera was creating huge murals, and he had to work on them a section at a time during a window of between six and eighteen hours before the plaster would dry.

This was where his assistants came in. Each day a section of the wall needed to be prepared for painting. Wet plaster was applied, and new pigments were mixed, matching exactly the pigments used the previous day. Often this meant working through the night so that everything would be ready when Diego arrived in the morning. As Jack explained, his responsibilities were to "grind colours, wash brushes, plaster walls, enlarge designs, do odd jobs generally, paint skies and unimportant parts of the background." It was an apprenticeship of a lifetime.

Though he was kept quite busy, given his new responsibilities, Jack never lost contact with the Morrises. He and Cristina would travel down to Monterey to visit with Ruth and Govie. Finally in April, when Govie was sufficiently recovered, the Morrises traveled up to San Francisco to see the murals; one was completed and the other was still in process.

For Ruth and Govie, the murals were a revelation. Even for sea-soned art lovers, the Rivera frescoes were something else again. Bold. Audacious. Almost overpowering. And the Morrises loved them. The artistry. The craftsmanship. The content.

Their unbridled enthusiasm was in no way dampened by the con-troversy surrounding the mural at the stock exchange, which bubbled up when the idea was first proposed. Respected painter Maynard Dixon captured the mood: "The stock exchange could look the world over without finding a man more inappropriate for the part than Rivera. He is a professed Communist and has publicly caricatured American financial institutions." To Ruth and Govie, though, Rivera's politics were entirely beside the point. They chose to view the fresco at the stock exchange, which Rivera called *Allegory of California*, strictly on its own terms, and what their eyes beheld was a vivid and beautifully rendered tableau of California's abundant and rich natural and human resources.

The face of a woman, modeled by Helen Wills Moody, is the dom-inant visual and seems to represent California itself, gathering around her the resources of the state. Her left hand overflows with fruits and vegetables and grains of various kinds, a symbol of the state's vast agricultural abundance. Oil rigs and dockyards sit behind her. Immediately below is a young man holding an airplane. To the left is Luther Burbank examining a bit of flora. Below his left shoulder sits James Marshall, the man who discovered gold in Sutter's Creek in 1848, and below him is a prospector mining for gold. The woman's right hand curls down to the bottom of the mural and tears back the earth itself to reveal two miners working below. Above the mine sits a tree stump, a redwood no doubt, above the tree stump sits a pressure gauge, and immediately behind the gauge sits an engineer talking to a tool operator. The colors are rich and vibrant, and it remains to this day a thing of beauty.

Rivera's second mural, then under way at the California School of Fine Arts, went in a different direction, appropriate to its setting. Called *The Making of a Fresco*, it is a mural about the making of a mural. We see the scaffolding and the boards supporting the creative team as they work on the project. We see back and side views of people. Diego Rivera himself, for instance, observing and directing the activities. On the level above and to the left we see a rear view of Jack Hastings, holding a plumb line, and to the right a three-quarters view of British artist Clifford Wight, the lead assistant, measuring a section of the wall. For his efforts Jack Hastings earned a tiny sliver of immortality: his image would remain permanently fixed on the wall, as it is to this day.

Rivera's decision to focus the second mural on the act of art creation delighted Govie, as he explained: "When Rivera was working on the decoration for the Art School, he had the idea that some of the students would seize the opportunity to learn how frescoing is done. He asked nothing better because he loves to help young things who are learning to draw and paint." Govie went on to describe how Diego Rivera "showed them how to grind color, how to mix plaster, and put it on, how to determine the golden sections, how and when to trace the design on the plaster, how to hold the brush, how to make the light, sure stroke, when to start, and when to stop."

By the time they returned home, Ruth and Govie had become unabashed fans of Diego Rivera and were favorably impressed with Frida Kahlo as well, and the feelings appear to have been mutual. In two separate letters to Cristina later that year, Frida Kahlo would ask that her fond regards be passed on to "Ruth and Mr. Morris."

Probably the clearest measure, though, of just how impressed Ruth and Govie were with the two murals is that they decided to commission one of their own. Diego Rivera was out of their price range at that point. Actually everyone was out of their price range at that point, but that did not stop them from commissioning Jack Hastings to create a fresco in the guest quarters just across the courtyard from the main house in Monterey, the same accommodations Alec Waugh had made use of during his first visit. For his services, Jack would receive food and shelter for himself and Cristina and all the painting supplies he needed, but he would also work by himself from beginning to end without any assistants, though it's safe to assume that Govie played that role at least informally.

For this mural, Govie would be the central figure. It is his image your eye is first drawn to, sitting in a chair and holding in the palm of his hand the small figure of a nude Tahitian woman, meant to symbolize that earlier idealized time in French Polynesia, as captured by Gauguin, when the islands were unspoiled and the women wore no clothes. Behind Govie is a stylized image of the Monterey mansion. To Govie's right is a Hollywood cameraman framing Govie in his shot. Glaring out from the middle of the fresco is Zupatina, the wild cat who drove Jack out of the Society Islands and into a job with Diego Rivera. Flying overhead is Ruth in a biplane, and looming below her is the RMS *Tahiti*, the ship that sank the previous summer. Dotted throughout are recognizable landmarks like the Carmel Mission and the Ferry Building in San Francisco. A steam engine chugs across the upper left corner of the mural. On the lower left sits the Statue of Liberty. All the elements tie together coherently, and the end result is quite striking.

In its finished form, the fresco would earn the ultimate compliment: Diego Rivera loved it. He never got to see it in person, unfortunately, but Jack Hastings sent him photographs. After giving them careful study, Rivera and Frida Kahlo were unreserved in their praise, and Rivera was inspired to offer Jack Hastings a job working on his next fresco project, which would take place in Detroit in 1932 and become Rivera's most famous project in America. Jack would become one of only two assistants who were paid and whose names appeared on the original contract. The other paid assistant was Clifford Wight. In later years, Hastings would paint other murals, only a few of which have survived to this day, but the mural Jack painted for Ruth and Govie was his first solo effort and the one that made all the others possible.

So pleased were the Morrises with Jack's fresco that they promptly arranged to have Clifford Wight, Rivera's principal assistant, come down to Monterey and create a second fresco in the back room of the guesthouse. The terms were the same: Wight and wife, Jean, were provided food and accommodations while Clifford worked on the project, and the Morrises picked up the tab on the costs of all materials. Where the two projects differed was in their subject matter and presentation. Rather than painting a number of disparate images, pulled together as a unified whole, Wight chose to create what more closely resembles a portrait. His subject? A group of African American jazz musicians caught in midperformance. It's a splendid piece.

A few years later Clifford Wight, who was British by heritage and primarily a sculptor by trade, would earn a measure of fame and generate a good deal of controversy with his five panels in San Francisco's iconic landmark Coit Tower. While four panels remain to this day and are held in high regard, the fifth was removed, following a huge uproar over its inclusion of a small hammer and sickle. For this bit of political theater, Clifford Wight was deported from the country and would live out the rest of his life a somewhat broken man.

With the frescoes by Hastings and Wight complete, Govie was inspired to add one more, and this time the artist would be closer to home: himself. After spending all that time watching Francis McComas create watercolors, and having been present as two murals blossomed on the walls of his guesthouse, Govie decided to put down his writer's pen for the moment and pick up a paintbrush. The result, which no doubt benefited from the able assistance of Clifford Wight, is a colorful and quite playful fresco featuring rabbits. It, like the other two murals, remains to this day.

While the three new works of art were wonderful aesthetic additions to the Morris property, they did nothing to help pay down the construction loan, which was hanging over them like a Sword of

Damocles, and they weren't going to be able to stave off the inevitable much longer.

Rather than sit home and stew about it, though, they would return once again to Tahiti. Ruth would go first. Govie would follow, and they would not stay long. Ocean voyages at this stage were extravagances they truly could not afford, forcing them to run up bills they didn't have the ability to pay. But they felt they had an obligation to go. They had invited friends to come stay at the plantation.

The bottom line was this: they had to keep up appearances.

CHAPTER SEVENTEEN

THE HARD-LUCK GIRL

There was much weighing on Ruth Morris's mind as the ship set sail from San Francisco in July 1931, but she had a great traveling companion: Marcella Gump. The two had a long history together and had supported each other through various romantic travails. On this trip, Marcella was to serve as Ruth's stand-in hostess, allowing Ruth to return home quickly, once she had greeted her guests.

The first to arrive in Tahiti were the wife of the chancellor of the University of Southern California, the spouse of another university official, and a USC professor. The professor had come for the express purpose of recovering Friedrich Murnau's sixty-five-foot yacht *Pali* and sailing it home. The USC party got its brief taste of paradise and then was gone.

The next wave of guests, however, was of much greater importance to the Morrises, and Govie had made a special trip down just to greet them. Particularly one guest: Lila Lee.

Of all the friends and acquaintances the Morrises would pull into their orbit over the years, Lila Lee would remain in a category by herself. Call her a special friend. Call her almost part of the family. Lila had known Ruth and Govie from their earliest days in Hollywood, back when she was briefly romantically linked with Charlie Chaplin. Most significantly, she was destined later to become a part of the Morris household during a crisis in their lives still to come, so hers is a life deserving closer examination.

A good place to start is her nickname, which may explain, in part, why the Morrises were so attached to her. Lila was known in Hollywood as the "hard-luck girl," and not without justification. For all the surface glamour of her life and the fan-mag fantasies about the world of celebrities, Lila's life had been painful and difficult.

She'd had her childhood stolen from her, in a way that to modern sensibilities sounds quite disturbing. Born Augusta Wilhelmena Fredericka Appel in 1901, she never aspired to be in show business. Her dream was to be a nurse, but someone else had other ideas.

That someone else was an ambitious promoter of "kiddie review shows" named Gus Edwards. When she was still a child, Edwards spotted her and immediately began a campaign to have her parents sign over legal guardianship to him so he could "exploit her cuteness and natural talents."

Why any parent would agree to such an arrangement is hard to fathom, but evidently they saw dollar signs. Mom and Dad signed on the dotted line, and young Augusta Wilhelmena Fredericka was handed over to Gus Edwards so that he could "exploit" her.

Soon he had her on stage performing under the nickname "Cuddles," effectively supplanting her father and mother as the parental figure in her life. By the time her parents finally came to their senses and tried to regain custody, Edwards had so established control over her that she sided with him in the battle with her parents. It was as though her parents had shipped her off to a cult and then discovered they couldn't deprogram her.

By the age of twelve, she had appeared in her first feature film, and it was then that Edwards came up with the stage name she would have for the rest of her life: Lila Lee.

Five years later in 1918, Lila arrived in Hollywood an ingénue with star potential. It wasn't long before she found success, and in 1922 she would become a fan-magazine-fixture celebrity when she starred as Carmen opposite Rudolph Valentino in *Blood and Sand*.

It all sounds quite glamorous, but the life she had endured as she was growing up had caused real damage. Gus Edwards's relationship with her had been almost that of a pimp. He had kept her under tight control, and that complicated her ability to deal with other men. After Edwards, she wasn't looking for tenderness. She wanted someone firm and controlling, and unfortunately she found him.

His name was James Kirkwood. He was an actor. His age: forty-eight. Her age: twenty-two. The difference in ages exceeded Ruth and Govie's by five years.

A baby boy, James Jr., followed a year later, and Lila dutifully took time off from her career, just as it was heating up, to care for her infant son. Had the twenty-three-year-old Lila been willing to remain home as a full-time wife and mother, Kirkwood might have been satisfied. But she had already come too far as an actress and was unwilling to give it all up.

In a rare act of independence, Lila resumed her career and began leaving young Jimmy in the care of a nanny, and as her success continued to grow, it overshadowed Kirkwood's more modest, journeyman-actor career, creating inevitable tensions.

But what really got under Kirkwood's skin was that Lila was developing a social life that involved people closer to her own age, and some of those friends were men. Worse, one of those men, actor and director John Farrow, was showing Lila special attention. It was a perfect recipe for marital discord, and in the case of Lila and James, it became grounds for separation, forcing Lila to seek refuge with the actress Bebe Daniels.

Eventually Kirkwood filed for divorce, and he took a hard shot at her in the divorce papers: "Lila Lee was so taken up with Hollywood parties and people that she did not have time to devote to the care of their five-year old son." To which Lila protested, "My baby was never neglected," pointing out that when she was tied up at the studio, "he was left in the most capable of hands," and she scoffed at the talk of Hollywood parties and her social friends, saying, "There is a great difference in the ages of Mr. Kirkwood and myself. Naturally, our friends would not be the same."

Lila had genuine reason to fear Kirkwood's line of attack, however, because if he was able to successfully make the case that she was a loose woman and an unfit mother, she would lose custody of her child, and the centerpiece of his legal action was a demand for full custody of young Jimmy.

Then things got more complicated. In the middle of all the divorce and custody drama, Lila was forced to check into a sanatorium in Prescott, Arizona, called Pamsetgaaf, which specialized in the treatment of tuberculosis.

One press report said, "Her physician has ordered her away for a complete rest of from three to six months." Another said that she had suffered a "nervous breakdown." When her press agent, Margaret Ettinger, was asked point-blank whether Lila was suffering from tuberculosis, she flatly denied it, saying, "Miss Lee is simply worn out with hard work and she has been ordered to rest."

Whether these reports were covering up tuberculosis, or whether later references to TB were covering up some breakdown, Lila would maintain later in life that she had been suffering from tuberculosis.

Whatever was going on, it was big news in the entertainment and gossip corridors of journalism. *Motion Picture* magazine breathlessly reported that John Farrow was paying her regular visits, noting, "Once a week or so a big plane leaves Hollywood for the Grand Canyon region, and Johnny's aboard. It carries him to see Lila Lee in the sanitarium in Prescott."

Needless to say, Lila's health issues did not help her legal battle with James Kirkwood, and, unsurprisingly, he got the divorce he sought and the full custody of young Jimmy he had demanded. In response Lila had the following to say: "I was simply not adult enough to know how to handle Jim."

As Lila Lee began trying to put her life back together following her release from the facility in Arizona, the Morrises stepped forward to offer a friendly hand. It came in the form of an invitation to Lila and her new man, John Farrow, to come to Tahiti and stay as guests of the Morrises at their plantation in Paea to relax and maybe enjoy a little romance.

It all seemed perfect until John Farrow got tied up at work and couldn't get loose for the trip, but he proposed a plan B: silent film actress Patsy Ruth Miller, who the Morrises had known going back to Max Linder's party back in 1921, could go with Lila in his stead.

So it was that Lila and Patsy sailed off together to Tahiti in the summer of 1931, and when they arrived in Papeete, Govie and Ruth were on the dock to greet them. After playing the role of dutiful hosts until the next ship to San Francisco arrived, the Morrises departed.

That was Marcella Gump's cue to take over as hostess, and she was well cast in the role. She was outgoing and funny, she knew how to have a good time, and she had no problem keeping Lila and Patsy occupied. One moment they were fishing with the natives on Bora Bora. The next they were walking across hot coals on Raiatea.

Marcella's playfulness, however, misfired on one occasion, when John Farrow showed up unexpectedly. In passing, Marcella happened to mention the charming young Frenchmen who had briefly been houseguests. All quite innocent, but there was just enough of the if-you-know-what-I-mean in her tone to light up every jealous cell in Farrow's body.

Suddenly the accusations were flying. Her alleged lovers. His alleged lovers. Tears mixed with recrimination. It was an ugly mess.

The following day, Lila stayed behind closed doors, and John fled to Papeete, returning well after dark.

That was when things got strange. As Patsy lay asleep in her bed, a sharp bump against the wall that joined her room with John Farrow's woke her up. Lighting a candle and walking soundlessly through the house, Patsy first roused Lila, and then the two of them moved slowly into John Farrow's room.

Patsy vividly recalled the scene: "The flickering light disclosed Johnny lying peacefully in bed, his eyes closed, a look of utter serenity on his face. The covers were pulled up to his chin, but one arm lay, palm up, on the outside and from the arm slow globules of blood were dropping rhythmically to the floor, landing with little clinking sounds on the knife with which he had slashed both his wrists."

Help was immediately sought, and John Farrow was saved. Peace between Lila and John was also restored. But the walk down the aisle everyone had been anticipating was now destined never to happen. Instead John Farrow married actress Maureen O'Sullivan, which means Mia Farrow may owe her existence at least partially to Marcella Gump.

Back in California the cocoon of denial Ruth and Govie had tightly wrapped around themselves was finally beginning to crack. The moment of truth seemed to have come when superior court judge Harry Falk slapped a judgment of $16,000 against the couple for failing to pay S. H. Hooke and W. E. Hooke for the addition on the house, an amount Ruth and Govie did not have the ability to pay.

One passage out of the legal documents is quite telling: "Mrs. Morris left Monterey on a trip to the South Seas a few days after construction commenced, but Mr. Morris continued to reside on the premises. He was very active in observing all details of construction and had very definite ideas as to what he desired. From time to time changes were made in the plans drawn by architect [Wesley] Hastings, and in a number of instances after certain portions of the work had been done in accordance with the directions of Morris he decided that something else was preferable and the work was done over. The conduct of Mr. Morris, as testified to by Hooke and by the subcontractors and material men, indicates that his insistence throughout was that everything, down to the smallest detail, should be exactly as he and Mrs. Morris desired it, and that said contractors and material men were warranted in inferring that price was not a major consideration."

At long last Ruth and Govie realized the lifestyle they had come to love was no longer sustainable. It had been a great ride while it lasted. The house. The plantation. The travel. The parties. The shopping. All things difficult to give up, but they simply weren't bringing in enough money to keep it going.

Worse, the country was now sinking further into what would become known as the Great Depression. Banks were failing. The GNP was plunging. And by the end of 1931, the unemployment rate had climbed to 15.9 percent, on its way to 23.6 percent the following year.

Thus the Morrises did what would have been unthinkable before. In early 1932 they packed up many of their things and moved out of their dream home. A home that had been built to their exacting specifications. That had been filled with furnishings and housewares they had collected in Spain. That contained two original frescoes created by assistants to Diego Rivera. That had accommodated so many famous and celebrated guests. And that contained within its walls a veritable constellation of memories.

They no doubt told their friends it was temporary. They probably even tried to convince themselves of the same thing. But it was not to be.

Within a year of losing her lover, Ruth Morris was losing her home, and she had to have been asking herself, What more could she possibly lose?

CHAPTER EIGHTEEN

HOLLYWOOD—
THE SEQUEL

Over the years Ruth Morris had experienced her share of triumphs and disappointments, shocks and thrills, but rarely had she felt as demoralized as she felt in early 1932. The fortune was gone. The mansion was going. And now she and Govie were back in Southern California with what amounted to hats in hand.

The Morrises would never have put it that way. Their savings might have vanished, but their pride was quite intact. So they would continue as best they could to keep up appearances, but truth be told, they really needed to start generating some income to contend with the stream of unpaid bills.

Finding a place to live, at least, proved relatively painless, but it always helps when you have connections, which were the one thing the Morrises had not lost. In this case, those connections led them to Herbert Manfred Marx. Or as movie fans know him, Zeppo Marx. It turns out that in addition to playing the straight man in movies like *The Cocoanuts*, *Animal Crackers*, *Monkey Business*, *Horse Feathers*, and *Duck Soup* with his madcap brothers, Zeppo was also the owner of an apartment building, and he conveniently had an apartment available for Ruth and Govie.

Once Ruth was settled in, she began looking for ways she could be productive, and though it seems counterintuitive, her sense of despair seems to have, at least initially, given her a kick in the butt. Rather quickly Ruth began coming up with writing and even film ideas, and for the first time in years, she saw some of these projects through to completion.

Ruth's first project was a writing assignment for *Variety* magazine with a crackerjack subject: director Frank Capra. Whether it was her idea or the magazine's, her timing was impeccable. Capra was just on the cusp of breaking out as a major motion picture director with a string of unforgettable classics. Just consider: *It Happened One Night*, starring Claudette Colbert and Clark Gable, would be released two years after Ruth interviewed him and would go on to sweep all five top Oscar categories. Capra would later win Best Director Oscars for *Mr. Deeds Goes to Town* and *You Can't Take It with You*, and he would receive Oscar nominations for *Mr. Smith Goes to Washington* and that perennial favorite *It's a Wonderful Life*.

Ruth's profile offers ample hints why Capra's success should have come as no surprise. Even then he had an uncanny finger on the pulse of American sensibilities as the Depression strengthened its brutal grip on the nation, asserting, "The Man in the Street has had so many dogmas crammed down his throat that he is prepared to revolt against the current under estimation of his intelligence. He's fed up. Politics, prohibition, patriotism, big business, high-powered advertising, are subjects ripe for ridicule."

Capra also expounds upon the importance of human emotion in filmmaking: "Emotional dramas will narrow down to small casts and concentrate on two human beings who find tender mitigations in the everyday problems of life." Not unlike what filmgoers would soon be seeing with Colbert and Gable in *It Happened One Night*. Capra expanded upon this point: "Good box office pictures must project some great love—not necessarily of one human for another. The love may be for nature, a career, an art, a country, but it must be deep and true, humanized by everyday occurrences that translate its basic truth to the average fan."

While Ruth was reengaging with creative projects, she took time out to meet with pal Lila Lee in Beverly Hills, an encounter that snagged the attention of a gossip columnist who dutifully reported that Ruth Morris and Lila Lee were spotted "lunching" at the Brown Derby and mentioned that the women were just back from Tahiti, where Lila Lee had been a guest of the Morrises. What they actually talked about would have been more interesting. John Farrow? Fire walking? Marcella Gump?

Another social engagement early in 1932 seems to have given Govie's prospects a slight boost as well. The Morrises were invited to a spring garden party by an old friend from the 1920s, Colleen Moore, whose career in the intervening years had only grown. It was Moore who had almost single-handedly popularized the flapper craze in America, thanks to her star turn in the 1923 movie *Flaming Youth*. When you think bobbed hair and slinky outfits, think Colleen Moore. As no less an authority than F. Scott Fitzgerald would proclaim, "I was the spark that lit up *Flaming Youth*, Colleen Moore was the torch. What little things we are to have caused such trouble." Later in the 1920s, Colleen Moore would reign as the number one box office star in America two years running.

"Party girl" might have been her image, but Moore was that rare starlet in Hollywood who managed to always keep her head on straight, and by 1932 she was living in a magnificent mansion with beautifully landscaped grounds in one of the toniest areas in Southern California: Bel Air.

The party to which the Morrises were invited was billed as "the tea party of the season," with a guest list dripping with boldface names. Gary Cooper. Jean Harlow. Mary Pickford. Harold Lloyd. Fredric March. Louie B. Mayer. Theda Bara. Hedda Hopper.

At first blush it seemed just like old times, until you considered how much had changed. The Morrises were living in an apartment now, not a mansion, and any explanation for why they had left Monterey would have required either painful honesty or complete applesauce. Still, with an A-list crowd like this on hand, it was an ideal environment for networking, and the evidence suggests that Govie's time at the party may have produced some results.

At least that is the reasonable supposition, given that shortly after Colleen Moore's party, at which Louis B. Mayer was in attendance, Metro-Goldwyn-Mayer announced that Gouverneur Morris would be doing some projects for the studio. The nature of those projects was left a little nebulous, but it was an opening of sorts, though with some challenges. Govie, after all, had never written a movie script before, so he would be learning on the job, as it were.

For his first effort, Govie teamed up with, of all people, Zeppo Marx, which was certainly a convenient pairing, given that they both lived in the same building, but also an odd one. The zaniness we associate with the Marx Brothers is such a departure from anything Govie had ever written, it's difficult to imagine where they found common ground. Govie, though, thought Zeppo made a great partner, precisely because they were so different, effectively complementing each other. Zeppo was, he said, "a lamb with a god given sense of the ridiculous."

All well and good, but the script Zeppo and Govie finally produced, called *Tom, Dick, and Harry,* which tells the hard-luck story of a Kansas farmer with three sons who loses his home and all the family's possessions, seems to have contained a few too many servings of the ridiculous. The executive at MGM who reviewed it said, "We found it interesting in the early part but it is our opinion that the story goes all hay-wire at the end. The coincidences pile on each other so thick that it could not be picturized."

Thus ended the short, happy life of the screenwriting team of Marx and Morris. Govie did manage to pick up the odd writing assignment on his own, and he wrote a piece about Diego Rivera that extolled the wonders of the fresco and argued for government funding of the arts, concluding, "Angelenos who love their city should visit San Francisco, and see the tremendous paintings at the Art School and the Stock Exchange. They will want the same things also, only bigger and more numerous, and if it is possible more beautiful." Still, what Govie was angling for was a staff job at a studio, and so far that had not come through.

Ruth, at this stage, had bigger ambitions. She wanted to produce two short movies, set in French Polynesia, taking a page straight out of the F. W. Murnau playbook. Once again she was swimming against the tide, because women's opportunities behind the camera were shrinking, not expanding, in the 1930s. Hollywood culture was becoming more business minded and more rigid about gender roles, but Ruth was operating as an independent producer outside the studio system.

Drawing on her extensive exposure to the warm, friendly people and the rich, vibrant culture of the Society Islands, Ruth wrote two stories and then turned them into shooting scripts, dusting off the skills she had perfected at Goldwyn Pictures.

Then she got quite lucky. She found a cinematographer, Glenn Kershner, who needed to capture footage in French Polynesia for a film in production at Universal, and he agreed to shoot her stories as well. In other words, she was able to piggyback on a major studio project. Given the shoestring nature of her budget, she probably couldn't have pulled it off any other way.

Ruth also managed to recruit Irvin Willat, a director from the silent era, who was starved for any kind of work he could get. With his hire, she had effectively mirrored the three-person professional crew arrangement Murnau had used. Not surprisingly, Ruth relied on an all-native cast for her two movies as well.

Housing was easy on this low-budget affair: Kershner and Willat simply stayed at the Morris plantation at Paea. And Ruth was also able to wear the extra hat of the film crew's liaison with the local community, as Kershner noted: "She being so well acquainted with and well liked by the island people extra privileges were granted us."

Ruth confined filming to Moorea and Tahiti, which simplified the logistics, and the shoots themselves came off without a hitch. Irwin, Kershner, and Ruth were all delighted with what they had created, and along the way, Ruth's cameraman and director became thoroughly enamored with French Polynesia, a now familiar pattern.

There is no happy ending, however. Whatever the merits of the films—and Kershner, for one, thought they were wonderful—they never found their way into release because of their length. Hollywood in the 1930s wanted feature-length films, not shorts, and wouldn't even consider distributing them. Sadly, Ruth's two movies are now lost forever.

Another part of Ruth's life was lost forever as well. When she boarded the ship for her return to California, she was saying good-bye to French Polynesia for the last time. With their need for cash, the Morrises would soon sell the plantation.

Meanwhile, Govie had finally nailed a studio job, thanks to Carl Laemmle Jr.—or Junior, as everyone called him—head of production at Universal Studios. And Govie's first assignment? To write a screen treatment of the H. G. Wells novel *The Invisible Man*. This was to be a star vehicle for Boris Karloff. But Karloff would have no part of the picture. And his objection? He would be invisible on-screen. No one would see him. Fortunately, Claude Rains had no such qualms, and the role would kick-start a career that would see him a few years later uttering those immortal words in *Casablanca*, "Round up the usual suspects."

Govie's career, however, received no such kick start from *The Invisible Man*. Somewhere along the line, other writers were brought onto the project. When the film was released in 1933, the screenplay was credited to R. C. Sherriff, and it was later revealed that Philip Wylie and Preston Sturges had also contributed to the script, though they went uncredited.

Govie continued plugging away at Universal, but the pattern would be repeated more than once. He would get an assignment. A press release would go out identifying him with a project. The movie would come out, and his name would be missing from the credits. His job was providing an income but could not have been providing much satisfaction.

While Govie was busy at his day job, Ruth embarked on yet another ambitious project: writing a novel. Drawing upon the people she had encountered in the Society Islands, the stories they had told, and the things she had observed, Ruth began developing a narrative. Real people from the islands became models for her characters, and she inserted some of her friends, like Jack and Cristina Hastings, into the story.

To Ruth's credit she finished the novel and even reached out to Clifford Wight for help illustrating the story, but this was in the depths of the Depression. Nothing came easy. Like her two short films, Ruth's novel is now gone forever, having never found a publisher.

With this latest setback, Ruth's creative drive began to falter, which had to have been particularly disheartening. She had for a time redis-covered at least some of the spirit of "the other Ruth," and there had been a focus and an ambition she had not displayed in years. In such a difficult economic environment, however, it was not something she could sustain.

Ruth would make halting attempts to write short stories in the years that followed, but she no longer had the drive to stay with it. Her stories would lay there, titled and half finished. Eventually Govie would find them, as he later admitted, finish them, and submit them for pub-lication. Under his name.

While circumstances for the Morrises were at best mixed during their return to Hollywood in the early 1930s, one pattern did emerge that reflects rather favorably on them both: even as they struggled pro-fessionally, on more than one occasion they helped others get ahead.

Take Richard Gump, brother of Marcella and son of the owners of Gump's in San Francisco. In the 1930s he came to Hollywood look-ing for a job, and it was Govie who made the key phone call that got him hired. It went to Cedric Gibbons, an important player at Metro-Goldwyn-Mayer. He was Louis B. Mayer's go-to guy for production design, a founding member of the Academy of Motion Picture Arts and Sciences, and a nominee for an Academy Award thirty-nine times. And here's the capper: Cedric Gibbons designed the golden statuette they give out at the Oscars. In other words, he was someone who could make things happen. All it took was one phone call from Govie, and Richard Gump was designing sets at MGM.

There is one other story, in particular, that stands out, mostly because of its historical significance. Call it a footnote, if you will, but it appears to have been a rather important footnote in the career of someone who would ultimately become quite famous.

It all started with an unsolicited script from an unknown writer, something Govie generally detested, which showed up in his mail one morning at his office at Universal. For some reason, on this particular occasion, he decided to read the script and found himself engrossed.

Unknown the author may have been, but she had crafted a story that held Govie's attention from beginning to end, not entirely surprising since the story contained a love triangle. Govie was a pushover for love triangles, as long as they were a part of a fictional story and not his own life. The love triangle in this instance, though, turned out to be the only conventional aspect of the script. In every other way, the story was fresh and original, thanks to its setting in the Soviet Union and its Russian characters. An opponent of the regime and a supporter vie for the attentions of a young woman, and if there were any doubts about which character would prevail in the end, it is telegraphed by the title: *The Red Pawn.*

Govie would later say it was "the first script sent to me by an unknown youngster which showed positive genius." He passed it along to the decision makers at Universal Pictures, and the studio bought it for $1,500. While the story would never find its way to the screen because of internal political concerns, it would mark a milestone for one young writer. *The Red Pawn* was the first script ever sold by Russian immigrant Ayn Rand.

What's interesting about this episode is that in the same year Govie gave Ayn Rand's writing career a critical boost, he also wrote his piece in the *Los Angeles Times* praising Diego Rivera as "kind, wise, witty, generous," and urging government funding for the arts. Here you had a passionate anti-Communist on one hand and a friend of Leon Trotsky on the other, and Govie found something worthy in each of them to support.

Ayn Rand's career would later receive one more critical boost from a member of the Morris household, and this time it would be from Ruth. After selling her first movie script, Rand wrote a play called *Woman on Trial* that contains an original plot gimmick. At its core, the play is a courtroom drama, but here's Rand's unique twist: each night the jury would be composed of members of the audience, and how the play ended depended upon how the jury ruled.

Ruth loved the play, and it became her personal cause to get it produced. At this, she was playing to her strong suit. Proving once more that she still had the power to persuade and get a man to do what she wanted, Ruth convinced E. E. Clive, one of the actors appearing in the film *The Invisible Man*, to stage the play.

Woman on Trial opened at the Hollywood Playhouse to positive reviews and enjoyed some success. Later it would move to Broadway under a new title, *Night of January 16th*, and would ultimately become a motion picture.

The success they helped others achieve somehow eluded the Morrises, however, and like ghosts from the past, reminders of their spending excesses kept coming back to haunt them in the newspapers, which all their friends read. The worst had to have been the *Times* story a few years earlier revealing that the St. Francis hotel, once their social headquarters in San Francisco, had secured a judgment against them.

Something else that may have surprised and possibly alarmed their friends was the news Govie shared privately that he had gotten mixed up in a get-rich-quick scheme involving the recovery of gold ingots in Mexico, which he claimed were worth billions. Whether it involved smuggling or shipwrecks, it all sounded dodgy.

Not surprisingly, no gold ingots appear to have been recovered, and soon the depressing news arrived that the Morrises had finally lost the mansion in Monterey to foreclosure, after a long, protracted legal battle.

Though it was small compensation, Ruth and Govie were able to move into a mansion, upgrading from an apartment, but they mostly had the Great Depression to thank for it. The mansion in question was located in Manhattan Beach, a sparsely populated beach community southwest of Los Angeles. It had just been completed when the cratering economy rendered it unsaleable. Eventually its owner, desperate for any income from the thing, rented it out at what the market would bear, which wasn't much, and the Morrises were able to return to mansion living—albeit in Manhattan Beach, not Beverly Hills, and with little more landscaping than the fruit trees and shrubs that had already been there.

That small bit of good news quickly soured, however, when Govie got slapped with felony drunk-driving charges, an ugly situation all the way around. He had not simply been driving while drunk. He had been driving while drunk and had injured someone. It happened May

23, 1935, on Western Avenue in Los Angeles between Washington Boulevard and Venice Boulevard, as he was attempting to maneuver into a parking place. It did not go well. Both his aim and his velocity were way off, and he ended up hitting a parked car, which caused a chain reaction involving two other cars.

At the precise moment the third car lurched back, L. E. Erickson stepped off the curb, and he was instantly pinned, fracturing both legs. Officers called to the scene determined that Govie was inebriated and arrested him for felony drunk driving, a charge he vehemently denied.

Needless to say, Govie's arrest did not go unnoticed by the news media, only adding to the string of unflattering notices that had of late greeted the Morrises.

Once Govie was in a courtroom and under oath, he fessed up. When asked what he had been drinking, he replied, "Call it gin." He pled guilty, and the judge gave him a $500 fine and threatened jail time if it wasn't paid. Govie paid.

It had been a hard five years for Ruth Morris since that fateful day she mixed up the envelopes and abruptly ended her relationship with Alec Waugh. Much more had gone wrong than had gone right in her life, and throughout all that time not a word had passed between the two of them. Ruth and Alec were now living very different lives in very different places, and it was difficult for either of them to have a sense of what the other one was doing or thinking or feeling.

While Ruth was busy trying to keep herself afloat in Southern California, Alec had married an Australian woman named Joan Chirnside, who would ultimately become the mother of his three children. How closely Ruth kept up with events in Alec Waugh's life in the 1930s is impossible to know, but about one thing we can be certain: she never forgot him.

Alec never forgot Ruth, either, as he would later recall: "Through the crowded 'thirties, though Ruth and I had gone out of each other's lives, I was always aware of her, there on the Pacific coast. I had one standard, one criterion, and it was this, a resolve that she should never hear of something I had done, or read something I had written, with a sense of shame, with the thought 'How could I have?' I vowed that she should stay proud of me."

As Ruth navigated through some particularly rough patches in 1935, she felt compelled to contact Alec one last time. Carefully she copied the words of an old poem by Ernest Dowson onto a piece of paper, and at the top she scrawled "Nor Many Waters," the title of the book Alec had dedicated to her on her birthday in 1928. When those words reached London, they would be the last from Ruth Morris to Alec Waugh:

By the sad waters of separation
Where we have wandered by divers ways,
I have but the shadow and imitation
Of the old, memorial days.

In music I have no consolation,
No roses are pale enough for me;
The sound of the waters of separation
Surpasseth roses and melody.

By the sad waters of separation
Dimly I hear, from an hidden place
The sigh of mine ancient adoration:
Hardly can I remember your face.

If you be dead, no proclamation
Sprang to me over the waste, gray sea:
Living, the waters of separation
Sever, for ever, your soul from me.

No man knoweth our desolation;
Memory pales of the old delight;
While the sad waters of separation
Bear us on to the ultimate night.

CHAPTER NINETEEN

DEATH AT THE MANSION

Friday, September 25, 1936, was the worst day in Ruth Morris's life. From its first moments it was a tragedy, which quickly mushroomed into an ugly, media-driven scandal. And no one save the victim would pay a higher price for what happened that day than Ruth herself.

It was also a mystery, complete with clues, some leading to answers and others leading only to confusion, and its unfolding came with more than its share of twists and turns. In the annals of Southern California scandals, this was one of the strangest.

It was also laden with emotion because Ruth's good friend, the actress Lila Lee, had only recently come to live with the Morrises in their Manhattan Beach mansion, and her twelve-year-old son, Jimmy Kirkwood, with whom she had just been reunited after years of separation, was with her. For the Morrises, these were two welcome additions to the household, and that such a happy reunion could so quickly take such a sobering turn was not something any of them could have foreseen. But on Friday, September 25, life in the Morris household changed forever.

In Ruth's telling as reported at the time, this was how the nightmare began. She received a phone call around midday. Victoria Russell, a distant relative of Govie's whom he had never met in person, was calling because she was worried about her twenty-eight-year-old son, Reid Russell, a frequent guest at the Morris residence. He had not come home the previous evening, and she wondered whether the Morrises knew of his whereabouts. Ruth answered that she did not but saw little reason to be concerned. After all, Victoria Russell had called with a similar question five days earlier, and Reid had turned up soon afterward.

As she was hanging up, Jimmy Kirkwood anxiously sought her attention. He had seen something she needed to know: Reid's car was parked down at the edge of the property. If Reid's car was around, then Reid was probably around, too.

Lila's son and Ruth hurried down to the spot where Jimmy had seen the car, and it was still there. Reid, though, was nowhere to be found. Next they looked in the barn. No Reid.

The pair returned to the house, and Ruth headed straight up to the second-floor balcony, which afforded a better view of the property. With binoculars, she made a visual sweep of the garden, coming to a sudden stop when she spotted something. Two legs were sticking out from the garden swing.

Startled by what she had seen, Ruth quickly roused Govie, who was squirreled away in his office. He in turn tracked down the gardener, John Munolo, and the two men rushed out into the garden, approached the swing, and made the grisly discovery. It was Reid Russell, with a gunshot wound to the head, a pistol in his hand, and no pulse.

Ruth would then explain that she made two phone calls. The first went to the Manhattan Beach Police Department. The second went to Victoria Russell, who collapsed when she heard the news.

Captain Percy Jones and Motorcycle Officer H. M. Eagles soon arrived, and they promptly botched the case. The problem was confirmation bias. They were operating under the assumption that it was a suicide, and they seemed to be looking for evidence that supported that theory. Russell had been shot at close range, and the pistol in his hand was a .32-caliber. Simple deduction. Gun in hand. Wound in temple. Suicide.

Typically, however, police officers test, or arrange to have tested, the decedent's hands for evidence of residue, which would confirm he had recently fired a weapon. They didn't bother, and by the time the coroner had cleaned up the body, it was too late.

It gets worse. When they found a bullet "lodged in a settee behind the lawn swing," they tossed it off into the grass, never to be seen again, because it was .22-caliber and didn't match the pistol in Reid's hand. So unimportant was this bullet that the officers never bothered to even mention it in their report. Their bad police work came to light only because Jimmy Kirkwood saw them toss the bullet.

Then there is the matter of the spent cartridge casing. If Reid Russell had fired the pistol, there had to have been a cartridge casing somewhere. But they could find no casing. That's a big deal. Under normal circumstances, the failure to find a key piece of evidence like that would prompt investigators to keep an open mind about what had happened, maybe pursue the matter further. Not so with this team. It was suicide. End of story.

In fairness to the officers, Ruth and Govie were pushing the theory of suicide hard. Here are Govie's first comments about the case: "I know that Russell was disconsolate because after having received a promotion only a few days previously, he was discharged from his job as an automobile salesman last Saturday." Ruth chimed in on the same theme: "He confided to us Thursday that he was reluctant to tell his mother, Mrs. Victoria Russell, that he had lost his position. And he had talked of jumping off the pier." While the state of Reid's frame of mind is important information, it did not negate the need for a full investigation.

Fortunately, the Los Angeles County Sherriff's Department gave the case a second look, and it proved more thorough, completely revisiting the case again and covering additional ground the Manhattan Beach officers had left untouched. For instance, the first thing Deputies Charles Bright and James Claxton did was pay a visit to the grieving mother, Victoria Russell, who did not believe her son had been responsible for his own death, arguing, "He was too brave for that." She did, however, confirm that the .32-caliber pistol found at the death scene was his, saying, "The gun was rusty, since Russell carried it in the car on several long trips."

When the sheriff's deputies examined the death scene, a couple of things didn't add up. Take the pistol, for instance. It did not appear to have been fired in a long time, and it was so rusty there was reason to question whether it could be fired at all. Then there was the hole in the canvas swing. Supposedly a bullet had gone through the canvas, but the hole did not line up with the path the bullet would have traveled.

Which brings us once again to the cartridge casing. Where was the shell casing? The two officers combed the area around the garden swing, but they could not find the casing anywhere.

Then there was this: "Both John Munolo, a gardener, and a maid employed by the Morrises, worked in the garden Friday, passed and repassed the swing where the body was discovered—and both declared Russell's remains were not there during the day." The deputies by this time were convinced the body had been dead for at least twenty-four hours when it was discovered.

Just to review: Witnesses had not seen the body in the swing in the hours before it was discovered, though the time of death was at least twenty-four hours earlier. The pistol found in Reid's hand did not appear to have been recently fired. And the bullet hole in the canvas swing did not line up with the wound in the body.

That was when one of the most powerful men in law enforcement circles, Los Angeles County district attorney Buron Fitts, weighed in on the case. In those wild and woolly days of Southern California law and order, Fitts was something of a legend. He had nailed high-profile bad guys like Rattlesnake James, a barber who had murdered multiple wives for the insurance money, and he had beaten the rap when he himself was charged with taking a bribe.

Then there was the show business angle. By all accounts, Fitts loved to pal around with folks in the industry, particularly the stars. And one episode, in particular, which took place a few years after the Russell case, captures how he operated. Fitts sent one of his deputies to Union Station to greet Mae West with a kiss and the message, "This is from Buron." To which Mae responded, "Is that a gun in your pocket, or are you just glad to see me?"

Not surprisingly, the talk around town was that Fitts would some-times bend to studio pressure and pull his punches when one of their own was in legal jeopardy. Whether Govie's show business connections colored Fitts's handling of this case is impossible to know, but Fitts was pretty adamant that he saw no point in pursuing the Russell case. He ordered the autopsy skipped, and the Russell death was treated as a suicide.

The matter would have ended there, but Victoria Russell, Reid's mother, was not buying the suicide story, and she retained legal counsel. On November 9, 1936, her attorney, Stanley Visel, met with the chief investigator in the district attorney's office, Captain Clyde Plummer, and demanded that he reopen the case.

And here's why: Victoria Russell believed her son had been mur-dered because "her 28-year-old 6 foot 1 inch handsome son had been carrying on a clandestine love affair with a wealthy married woman." Jealousy was the motive, she asserted, but precisely who was jealous of whom and for what reason was not stated. Nonetheless, Mrs. Russell was convinced that there had been foul play afoot.

Attorney Visel then raised the following questions: (1) Why did the gun "show no apparent indication of having been fired for a long time?" (2) "Was a strand of hair found on the tip of the gun barrel and turned over to the Coroner's office given a scientific examination and was it determined to have been from the head of her son?" (3) "Why were the boy's hands washed" before a test could be conducted for gunshot residue?

Victoria Russell's attorney went on to question why there had been "no inquest into the boy's death" and to point out that no suicide note had been found. Concern was also expressed that no cartridge casing or spent bullet had been recovered.

The following day the story hit the papers, and one day after that, Victoria Russell alerted authorities that she had received a death threat. The caller had been a woman, and her message was chilling: "I've read about the story, and I'm interested in the case—as a mother. Some harm might befall you if you continue to push the investigation into your son's death."

That phone call changed everything. For one, it raised the obvious question: If this was a suicide, why was someone making death threats about the case? It also prompted two other questions: Who was the woman caller, and what was her interest in the case?

The story was now all over the newspapers, and the public was engaged. A grieving mother was demanding justice, and there could be little doubt where public sympathies would fall. How could District Attorney Fitts not reopen the case? The short answer was, he had to.

Quickly the announcement came that Captain Plummer, acting on behalf of DA Fitts, was assigning Everett Davis, one of his key investigators, to the case. Then he dropped the hold-the-presses news: he had just paid a "surprise visit" to the Morris home in Manhattan Beach, and that surprise visit had produced a surprise revelation—there was a suicide note.

Now, after an attorney tries to reopen the case and cites the lack of a suicide note as one of the reasons, a suicide note miraculously appears. Or did it?

During the visit to the Morris mansion, Ruth had told Captain Plummer that she had found a suicide note shortly after Reid Russell's death. But had she turned over this critical piece of evidence, which supported the theory of suicide, to authorities? No, she burned it. Or to be more precise, she destroyed evidence—in this case, evidence that would seem to support her prior claims. Why would she do such a thing? Second, why would she admit to doing such a thing?

If Captain Plummer's surprise visit to the house was intended to catch Ruth off guard, leading her to reveal more than she intended, he certainly succeeded. With no attorney present, there was no one to restrain her from exercising astonishingly bad judgment. Had she been drinking?

Then, if such a thing is possible, Ruth made matters worse. She brought up a bizarre story about how she had made a bet that Reid would commit suicide. Why would anyone make a bet like that? And why would anyone admit making a bet like that?

For almost all of Ruth Morris's adult life she had been a master of handling herself in difficult situations. She had been a talker extraordinaire, able to charm her way out of almost anything, and powerfully persuasive when advancing a cause. Where others would be bathed in sweat, she would not even blink. But now she had mishandled a situation with real legal implications on a scale that defies imagination.

That she was now in the legal crosshairs goes without saying. Before Captain Plummer departed, he made clear he wanted to question Ruth, Govie, and Lila further.

The following morning it was announced that Ruth Morris, Gouverneur Morris, and Lila Lee had voluntarily offered to come downtown to the district attorney's office to provide statements.

If September 25, 1936, was the worse day of Ruth Morris's life, then November 14, 1936, was the second worst. Her second nightmare would begin when she navigated the media swarm as she entered the district attorney's office, and citizens all over America would learn the next day that Mrs. Morris had arrived wearing a sport coat, blue slacks, and a headband sweeping back her hair. They would also be treated to a photo of her sitting at the interview table with Lila Lee to one side, Govie behind her, and Captain Plummer, the lead investigator, to her other side.

Captain Plummer began by questioning Ruth about her claim that she made a ten-dollar bet with Guy Tano, the owner of an Italian restaurant in Redondo Beach, that Reid Russell would commit suicide, and she responded:

> *Reid had been talking about killing himself because he had lost his job as an automobile salesman. More a joke than anything else, I made the bet with Tano.*

Setting aside the tastelessness of her testimony, Ruth had immediately placed her credibility on the line because she had invoked the name of Guy Tano, a restaurant owner, as a party to this alleged bet. It would only be a matter of time before Tano would go on record denying any such conversation ever occurred, but Ruth wasn't finished shredding her credibility.

> *Reid told me after he heard the bet had been made that he guessed he'd have to commit suicide so I'd win the bet.*

Captain Plumber then zeroed in on Ruth's claim that she found a suicide note from Reid Russell. Now visibly "pale and nervous," she began reciting, allegedly from memory, the contents of the note she claimed to have found and later destroyed:

> *Dear Ruth: You thought I would not do it but now you know. This has been the happiest vacation I have had in a long time. Thanks a lot for everything. I hope you don't think I didn't keep my chin up. Goodbye. Reid.*

And then *boom*—Ruth collapsed.

Quickly, Captain Plummer called for help, and two women from the office staff rushed into the interview room. Carefully they walked Ruth to the ladies' room, where they gave her a blast of smelling salts to bring her around.

Eventually Ruth composed herself somewhat and was able to continue with her story:

> *I was in my boudoir. I opened my jewel case, which I had not touched since Reid's death. I saw the note in Reid's handwriting. Lila came into the room as I held the note in my hand. I read it to her. Then, impulsively, I walked over to an ash stand, held a match to the note, and watched it burn.*

Lila Lee, who sat beside Ruth during her testimony, described the scene when she entered Ruth's bedroom:

> *Her hand was trembling. I asked what was the matter. She said, 'Oh, my God, it's a note from Russell.' I asked what it said. She said it told how he was going to commit suicide. Then she struck a match and burned the note.*

What's striking about this testimony is that in Lila's telling, she never actually read the note, which means, amid all Ruth's theatrics, Lila is relying on what Ruth said, not anything she herself read. Assuming any of this actually happened, loyal friend Lila certainly has Ruth's back here.

That is true throughout, most notably when Lila voiced her unwavering belief that Reid had suicide on his mind:

In fact, he talked about it incessantly. I had a long talk with him in the kitchen a week before he died and he told me he was in trouble with the automobile company that employed him, involving money, and he threatened then to commit suicide.

A few additional facts were shared during this difficult day for the Morrises. Ruth claimed that Reid was carrying nineteen dollars in his wallet the last time she saw him. When his body was found, his wallet was empty. Why she thought he had nineteen dollars was not immediately explained.

Georgia Jones, the maid in the Morris household, testified that two days before Reid's body was found, Reid had said to her, "I only have three hours to live."

Ruth, Govie, and Lila were all asked about reports from neighbors that gunshots were heard inside the Morris residence the night before Reid's body was found. All three were home that evening, and all testified that they heard no gunshots.

One other interesting fact emerged: Reid Russell, "who was thought to be a bachelor, had talked privately about having a divorced wife and a son in Texas." Ruth, Govie, and Lila confirmed that Reid had mentioned his ex-wife and son but had offered no details.

When Lila, Georgia, and the Morrises finally made it back to Manhattan Beach, Ruth was "in a state of nervous collapse." She immediately took to bed, and two nurses were brought in to stay by her side through the night.

The following morning the household would wake up to discover that a letter Govie had sent to Victoria Russell shortly after her son's death had been leaked to the newspapers. Here is the letter, which one paper printed in full:

Dear Mrs. Russell—
This letter will be typewritten because my handwriting is too difficult to read.

Your boy had my affection and I think that I had his. I like young things, and encouraged him to come down here when he could, because the rented house and grounds are charming and he liked them, and because we are easy-going people who like to be liked and like back. He and my nephew, Richard Bonsal, who was here in August got on famously. They were the same age and understand each other.

I think that your boy adored my sister, Mrs. Stephen Bonsal (if he didn't he was an exception), and when my brother-in-law recounted and anecdoted about the world and the people in it during the last fifty years, he listened as devoutly as I did. And we both laughed and thrilled at the same things.

Your boy had dignity, reticence and pride. I wish that I had always as much. He had a beautiful courtesy and thoughtfulness. I noticed that when Georgia, the colored maid, and her husband were away and dishes had to be washed by amateurs, they were always more quickly and efficiently washed when he was among the present.

Jimmy Kirkwood, the beautiful Lila Lee's 12-year-old son, while not sure that your son or my nephew made the world perhaps thinks it would be a better world if they had.

Jimmy was the last one of us to see Reid alive. Reid's car back-fired a lot on the way to the front gate and then stalled. Jimmy ran down the little declivity to see what was up and found Reid giggling and laughing.

Just before, Reid and my dear little wife and I had an open air lunch of grilled lamb chops and potatoes and things, and there had been two or three annoying house flies and my Ruth would think that she had one in her hand, and when Reid and I dared her to open her hand and show us, she would finally open the hand and there wouldn't be any fly. Reid and I teased her about her optimism and faulty technique, and laughed our heads off.

That was Thursday. Reid left for town at about 4 o'clock. He was to deliver two manuscripts for me, mail a special delivery letter, and then go straight home to you. The last thing I remember saying to him was something like this: "Now, you look here, Reid. I don't want any slip-up. You promised to bring your mother—my cousin Victoria—to lunch Sunday," and he promised that there would be no slip-up.

We looked forward to meeting you because of the sweet admiring things that Reid so often said about you. We thought that we could repeat the lamb chops and potatoes in the open air and possibly duplicate the fly episode.

Tuesday night I came home after dinner to find my family and Reid and another young man that we like, and are trying to be affectionate with and kind to, playing rummy. As I came in I laid my hand on your boy's shoulder, affectionately, because that was the way I felt, and said something like this: "There's an awful fog, and I don't like any friend of mine to drive in a fog. Now you stay with us tonight. We can put you up without any trouble at all." I think he was touched and pleased that I should be the one to ask him instead of the younger people.

I had a speaking engagement Wednesday night, and while I was filling that, Reid took Ruth and Jimmy Kirkwood to Redondo where they ate hamburgers and rode the merry-go-round. They got back here just before I did.

Thursday I learned from the recipients that the two manuscripts had been delivered. I think we were a little surprised, though, not to hear from Reid directly.

The rest of the story you know. He must have come here in the middle of Thursday night, or early Friday morning and shot himself.

There is no point I can see in a handsome, healthy young man doing a thing like that. But I am not going to judge the intensities of another man's failures by the philosophy or even the levity with which I must meet my own.

He looked extraordinarily peaceful in that first stage of last sleep. His face composed, his handsome strong hands folded. If it had not been for this and that, the gardener and I, who were the first to see him, must have thought him asleep.

Why he came here to end his troubles, I cannot know. He was always so courteous and considerate. But surely he was old enough to know that he was letting people who had been kind to him in for slander, scandal, suspicion and God knows what.

He had promised to go straight home to you after he had executed his commissions. Instead he comes back here and makes a lot of grief and ghastly trouble for us. The grief we would have felt in any case. But we had done nothing to deserve the notoriety and the endless blunderings and stupid intrusions upon our privacy by the police and the press.

Surely, he can't have been in such serious difficulties that he couldn't have gone to his own mother with them and talked them over with her until they seemed less serious. I do so wish that he had done that.

I have written this long letter in the thought that every detail of her boy's last hours is of interest to the boy's mother.

I have told you all that I know. But I cannot tell you how very sorry I am. Most unhappily yours, Gouverneur Morris.

Ruth had never been in a situation like this before. She was getting the just-the-facts-ma'am treatment from the DA's office, and the media scrutiny and exposure were heading ominously close to Roscoe Arbuckle territory.

Sensing his wife's growing vulnerability, Govie whisked her off to a five-thousand-acre cattle ranch near Fresno, the historic Fort Miller Ranch, for some hoped-for respite.

In the short run it worked. Ruth loved to ride and sat a good saddle, so each morning during her stay, she and Pop Charlie, the ranch boss, would ride the range, chasing around twenty-odd head of cattle.

The Zen of the ride helped settle her mind a bit and spared her, if only briefly, from the next headline that hit the newsstands: "Sleuth Brands Russell Death Love Murder."

Victoria Russell had come forward with yet another sensational disclosure, and this one proved irresistible for the media: about phone calls "a woman made to the Russell apartment, declaring that the handsome young man had failed to keep an engagement with her and begging the mother to disclose her son's whereabouts."

Captain Plummer responded with all the reserve and measured tone of a Page Six editor: "This is a love slaying and not a suicide. We have eliminated the suicide theory. As for the love slaying theory, all I can say now is that I have information to support it."

District Attorney Fitts was all in on the investigation, approving the exhuming of the body and authorizing Plummer to state categorically that "the gun found in Russell's hand had not been fired in at least a year." As for the missing cartridge casing, "either the shell was deliberately taken away or the fatal shot was fired at some other point than the one at which the body was found."

Now the race was on for newspapers to answer the question on everyone's mind: Who was the woman making the calls? It didn't take long to come up with the most circulation-boosting speculation: Lila Lee.

But Lila was having none of it. Her response was clear and unequivocal: "I knew young Russell only as a friend. A friend in the Morris home where I met him. He was a nice, personable young man whom Mr. and Mrs. Morris befriended. How can any mature person entertain such an idea? Why, Jimmy (James Kirkwood, her 12-year-old son) lives right here with me. I saw Reid only as a guest—and at home here, where he came occasionally to play bridge or spend the evening. If he was interested in the least in me, he certainly did not show it. He didn't show it by looks, or by words, or by actions. Don't you think a woman can tell when someone is interested? If I thought he had been interested in me, I certainly would tell you."

When asked if she had ever been with Reid alone, she replied, "No, I did not. Oh, I went to the village (Manhattan Beach) perhaps a couple of times—but never out alone at night. On several occasions, when Reid was over, I wasn't even at home. I had other engagements and also my studio work."

Captain Plummer decided to question Lila at length in private, and after three hours of questioning, Plummer became convinced that there was no romantic involvement between Lila Lee and Reid Russell, which was a theory that never made much sense anyway. Reid Russell hardly fit the profile of a potential Lila Lee suitor, and besides, why in the world would Lila be fooling around when she had just gotten her son back? Suggestions that she was a loose woman had cost her custody of him in the first place. It just did not make sense that she would jeopardize her relationship with her son in order to have a fling with a car salesman.

Throughout the scandal, Lila Lee and her son remained at the Manhattan Beach mansion, but Lila ceased to be of much interest to law enforcement. She continued with her studio work and seems to have avoided the kinds of meltdowns and erratic behavior her close friend Ruth had displayed.

With Lila now scratched off the list, Plummer vowed to make a "microscopic examination of Russell's love life" and added "other women with whom Russell was acquainted were being listed and catalogued as to the closeness of their relationship with the man." The search for other women drove one reporter to make the trek to Fort Miller.

As Ruth arrived back at the stable after a long run in the pasture, the reporter was waiting for her. Her response was brief: "I happen to know that the young man was gravely worried over financial troubles with which he found himself beset. He wasn't thinking about any love affair, and he wasn't as far as I know, paying fervent court to any woman. But his financial difficulties preyed terribly on his mind, and the fact that he did slay himself was not a great surprise to me."

Back in Southern California, Reid Russell's body was exhumed from its resting place in Calvary Cemetery and was examined by Assistant County Autopsy Surgeon Frank Webb and Coroner Frank Nance. Their examination confirmed that Reid had been killed by a .32-caliber bullet. Webb "found powder burns inside the scalp and at the entrance to the wound; and he found that the course of the bullet had been horizontal, indicating that the gun was held against Russell's head." The examiners continued to believe that the wound was self-inflicted.

Investigator Everett Davis disagreed, however, and offered the following evidence: an abrasion on Reid's right temple. Davis asserted, "Tests showed that it could not have been caused by ordinary pressure of a gun barrel against the human flesh. It would only have resulted from the sudden, powerful jamming of a gun against the head."

One other voice was heard from, supporting the suicide theory: Reid's ex-wife, Lorraine Crockett Russell. Reached at her home in El Paso, Texas, Lorraine had this to say: "He was the moody type who brooded a great deal and would be likely to take his own life if he became too despondent. I believe he shot himself."

Moody he may have been, but where was the missing cartridge casing and the missing bullet? More important, how did he kill himself with a gun that had not been fired in over a year? Finally, why had someone been making threatening phone calls about the case?

Which brings us to the final twist. It turned out there was more going on in Reid Russell's life than had previously been revealed. Los Angeles detective lieutenant Harry Leslie Hansen came forward with an astonishing story.

On Saturday night, September 19, 1936, Detective Lieutenant Hansen had talked to Reid Russell during an evening of wild partying. As he described, "At the climax of a party that began Saturday, September 19, and ended Sunday morning, September 20, and in which Russell, my wife, Norma, and myself, and another couple participated, Russell said to me suddenly: 'Harry, I'm sick of working for

$100 a month as an auto salesman. I'm going to quit my job—in fact, I've already quit. I'm going to do something that has plenty of excitement and plenty of dough connected with it."

Initially Reid was coy about what he was up to, and when Hansen pressed him, he first demurred, saying it was "dangerous to talk." Eventually, Hansen loosened his tongue, and Reid explained, "Well, it has to do with delivery of guns to some foreign port. It is a port in Mexico or China. I don't know which. I have been ordered to board a speed boat, which will take me to the gun running ship, which is lying off shore at an undisclosed port. I'm going to get $300 a month and a big bonus—and that's all I'm going to tell you."

It turns out investigators had known about the possibility Russell was involved in gun smuggling much earlier but had not made the information public. Early in the investigation Victoria Russell had told investigators that "Reid was mixed up with some gun-runners, with whom he became involved through a woman."

More collaboration of the detective lieutenant's story was soon forthcoming. One of the women who had been with Reid the Saturday night before he died, Frances Patten, recounted her experience:

My friend, Tony Coombs, called me and said he wanted me to go to a party with him that Saturday night. We first went to the home of Detective Lieutenant H. L. Hansen. Soon after our arrival Reid Russell came. He brought with him two bottles of champagne.

From there we went to the Biltmore Bowl where we drank more champagne. It seemed that everywhere we went Reid was buying champagne and in several night clubs, the bottles he bought were left untouched. Reid was in an exceptionally jovial mood. When one of the party protested against his lavish expenditures, he laughed gayly. "Why, I've got several hundred on me," he replied.

Early in the morning we wound up in a Wilshire cafe for breakfast. It was there that Reid spoke briefly about his mysterious plan to build up a fortune. He did not say specifically

*what he meant. I remember he and Detective Hansen spoke of
some "plan."*

According to Frances Patten, later that Sunday "Reid called her and
asked that she meet him and some more friends at a cocktail lounge."
Patten, who was a radio artist, begged off because she had professional
obligations that afternoon.

Now the district attorney's office had a new theory of the case: that
Reid had been pulled into this dodgy activity by "a rich and beautiful
woman," and "because during a night of revelry in Los Angeles' and
Hollywood's gayest 'hot spots,' he was seen in the company of a detective lieutenant, suspected of the 'double cross,' and death was decreed
for him."

The mind-numbing cascade of new information now had the district attorney's office fully engaged. District Attorney Fitts seemed
determined to make sure every lead was pursued, and he even began
reaching out to other government agencies to address the potential
international scope of a gun-running operation. A decision was also
made to subpoena bank records "not only of the dead youth but of a
number of other figures in the case." Could the reference to "other figures in the case" possibly include Ruth and Govie?

Which brings us to some big questions. Exactly what did Ruth and
Govie know about all of this? Were they completely duped by a young
man who was leading a double life? Was all his time spent at the Morris
home just about bridge games and burgers? Or had the Morrises in
a moment of financial desperation gotten involved in another one of
Govie's ill-considered get-rich-quick schemes? Finally, why had this
car salesman become such an important part of their lives anyway?

At this point it is impossible to know. What seems clear, though, is
that both Ruth and Govie were extremely determined that the case be
treated as a suicide and not a homicide. So determined that Ruth made
dubious claims that shattered her credibility.

The spectacle of Ruth collapsing under questioning suggests at the
very least she was feeling deeply troubled about something, possibly
even feeling guilty about it. Her behavior throughout the whole saga

suggests she felt responsible in some way for Reid Russell's death. How and why we will never know, but the suspicion is inescapable.

Clearly the district attorney's office had its suspicions as well. When Ruth and Govie returned from Fort Miller, Captain Plummer was waiting for them with another round of questions.

The Morrises, though, were done. With the help of their attorney, C. P. von Herzen, Govie issued a statement demanding that Fitts back off: "No matter what they do or how long they keep up this asinine investigation, they'll learn only one thing—and that is that the unfortunate young man killed himself. We have given officers the names of five people to whom Russell had declared he intended to commit suicide. I'm sick and tired of being hauled out of bed at all hours to answer questions I've already answered, and if this thing continues I'll take legal action to stop the District Attorney's office from making a public show of me."

Then came the final surprise: District Attorney Buron Fitts shut down the investigation. For what reason we will never know. Maybe one of the studio bosses had given him an earful. Or maybe the new scope of the investigation made other powerful people nervous. Whatever the reason, Fitts called off the hounds.

As for Reid Russell, the cause of death was now official: suicide.

Case closed.

CHAPTER TWENTY

––––––––

SUNSET IN THE SOUTH SEAS

Two and a half years later, Ruth Morris would be dead. Not from a gunshot wound. Or a car accident. Or a fatal illness that showed up in a lab test. Instead her death came on slowly with each glass of gin she drank. First it had been social. Over time it became medicine. And by the end it was a numbing agent. Glass after glass after glass. Numbing the pain. Numbing the guilt. Numbing the despair.

What first had been pleasure eventually became poison. Ruth was a small woman, "a mere slip of a thing," and her body's tolerance for alcohol was lower than most. Eventually the sustained concentrations of alcohol begin to destroy vital organs, and it becomes only a matter of time before the ability of the body to continue functioning completely gives out.

By late 1936, Ruth's doctor started sounding the alarm. She was not doing well, and if she stayed in Southern California it would only get worse. There were too many bad associations. Too many reminders. Too many excuses to pick up another glass.

The Morrises were done with Southern California anyway. With Hollywood. With the whole crazy mess. So Govie looked around for the most un-Hollywood place he could find, and he found it in rural

New Mexico. Then like the Joad family in reverse, they packed up their belongings and headed east on Route 66. And their destination? Not Taos or Santa Fe, but rather a little patch of cactus and sandstone called Coolidge, some twenty-two miles east of Gallup, and light years away from the Hearst beach house and the Del Monte Lodge.

Instead of a mansion, they now had a one-thousand-square-foot apartment in what had once been a high-desert trading post called Casa de Navajo. Simple wooden furniture filled the room, Navajo rugs covered the floors, and a rough-hewn open-beam ceiling and polished logs held the place together. Outside they were surrounded by a rugged, sparse high-desert landscape that extended out to a stark red sandstone mesa.

Culturally, the area was defined by its dominant neighbor, the Navajo Nation, which occupied a large tract of land to the north, and by a smaller tribal contingent, the Zunis, to the south. In its own way, Coolidge, New Mexico, was as remote and otherworldly as the Society Islands. Native languages were still spoken, and craft traditions like rug weaving and jewelry making were still widely practiced.

It was a peaceful refuge in many ways, but the problems Ruth brought with her from California never went away. Her once lovely voice had become little more than a raspy slur, and she was now almost perpetually drunk.

As the year 1939 rolled around, the Morrises received the tough news that their special pal from their Monterey days, Francis McComas, had died of a heart attack on December 27, 1938. By this point only Govie was in any condition to respond, so he called up Western Union in Gallup and sent this message: "Have just heard the news about Frank by letter in this far off place. But men like that don't die they become legends. I loved and admired him without capitulation and I always will. Love from us both. Gouverneur Morris."

By springtime, Ruth's mental stability was faltering, and she began acting out, sometimes quite violently. Faced with a situation he could no longer manage, Govie had no choice but to seek professional help, and the initial diagnosis was brutal: Ruth was found to be "violently insane." Once she was placed in the care of the Nazareth Sanatorium in

Albuquerque, the underlying issue immediately became apparent: "she was found to be pretty well putrefied. Alcohol, primarily."

The end came soon after, and it was Ruth herself who played the final hand, with an intentional overdose of pills. She was pronounced dead on April 19, 1939, at age forty-one.

Only twenty-one years had passed since she had driven at Ascot. Only fourteen since she had fought the bull in Spain. And only seven since she had produced two movies in Tahiti. It had all gone by so quickly. And then she was gone.

For Govie, her death was particularly difficult. Within days he was involved in a nasty auto accident, and it would take months for him to pull himself together. Eventually he was able to fulfill a final promise he had made to "the most fascinating little person that ever was on sea or land," though he no longer could afford to do it himself.

Ruth's last wish had been to have her ashes scattered in the South Seas, near Tahiti, a spot more than any other that held a special place in her heart, for reasons that are best captured in a passage Ruth was fond of from Alec Waugh's book *Hot Countries*:

> *I shall remember the long curve of that little harbour with the nestling schooners and the painted bungalows, and across the lagoon the many pinnacles of its sister isle. I shall remember the gentle manners of its people, the dark-skinned Polynesians, the French officials, the Chinese traders. I shall remember their soft singing and the glimmer on the water at nightfall of the torches by which they fish. I shall remember their cool verandahs, the red and white of the hibiscus, the yellow amanda flower and the purple of the bougainvillea; I shall remember how the sun shines and the earth is fertile and nobody is sad.*
>
> *And I shall know that were I to return there, I should find the same merrily laughing group drawn up along the wharf. . . . There would be the hailing of a remembered face. "Ia ora na," they would shout to me. They would wave their hands. There would be a drifting towards the café, a laughing together over ice-cream sodas. And after the sun set, a miracle of golden lilac behind Moorea, there would be a wandering to the Chinese*

restaurant for a chop suey, with afterwards a riding out along the beach with the moon shining upon the palm trees, and the warm air scented with the white bloom of the tiare. There would be the singing, the laughter and the dancing, a sense of unity with primeval forces.

And ultimately that is, I suppose, what death will prove to be: a stepping away from what is transient into the waveless calm of an eternal rhythm.

Later that year Ruth and Govie's longtime friends, Gladys and Medford Ross Kellum, traveled back to the Society Islands with Ruth's ashes, and somewhere in the South Seas along a route Ruth had traveled so many times, and where she had met a certain young British writer, her final remains were released over the open sea and entered "the waveless calm of an eternal rhythm."

EPILOGUE

One of the first people Govie notified following Ruth's passing was his dear friend Gene McComas, who herself was grieving the loss of her beloved husband, Francis. She responded with a letter than contains these lovely words: "Our wild birds have flow away." Touched and even inspired, Govie wrote back with a suggestion of his own. He recalled a short story Ruth had begun writing some years back, entitled "Bright Wings Are Folded," which she had not been able to complete. He finished the story, and it appeared in the February 1936 issue of *Good Housekeeping* under his name. Why not, he suggested, express the line this way: "Our wild birds have flown away and bright wings are folded."

A year later Gene McComas would write to Alec Waugh to share with him the news about Ruth, and he would reply, "As you've probably known she meant to me things that no one else has ever meant, as no one else can ever mean again . . . and a few days ago I was reading *Macbeth*'s 'she should have died hereafter . . .' At the same time I can't help feeling that for her sake it's better the way it is. She'd have so hated being old."

For Alec at that moment, his greatest writing success was still ahead: the publication in 1955 of his novel *Island in the Sun*. A story of interracial romance on a Caribbean island, it would become an international bestseller and a Hollywood movie, boasting an all-star cast, including James Mason, Joan Fontaine, Harry Belafonte, Joan Collins, Dorothy Dandridge, and Michael Rennie.

Ruth's mother, Lulu, who had been living quietly in retirement in Pacific Grove, received the devastating news about her only child in a long letter from Govie. She would die within a year, and it's hard not to imagine that Ruth's death hastened her own.

Others who were close to Ruth simply had to carry on. Govie's two daughters had by then relocated to Southern California. Patsey married a retired British military officer who served as a technical advisor on Hollywood war movies. Bay would never marry, and neither daughter would ever have children, though Patsey would have two stepchildren.

Lila Lee would continue to act, mostly landing small parts in low-budget films and early television soap operas. She would have one final chance to visit with Govie in the 1940s when she came to Gallup, New Mexico, for a location shoot. To the very end, Lila was an unwavering friend of the Morrises.

As for Jimmy, later James Kirkwood Jr., he would establish a successful career as a writer and would win the Pulitzer Prize for Drama as cocreator of the landmark Broadway musical *A Chorus Line*.

For his final years, Govie would live a simple life in Coolidge, New Mexico, making jewelry, which he learned from his Native American neighbors, and painting watercolors of the desert landscape, as he had learned from his friend Francis McComas.

On the occasion of the fiftieth anniversary of the graduation of the class of 1898 at Yale University, he was asked to write an account of his life for inclusion in a special yearbook, but he demurred. He didn't feel he could write an honest account. Besides, he said, if he were ever to write anything biographical, it would be about his late wife, Ruth. Her life, he believed, was the more interesting one.

On August 14, 1953, Gouverneur Morris died of a massive heart attack, a day before the fifty-sixth anniversary of Ruth Wightman Morris's birth.

ACKNOWLEDGMENTS

One of the rewards of a project like this is that you meet so many wonderful people along the way who are so generous with their help and assistance, and I wish to acknowledge those who have been particularly kind to me.

First, I must extend special thanks to Selina Hastings, who shared with me detailed information about her father, Lord Hastings, and his relationships with the Morrises, Diego Rivera, and others. She was also a great sounding board and source of constructive advice, and she went the extra step of introducing me to members of the Waugh family. Quite simply, this book would not have been the same without Selina's help and support.

I wish to acknowledge the gracious support of the late Peter Waugh, Alec Waugh's son, who sadly did not live to see the publication of this book. He was always encouraging and helpful. I send thanks as well to Alexander Waugh, Evelyn Waugh's grandson, who introduced me to Jonathon Waugh, Peter Waugh's nephew and the person now managing permissions for Alec Waugh's estate. I extend special thanks to Jonathon for granting me permission to quote from Alec Waugh's books and private correspondence.

Special thanks to all the wonderful people at Girl Friday Productions, who proved an essential production resource for Hawk Tower Press. Special projects editor Emilie Sandoz-Voyer, developmental editor Shannon O'Neill, copyeditor Mark Steven Long, cover designer Connie Gabbert, interior designer Rachel Christenson, director of publishing partnerships Meghan Harvey, and vice president for editorial Christina Henry de Tessan. This is an awesome group, and each earns my heartiest endorsement.

Special thanks to Maggie Riggs, formerly an editor at Viking and at New York Editors, who read an early draft of my manuscript and asked thoughtful questions and provided cogent advice.

There are many other people I wish to thank as well.

Michael Larsen, literary agent, who offered encouragement but also an honest assessment of the challenges today's publishing world would present.

Stephen Bonsal and Louis Bonsal Osler, Gouverneur Morris's grandnephew and grandniece, who were able to provide personal information about their uncle, Gouverneur Morris.

Shirley Newcomb of Gallup, New Mexico, who is the one person I interviewed who had known Ruth Morris when she was alive. Shirley was able to provide unique and valuable information about my subject.

Ernie Bulow, a writer from Gallup, New Mexico, who helped arrange my interview with Shirley Newcomb.

Gloria A. Anderson, village clerk in Falconer, New York, who located the original birth records for Ruth Wightman.

The staff at the Howard Gotlieb Archival Research Center in Boston, particularly archivist Charles Niles, who assisted me in discovering the many letters Ruth Morris had written to Alec Waugh, which Alec had carefully saved over all the years.

Neal Hotelling, historian for the Pebble Beach Company, who helped me locate an unpublished biography of Charlie Chaplin.

Dennis Copeland, historian and librarian for the City of Monterey, who helped me navigate the archive in the California History Room.

Caroline Cox at the University of the Pacific, who helped me obtain photographs from the 1918 auto race in Stockton.

Valerie Hemingway, Ernest Hemingway's secretary and posthumously his daughter-in-law, for taking the time to look through her files on my behalf.

Jan Prince, writer and resident on the island of Moorea, who provided information about the Morris plantation on Tahiti.

Muriel Feiner, writer and resident of Madrid, Spain, who provided context about the significance of Ruth Morris's experience with a bull.

Harold Osmer for providing a photo of Ruth Wightman in a race car.

Mary Ann Pruett for providing photos of the Stockton auto race from her grandfather, Bill Pruett, who had been Ruth Wightman's mechanician.

Freda Hamric, researcher based in Austin, Texas, who located an important Sinclair Lewis letter in the archives of the Harry Ramsom Center.

Jenny Romero at the Margaret Herrick Library, Beverly Hills.

Kristine Krueger and Jeff Thomas at the San Francisco Public Library.

Brandon Westerheim at the New York Public Library.

Melissa Hayes and Dacey Taube at the University of Southern California Library.

Lise Brown at the Syracuse University Library.

Jim Orr at the Henry Ford Library.

Kira Graybill at the California State Library.

And finally, all the staffers at the Monterey Museum of Art, both current and past, who have assisted me through the years on this project, but particularly John Rexine, the registrar, who has helped me in the archive, and Helaine Glick, former assistant curator, who encouraged Selina Hastings (who had contacted the museum while researching her own book project) to get in touch with me.

NOTES

ABBREVIATIONS

AW	Alec Waugh
BLCU	Butler Library of Columbia University
GM	Gouverneur Morris
HGARC	Howard Gotlieb Archival Research Center
HL	Huntington Library
HRC	Harry Ransom Center
MHL	Margaret Herrick Library
MMA	Monterey Museum of Art
NYPL	New York Public Library
RWM	Ruth Wightman Morris
SUL	Syracuse University Library

PROLOGUE

1. The primary source for the prologue is Alec Waugh's memoir entitled *The Early Years of Alec Waugh* (New York: Farrar, Straus, 1962), in which he devotes three chapters to his affair with Ruth Morris.

CHAPTER ONE: THE LITTLEST REBEL

1. "Should Vote on Street Speaking," *San Diego Sun*, January 11, 1912.
2. "'Water Cure' Given I.W.W. by Police," *San Diego Union*, March 11, 1912.

3. "Disperse Mob with Fire Hose," *Los Angeles Times*, March 11, 1912.

4. "The Big Noise: The Free Speech Fight of 1912," *San Diego Reader*, June 13, 2012.

5. Emma Goldman, *Living My Life*, vol. 1 (New York: Alfred A. Knopf, 1931), 494–501.

6. Theodore Schroeder, *Free Speech for Radicals* (Riverside, CT: Hillacre Bookhouse, 1916), 115–190.

7. Davey Jones, "A Fight for Free Speech in San Diego," *San Diego Indymedia*, January 21, 2005.

8. "Liberty's Flag with Anarchy," *Los Angeles Times*, May 14, 1912.

9. RWM's birth certificate is important, because documents from other sources are inconsistent about her correct age. Official records on file in Falconer, New York, confirm that Ruth Wightman was born on August 15, 1897, to parents John and Lulu Wightman. Her mother is listed as twenty-four years old and her father as thirty-two years old.

10. Bert Haloviak, "A Place at the Table: Women and the Early Years," in *The Welcome Table: Setting a Place for Ordained Women*, ed. Patricia A. Habada and Rebecca Frost Brillhart (Langley Park, MD: TEAM Press, 1995), available online at SDAnet, http://www.sdanet.org/atissue/wo/haloviakchapter.htm.

11. Josephine Benton, "Minister to Legislatures: Lulu Wightman," in *Called by God*, SDAnet, http://www.sdanet.org/atissue/books/called/whole-book/benton-03.htm.

12. Bert Haloviak, "Ellen White and the Ordination of Women," sermon, October 15, 1988.

13. "Lulu Wightman," Adventist History Library.

14. Lulu Wightman, *Great Questions of the Hour* (Reno, NV: self-published, 1914).

15. "Gospel Tent Meetings," *Westfield Republican*, June 1, 1898.

16. "Lulu Wightman Will Hold Revival Meeting," *Geneva Daily News*, March 23, 1899.

17. Frank Morton Todd, *The Chamber of Commerce Handbook for San Francisco, Historical and Descriptive: A Guide for Visitors* (San Francisco: San Francisco Chamber of Commerce, 1914).

18. RWM recalls her encounters with Jack London in a letter to Alec Waugh, October 1927.

19. RWM court appearance reported in "Mother and Daughter Fight Together for Personal Liberty," *Sacramento Star*, January 29, 1914.

20. Jack London, "The March of Kelly's Army. The Story of an Extraordinary Migration," *Cosmopolitan*, October 1907.

21. "How Kelly Traveled on Sympathy," *San Francisco Chronicle*, August 29, 1894.

22. "Leader of Unemployed Tells the Truth About Dr. Pardee," *San Francisco Chronicle*, October 18, 1902.

23. Rumeana Jahangir, "Secrets of the Wizard of Oz," *BBC News Magazine*, March 17, 2009.

24. "Oakland Consents to Feed Workless," *San Francisco Chronicle*, March 5, 1914.

25. "When the Army Arrives in Ogden," *Ogden Standard*, March 6, 1914.

26. "Trans-River Sandlots Seem to Suit 'Hikers': Many Cops on Guard," *Sacramento Star*, March 9, 1914.

27. Elizabeth S. Nichols, "The Battle of M_ St. Bridge," *Coming Nation*, April 1914.

28. Lulu Wightman, *The Menace of Prohibition* (Los Angeles: Los Angeles Printing, 1916).

29. *Wine and Spirit Bulletin* 30 (1916): 39–40.

30. "Love of Liberty Is Echoed by Speaker," *Oakland Tribune*, November 2, 1916.

31. RWM bronco riding mentioned in "The Speederettes Are All Coming," *Stockton Record*, February 16, 1918.

32. RWM encounter with Lincoln Beachey mentioned in "Ruth Wightman Arrives Here," *Stockton Record*, February 18, 1918.

33. Lincoln Beachey stunts described in "Beachey Loops Loop at Emeryville Track," *Oakland Tribune*, November 16, 1914.

34. C. O. Prest praised RWM in *Aerial Age Weekly*, June 18, 1917.

35. "Riverside School Instruct U.S. Flyers," *San Bernardino County Sun*, July 25, 1917.

36. "Prest Will Fly Six Weeks at Seal Beach," *San Bernardino County Sun*, August 1, 1917.

37. "Government Official 'Discovers' Expert Aviatrix in School at Riverside," *Los Angeles Examiner*, October 23, 1917.

38. "The Wright-Martin Model 'V' Reconnaissance Biplane," *Aviation*, March 22, 1917.

CHAPTER TWO: THE FASTEST WOMAN ALIVE

1. "Girl Aviator Offers a Prize for Women Racers," *Los Angeles Times*, January 24, 1918.

2. Katherine Stinson is extensively profiled in Eileen F. Lebow, *Before Amelia* (Washington, DC: Brassey's, 2002).

3. "Ascot Races Will Be Carnival of Femininity," *Los Angeles Times*, January 27, 1918.

4. "Women Race Drivers Will Fill Program at Speedway," *Los Angeles Examiner*, January 27, 1918.

5. "Policewomen Will Guard Ascot Course," *Los Angeles Times*, January 29, 1918.

6. "Hangs Up .57 in Ascot Dash," *Los Angeles Times*, January 31, 1918.

7. "Mrs. Wofelt Goes Mile in 57 Sec.," *Los Angeles Examiner*, January 31, 1918.

8. "Fair Speeders Qualify Today," *Los Angeles Times*, February 1, 1918.

9. "Woman Race Driver Crashes Through Fence at Ascot Speedway," *Los Angeles Times*, February 2, 1918.

10. "Fence Smashed by Woman Pilot," *Los Angeles Examiner*, February 2, 1918.

11. A special profile of Ruth Wightman appears in "Ruth Wightman Tells How to Become a Speederette," *Los Angeles Times*, February 3, 1918. A separate story about the upcoming race appears in the same issue.

12. "Fair Pilots Give Thrills," *Los Angeles Times*, February 4, 1918.

13. "Woman Speed Marvel Sets World Record," *Los Angeles Examiner*, February 4, 1918.

14. "Woman Racers Make Fast Time," *San Francisco Chronicle*, February 4, 1918.

15. Sonja Harris, "Roaring into the Twenties: The Story of the Speederettes, Female Automobile Racers of the 1910s and 1920s," University of the Pacific essay, 2003.

16. Harold Osmer, "Speederettes at Ascot," 1996.

17. Todd McCarthy, *Fast Women: The Legendary Ladies of Racing* (New York: Hyperion, 2007), 72–74.

CHAPTER THREE: A TIME FOR TEARS

1. "A Woman Auto Racer Coming," *Stockton Record*, February 14, 1918.

2. "The Speederettes Are All Coming," *Stockton Record*, February 16, 1918.

3. "Ruth Wightman Arrives Here," *Stockton Record*, February 18, 1918.

4. "Stockton Fans Are Enthusing over Coming Races of the Speederettes," *Stockton Record*, February 19, 1918.

5. An ad promoting the race appears in the *Stockton Record*, February 23, 1918.

6. "Speederettes Are Tuning Up," *Stockton Record*, February 25, 1918.

7. "Women Racers Arouse Spectators to Wild Cheers in Practice Spins," *Stockton Record*, February 28, 1918.

8. "Speederettes Are Ready for Starting Gun," *Stockton Record*, March 2, 1918.

9. "Miss Vitagliano 'Speederette,' Says Women Can Drive in Races as Well as Men," *Stockton Record*, March 3, 1918.

10. "Six Feminine Daredevils to Race in South," *San Francisco Chronicle*, March 3, 1918.

11. "Nina Vitagliano Is Killed in Auto Races on Local Track," *Stockton Record*, March 4, 1918.

12. "Woman Driver Killed in Automobile Race," *San Francisco Chronicle*, March 4, 1918.

13. "Italians Pay a Tribute to Dead Driver," *Stockton Record*, March 5, 1918.

14. "'Bud' Currie, Mechanician, Is Second Victim," *Stockton Record*, March 6, 1918.

15. "Third Victim of Auto Race Dies," *Stockton Record*, March 8, 1918.

16. An announcement that women were again banned from auto racing appears in *Motor Age*, March 7, 1918.

CHAPTER FOUR: REWRITING THE SCRIPT

1. John S. Wightman was reported as "seriously ill with tuberculosis" on April 14, 1918, by the Adventist History Library, and he would die two months later.

2. RWM's version of how she met Gouverneur Morris is reported in Alec Waugh, *The Early Years of Alec Waugh* (New York: Farrar, Straus, 1962), 251–252. Gouverneur Morris's own recollections about how they met, which appear in the article cited in note 10, suggests a slower time line, with them first becoming boss and employee before becoming a couple.

3. Details about the life of Gouverneur Morris's great-grandfather come from Richard Brookhiser, *Gouverneur Morris: An Independent Life* (New Haven: Yale University Press, 2014).

4. Gouverneur Morris shared his life story with newspaper columnist Lee Shippey, who wrote about it in "Personal Glimpses of Famous Folks," *Los Angeles Times*, October 23, 1932.

5. "Morris-Waterbury Wedding," *New York Times*, May 23, 1905.

6. "Daughter Born to Mrs. Morris," *New York Times*, June 17, 1910.

7. In a phone conversation on March 8, 2012, Gouverneur Morris's grandnephew Stephen Bonsal stated that Gouverneur Morris had been "the highest-paid writer per word in America."

8. Gouverneur Morris, "French Make Beauty Spots of Captured German Towns," *San Francisco Examiner*, December 10, 1915.

9. A photo Gouverneur Morris took of an ambulance in France during World War I, from the private collection of Shirley Newcomb.

10. GM's explanation for the breakup of his marriage appears in "Novelist's Plots Outdone by His Own Wrecked Romance," *San Francisco Chronicle*, September 9. 1923. The same article also presents his version of how he and RWM met.

11. "Eminent Authors Pictures Formed," *Moving Picture World*, June 7, 1919.

12. "Goldwyn Purchases Triangle Studios," *Moving Picture World*, June 7, 1919.

13. "Gouverneur Morris Arrives to Film Tales," *Los Angeles Times*, January 3, 1920.

14. The *Wid's Daily* issue dated September 3, 1920, reprinted an editorial from the *Los Angeles Examiner* that goes into detail about box office receipts, attendance, and revenue for the motion picture industry in 1920.

15. Hilary Hallett, *Go West, Young Women!: The Rise of Early Hollywood* (Berkeley: University of California Press, 2013).

16. Kevin Alexander Boon, *Script Culture and the American Screenplay* (Detroit: Wayne State University Press, 2008).

17. Joseph Ashurst Jackson, "Author! Author!," *Screenland*, December 1920.

18. Elmer Rice, *Minority Report: An Autobiography* (New York: Simon and Schuster, 1963), 170–175.

19. Mary Roberts Rinehart, *My Story* (New York: Farrar and Rinehart, 1931), 291–297.

20. Gertrude Atherton, *Adventures of a Novelist* (New York: Blue Ribbon Books, 1932), 543–544.

21. "High Hopes for 'Penalty,'" *Wid's Daily*, August 7, 1920.

22. "Goldwyn Has Four Big Dramas," *Wid's Daily*, August 14, 1920.

23. "Goldwyn Frank," *Wid's Daily*, August 23, 1920.

24. Gouverneur Morris, *The Penalty* (New York: Charles Scribner's Sons, 1913).

25. *The Penalty*. Produced by Samuel Goldwyn, directed by Wallace Worsley, story by Gouverneur Morris, scenario by

Charles Kenyon and Philip Lonergan. Hollywood, CA: Eminent Authors Pictures and Goldwyn Pictures, 1920.

26. "'The Penalty'—Goldwyn Capitol," *Wid's Daily*, November 16, 1920.

27. "Lon Chaney's Work Lifts This One," *Wid's Daily*, November 21, 1920.

28. "'A Tale of Two Worlds'—Goldwyn Capitol," *Wid's Daily*, March 16, 1921.

29. "Good Production and Well Acted," *Wid's Daily*, March 20, 1921.

30. "Tale of Two Worlds," *Los Angeles Times*, March 21, 1921.

31. Charlie Chaplin, *My Autobiography* (New York: Simon and Schuster, 1964).

32. Samuel Goldwyn, *Behind the Screen* (New York: George H. Doran, 1923), 175–178.

CHAPTER FIVE: A NAME IN THE CREDITS

1. A head shot taken of Gouverneur Morris for publicity purposes, circa 1920, MHL.

2. A photo taken at Goldwyn Pictures of Gouverneur Morris and RWM with an actor dressed as a policeman, circa 1921.

3. *The Ace of Hearts.* Produced by Samuel Goldwyn, directed by Wallace Worsley, story based on "The Purple Mask" by Gouverneur Morris, scenario by Ruth Wightman. Hollywood, CA: Goldwyn Pictures, 1921.

4. "The Ace of Hearts," *Wid's Daily*, December 3, 1921.

5. A. Scott Berg, *Goldwyn* (New York: Riverhead Books, 1998), 91–103.

6. "Celluloid Celebrities and Their Doings," *San Francisco Chronicle*, October 21, 1921.

7. "Producers Work upon Story Plays," *San Francisco Chronicle*, October 23, 1921.

8. "Katherine MacDonald," *Wikipedia*, https://en.wikipedia.org /wiki/Katherine_MacDonald.

9. "Just Wait Till You See Her New Series!" *Wid's Daily*, December 31, 1921.

10. "Katherine MacDonald Exhibits Versatility," *Logansport Pharos-Tribune*, January 1922.

11. "Vaudeville and Feature Films at the Olympia," *Boston Globe*, January 17, 1922.

12. "Doings of the '400' Shown in New Film, *Santa Cruz Evening News*, November 8, 1922.

13. "Credit Index, Feature Films, 1921–1930," *American Film Institute Catalog of Motion Pictures*.

14. "Author Fights Blue Law Plan," *Los Angeles Examiner*, March 17, 1921.

15. Gouverneur Morris published a letter to the editor in the *Los Angeles Times* of June 30, 1921, defending the anti-Prohibition movement.

16. "Arbuckle Is Not Guilty, Jurors Decide Quickly," *Los Angeles Times*, April 13, 1922.

17. Andy Edmonds, *Frame-Up!: The Untold Story of Roscoe "Fatty" Arbuckle* (New York: William Morrow, 1991).

18. Greg Merritt, *Room 1219: The Life of Fatty Arbuckle, the Mysterious Death of Virginia Rappe, and the Scandal That Changed Hollywood* (Chicago: Chicago Review Press, 2013).

19. Gouverneur Morris, "The Arbuckle Case: An Open Letter to the Editor of Screenland," *Screenland*, November 1921.

20. "Max Linder Busy," *Los Angeles Times*, August 9, 1921.

21. "Les 'Three Must Get There' de Max Linder," *Cinemagazine*, June 16, 1922.

22. Eve Golden, *John Gilbert: The Last of the Silent Film Stars* (Lexington, KY: The University Press of Kentucky, 2013), 56–57.

23. "Barbara Bedford (Actress)," *Wikipedia*, https://en.wikipedia.org/wiki/Barbara_Bedford_(actress).

24. "Bessie Love, Silent Screen Actress Discovered in 1915, Dies at 87," *Los Angeles Times*, April 29, 1986.

25. Patsy Ruth Miller, *My Hollywood: When Both of Us Were Young* (O'Raghailligh Publishers, 1988), 19–30.

26. RWM's engagement ring is mentioned in "Hollywood Hears," *Oakland Tribune*, January 29, 1922.

27. Her ring is also mentioned in "News Notes from Movieland," *Olean Evening Herald*, February 2, 1922.

28. GM received a large inheritance from his aunt, Anne Baldwin Schultze, on February 27, 1922. The details of that inheritance came to light in legal documents filed in the case of *Cleveland Trust Co. v. McQuade*, decided on April 26, 1957, following the death of GM.

29. Ruth Wightman, "In Defense of the Author," *Los Angeles Times*, January 29, 1922.

30. A grant deed recorded in Salinas, California, on May 9, 1922, indicates that Frances Diaz Tucker deeded property in Monterey, California, to Ruth J. Wightman, a single woman. This is the only legal document in RWM's entire life that includes a middle name or initial. No middle name or initial appears on her birth certificate.

31. "Noted Playwright Sues," *Los Angeles Times*, May 10, 1922.

CHAPTER SIX: LIVING IN SIN

1. Marilyn Coleman, Lawrence H. Ganong, and Kelly Warzinak, *Family Life in 20th-Century America* (Westport, CT: Greenwood Press, 2007), 12.

2. Edna E. Kimbro, *Historic Preservation Report: Guesthouse, Caretakers Quarters and Garden Wall*, 720 Via Mirada, 2001.

3. J. D. Conway, *Monterey: Presidio, Pueblo, and Port* (Charleston, SC: Arcadia, 2003).

4. Scott A. Shields, *Artists at Continent's End: The Monterey Peninsula Art Colony, 1875–1907* (Sacramento: University of California Press, 2006), 23–31.

5. Robert Louis Stevenson, "The Old Pacific Capital," in *Across the Plains* (London: Chatto and Windus, 1915).

6. Stephen and Robin Larsen, *Joseph Campbell: A Fire in the Mind* (Rochester, VT: Inner Traditions, 2002), 162. First published

by Doubleday in 1991 as *A Fire in the Mind: The Life of Joseph Campbell.*

7. *Santa Cruz Evening News*, January 14, 1922.
8. "The Rambler," *Book Buyer* 18, no. 4 (May 1899). This column describes the relationship between Robert Louis Stevenson and Jules Simoneau during Stevenson's stay in Monterey in 1879.
9. Gouverneur Morris, "First Visit to Peninsula Is Described by Noted Novelist," *San Francisco Chronicle*, August 20, 1922.
10. Gouverneur Morris, "Noted Writer Lauds Beauty of Monterey," *San Francisco Chronicle*, September 2, 1922.
11. *From Baltimore to Bohemia: The Letters of H. L. Mencken and George Sterling*, ed. S. T. Joshi (Madison, WI: Fairleigh Dickinson University Press, 2001), 242.
12. Pola Negri, *Memoirs of a Star* (New York: Doubleday, 1970), 220–224.
13. "Chaplin May Wed Today," *New York Times*, January 28, 1923.
14. "Star's Visit Is a Big Boost to the Peninsula," *Monterey Herald*, January 29, 1923.
15. "When Pola and Charlie Met at Del Monte," *Los Angeles Times*, January 30, 1923.
16. "Pola Negri Has Left Del Monte," *Monterey Herald*, February 1, 1923.
17. Alec Waugh had a number of opportunities to observe RWM and GM in social situations, which he details in *The Early Years of Alec Waugh* (New York: Farrar, Straus, 1962).
18. "Degree for Noted Author," *Los Angeles Times*, July 21, 1923.
19. "Author's Aide Denies Match," *Los Angeles Examiner*, July 22, 1923.
20. "Author Morris Miss Wightman Tell Betrothal," *San Francisco Call*, July 26, 1923.
21. "Secretary and Author to Be Wed," *Los Angeles Times*, July 27, 1923.
22. "Gouverneur Morris to Wed Secretary," *Los Angeles Examiner*, July 27, 1923.

23. "Ruth Wightman Wins in Women's Tourney," *Oakland Tribune*, December 3, 1923.

24. "Entertained at Point Lobos," *Santa Cruz Evening News*, December 16, 1924.

25. The encounter between reporters and Roscoe Arbuckle is detailed in legal documents from the libel case of *Sydney v. MacFadden Newspaper Publishing Corp.*, which was decided on March 2, 1926, by the New York Supreme Court.

CHAPTER SEVEN: COLLECTING BULLFIGHTERS

1. Muriel Feiner, *Women and the Bullring* (Gainesville, FL: University Press of Florida, 2003), 34.

2. Donald Ogden Stewart, *By a Stroke of Luck!: An Autobiography* (New York: Paddington Press, 1975), 131–133.

3. James R. Mellow, *Hemingway: A Life Without Consequences* (New York: Houghton Mifflin, 1992), 259–262, 298–311.

4. Ellis O. Briggs provides a colorful description of Alexander Moore in "No Charge for the Extra Buttons," *Foreign Service Journal*, December 1961.

5. Letter from RWM to Gene McComas, April 20, 1925, HL.

6. Letter from RWM to Gene McComas, May 28, 1925, HL.

7. Letter from GM to Gene McComas, circa June 1925, HL.

8. "Envoy Moore Is Home from Spain," *Scranton Republican*, January 15, 1925.

9. "Gouverneur Morris," *Fifty-Year Report—Class of 1898—Yale University*, 79. From the private collection of Shirley Newcomb.

10. "Elinor Glynn's Thoughts on a Real Bull-fight," *Cosmopolitan*, January 1921.

11. "Bulls Are Only Year Old, but Then She's Petite Toreadoress," *San Francisco Call*, June 20, 1925.

12. "Author's Wife Makes Fad of Bull Fighting," *Oakland Tribune*, June 21, 1925.

13. "Author's Wife in Bull Ring," *New York Times*, June 30, 1925.

14. "Morris Home from Spain," *San Francisco Examiner*, January 26, 1926.

15. Kenneth William Purdy, "Blood Sport," *Saturday Evening Post*, July 27, 1957.
16. Harold Loeb, *The Way It Was* (New York: Criterion Books, 1959), 279–298.
17. Ernest Hemingway, *The Sun Also Rises* (New York: Charles Scribner's Sons, 1926), 175–176.

CHAPTER EIGHT: A NOT-SO-CASUAL FLIRTATION

1. A major source for chapter 8 is Alec Waugh, *The Early Years of Alec Waugh* (New York: Farrar, Straus, 1962).
2. RWM reveals the name of the man she calls "the Lad" in a letter to Alec Waugh, dated January 6, 1928, HGARC.
3. "Novelist Here After Sojourn in Spain," *Los Angeles Times*, January 23, 1926.
4. The schedule of ports of call of the *Lochgoil* are found at Maritime Timetable Images, http://www.timetableimages.com /maritime/images/rml.htm. This information helps explain the sequence of events following RWM's return.
5. "U.S. Route 101 in California," *Wikipedia*, https://en.wikipedia .org/wiki/U.S._Route_101_in_California.

CHAPTER NINE: STANDING UP VALENTINO

1. Isabel Stuyvesant, "Society of Cinemaland," *Los Angeles Times*, February 21, 1926.
2. John Wolfenden, "Mrs. McComas' Murals," *Monterey Herald*, February 14, 1968.
3. Sinclair Lewis was surprisingly candid about his encounter with Pola Negri in a letter to his former wife, Grace, November 9, 1926, HRC.
4. Richard Lingeman, *Sinclair Lewis: Rebel from Main Street* (New York: Random House, 2002), 272.
5. *From Baltimore to Bohemia: The Letters of H. L. Mencken and George Sterling*, ed. S. T. Joshi (Madison, WI: Fairleigh Dickinson University Press, 2001), 226–227.

6. Emily W. Leider, *Dark Lover: The Life and Death of Rudolph Valentino* (New York: Faber and Faber, 2004), 370–396.
7. "Pola Negri Prostrated," *Los Angeles Times*, August 24, 1926.
8. "Scores Injured in Battle to See Valentino Body," *Los Angeles Times*, August 24, 1926.
9. "Pola Prays at Casket," *Los Angeles Times*, August 30, 1926.
10. "Sterling Death Mystery," *Los Angeles Times*, November 18, 1926.
11. H. L. Mencken, *Thirty-Five Years of Newspaper Work: A Memoir*, ed. Fred Hobson, Vincent Fitzpatrick, and Bradford Jacobs (Baltimore: Johns Hopkins University Press, 1994), 161.
12. Robert Louis Stevenson, *In the South Seas* (London: Chatto and Windus, 1908).

CHAPTER TEN: THE OTHER MAN

1. A major source for chapter 10 is Alec Waugh, *The Early Years of Alec Waugh* (New York: Farrar, Straus, 1962).
2. Another important source was Alexander Waugh's *Fathers and Sons: The Autobiography of a Family* (New York: Broadway Books, 2007).
3. Alec Waugh, *Kept* (London: A. C. Boni, 1925).
4. W. Somerset Maugham, "The Fall of Edward Barnard," in *The Trembling of a Leaf: Little Stories of the South Sea Islands* (New York: Doubleday, Doran, 1921).

CHAPTER ELEVEN: SIX LONG MONTHS

1. An important source for chapter 11 is Alec Waugh, *The Early Years of Alec Waugh* (New York: Farrar, Straus, 1962).
2. Letter from RWM to AW, February 21, 1927, HGARC.
3. Telegram from RWM to AW, February 25, 1927, HGARC.
4. RWM discussed the benefits of writing in a letter to AW, January 6, 1928, HGARC.
5. RWM discussed working on a novel in a letter to H. L. Mencken, March 30, 1922, NYPL.

6. Telegram from RWM to AW, March 4, 1927, HGARC.

7. Letter from RWM to AW, March 6, 1927, HGARC.

8. Marion Davies, *The Times We Had: Life with William Randolph Hearst* (New York: Ballantine Books, 1975), 139–155.

9. A docent at Hearst Castle discussed Marion Davies's strategies for hiding liquor during a tour of the family quarters on February 5, 2015.

10. "Literary Gossip," *Los Angeles Times*, January 23, 1927.

11. Richard P. Buller, *A Beautiful Fairy Tale: The Life of Actress Lois Moran* (Pompton Plains, NJ: Limelight Editions, 2005), 109.

12. "Rumor Connie's Engaged to Famous Author," *Des Moines Register*, June 25, 1925.

13. Jeffrey Meyers, *Scott Fitzgerald: A Biography* (New York: Harper-Collins, 1994), 168–172.

14. Letter from RWM to AW, March 7, 1927, HGARC.

15. Letter from RWM to AW, March 20, 1927, HGARC.

16. Letter from RWM to AW, March 26, 1927, HGARC.

17. Letter from RWM to AW, April 3, 1927, HGARC.

18. Letter from RWM to AW, April 17, 1927, HGARC.

19. Ernestine Black, "First Domingo Paintings in S.F.," *San Francisco Call*, January 30, 1926.

20. Letter from RWM to AW, May 7, 1927, HGARC.

21. Letter from RWM to AW, May 14, 1927, HGARC.

22. Letter from RWM to AW, May 20, 1927, HGARC.

23. Letter from RWM to AW, May 24, 1927, HGARC.

24. Letter from RWM to AW, May 27, 1927, HGARC.

25. Telegram from RWM to AW, June 8, 1927, HGARC.

26. Gossip column from the *San Jose News*, August 9, 1927.

27. "With These Charming People," *Game and Gossip*, September 1927.

28. Cari Beauchamp, *Without Lying Down: Frances Marion and the Powerful Women of Early Hollywood* (New York: Scribner, 1997), 212.

29. Gary Carey, *Anita Loos: A Biography* (London: Bloomsbury, 1988).

30. Letter from GM to Gene McComas, August 20, 1927, HL.

CHAPTER TWELVE: NINE PERFECT DAYS

1. Letter from RWM to AW, circa August 1927, HGARC.
2. Tahiti Message No. 1 from RWM to AW, circa August 1927, HGARC.
3. An important source for chapter 12 is Alec Waugh, *The Early Years of Alec Waugh* (New York: Farrar, Straus, 1962).
4. Tahiti Message No. 2 from RWM to AW, circa August 1927, HGARC.
5. Tahiti Message No. 3 from RWM to AW, circa August 1927, HGARC.
6. Caroline Guild, *Rainbow in Tahiti* (London: Hammond, Hammond, 1951), 65–83.
7. Victor J. Bergeron, "Let's Set the Record Straight on the Mai Tai," oaklandish.com, February 22, 2011.
8. Malcolm Peaker, "Tahiti-Introduced Birds," www.zoologyweblog .blogspot.com, June 2012.
9. Tahiti Message No. 4 from RWM to AW, circa September 1927, HGARC.
10. Tahiti Message No. 5 from RWM to AW, circa September 1927, HGARC.
11. Tahiti Message No. 6 from RWM to AW, circa September 1927, HGARC.
12. Tahiti Message No. 7 from RWM to AW, circa September 1927, HGARC.
13. Tahiti Message No. 8 from RWM to AW, circa September 1927, HGARC.
14. Tahiti Message No. 9 from RWM to AW, circa September 1927, HGARC.
15. Tahiti Message No. 10 from RWM to AW, circa September 1927, HGARC.
16. Tahiti Message No. 11 from RWM to AW, circa October 1927, HGARC.
17. Tahiti Message No. 12 from RWM to AW, circa October 1927, HGARC.

18. Margaret Curtis, *Planter's Punch* (New York: Appleton-Century-Crofts, 1962), 195.

19. An important source for information about Lord Hastings is his daughter Selina Hastings, both through e-mail and personal conversation. She first shared information about how her father came to Moorea in an e-mail dated December 1, 2012.

20. "World's Most Romantic Honeymoon," *Sunday Tribune* (Providence, RI), February 12, 1928.

21. "Notables Arrive in S.F. from South Seas," *San Francisco Examiner*, October 29, 1927.

22. "Hastings Go to Pebble Beach," *San Francisco Examiner*, November 1, 1927.

23. Tahiti Message No. 13 from RWM to AW, October 15, 1927, HGARC.

CHAPTER THIRTEEN: THE JUGGLING ACT

1. Records for the United States Customs Service indicate that on February 15, 1927, RWM listed her age as twenty-nine upon arrival at the Port of San Francisco.

2. Records for the United States Customs Service indicate that on November 25, 1927, RWM listed her age as thirty-one upon arrival at the Port of San Francisco.

3. An important source for chapter 13 is Alec Waugh, *The Early Years of Alec Waugh* (New York: Farrar, Straus, 1962).

4. "Morris Favors Tahiti Sojourn," *San Cruz Evening News*, November 25, 1927.

5. A clipping from an unidentified San Francisco newspaper that RWM mailed to AW, November 26, 1927, HGARC.

6. Letter from RWM to AW, circa November 25, 1927, HGARC.

7. Letter from RWM to AW, November 27, 1927, HGARC.

8. A second letter from RWM to AW, November 27, 1927, HGARC.

9. Letter from RWM to AW, December 2, 1927, HGARC.

10. Telegram from RWM to AW, December 27, 1927, HGARC.

11. Letter from RWM to AW, January 6, 1928, HGARC.

12. Letter from RWM to AW, circa January 1928, HGARC.

CHAPTER FOURTEEN: CONTROLLING THE BURN

1. Photo of RWM with AW and Marcella Gump at a polo match in Pebble Beach, *Game and Gossip*, April 1928.
2. Letter from RWM to AW, March 10, 1928, HGARC.
3. Letter from RWM to AW, April 7, 1928, HGARC.
4. Letter from RWM to AW, May 14, 1928, HGARC.
5. Alec Waugh, *Nor Many Waters* (London: Chapman and Hall, 1928).
6. Thank-you letter from RWM to AW, circa August 1928, from the personal collection of Peter Waugh.
7. Letter from RWM to AW, November 7, 1928, HGARC.
8. Letter from RWM to AW, May 10, 1929, HGARC.
9. John Wolfenden, "Mrs. McComas' Murals," *Monterey Herald*, February 14, 1968.
10. Photo of Gene McComas and GM aboard *The Temptress*, circa October 1929, from the private collection of Shirley Newcomb.
11. RWM discussed her surgery in a letter to H. L. Mencken, circa March 1930, NPL.
12. GM referred to the surgery in a letter to AW, dated July 12, 1930, MMA.
13. Mark Schorer, *Sinclair Lewis: An American Life* (New York: McGraw-Hill, 1961), 531–533.
14. Letter from Dorothy Thompson to friends Bill and Helen, February 21, 1930, SUL.
15. Letter from Dorothy Thompson to friend Helen, October 9, 1930, SUL.
16. Vincent Sheean, *Dorothy and Red* (Greenwich, CT: Fawcett, 1963), 154–166.
17. "Lindberghs Here for Glider Test," *Monterey Herald*, March 4, 1930.
18. "Flight May Take Noted Plane Pilot Many Miles," *Monterey Herald*, March 5, 1930.
19. Evelyn Waugh, *Vile Bodies* (Boston: Little, Brown, 1930).

20. Letter from RWM to AW, April 22, 1930, HGARC.

21. Letter from RWM to AW, May 30, HGARC.

22. Note card that accompanied Ming box, circa June 1930, HGARC.

CHAPTER FIFTEEN: BAD RUN OF LUCK

1. Letter from RWM to AW, circa June 1930, MMA.

2. Letter from GM to AW, July 12, 1930, MMA.

3. Telegram from AW to GM, August 3, 1930, MMA.

4. Alastair Sooke, "Matisse's Cut-Outs: A South Seas Voyage into History," BBC, November 17, 2014, http://www.bbc.com /culture/story/2014117-the-tahiti-trip-that-changed-art.

5. Lotte H. Eisner, *Murnau* (Berkeley: University of California Press, 1973), 202–220.

6. "The Making of F. W. Murnau's *Tabu*: The Outtakes Edition," Deutsche Kinemathek—Museum für Film und Fernsehen, https://www.deutsche-kinemathek.de/en/publications /general-information.

7. "Mr. Murnau's Last Picture," *New York Times*, March 19, 1931.

8. Shaun McGuire, "'Tabu': When Art Imitates Bora-Bora," Florida International University, http://www2.fiu.edu/~harveyb/filmsx1 .html.

9. Letter from David Flaherty to Robert Flaherty, March 19, 1931, BLCU.

10. Margaret Curtis, *Planter's Punch* (New York: Appleton-Century-Crofts, 1962), 130–131.

11. "Believers in South Seas Legends See Operation of Ancient Curse in the Passing of American Movie Director," *Milwaukee Journal*, September 9, 1934.

12. Edwin Schallert, "Far Places Provide Scenes," *Los Angeles Times*, November 23, 1930.

13. "F. W. Murnau Hurt as His Car Upsets," *Los Angeles Times*, March 11, 1931.

14. "Director's Body Rests in Film City," *Los Angeles Times*, March 12, 1931.

15. "Filming in South Seas Presents Difficulties," *Los Angeles Times*, March 15, 1931.

16. "Murnau's Farewell Poetic," *Los Angeles Times*, April 19, 1931.

17. "Great Cinematographers: Floyd Crosby," Internet Encyclopedia of Cinematographers, http://www.cinematographers.nl/GreatDoPh/crosby.htm.

18. *Tabu: A Story of the South Seas.* Produced by David Flaherty, Robert J. Flaherty, and F. W. Murnau; directed by F. W. Murnau; written by Robert J. Flaherty, F. W. Murnau, and Edgar G. Ulmer. Hollywood, CA: Murnau-Flaherty Productions.

19. Information about the character inspired by Lord Beauchamp comes in an e-mail from Selina Hastings, dated April 15, 2015.

20. Letter from David Flaherty to Robert Flaherty, August 18, 1931, BLCU.

21. Letter from RWM to GM, circa August 1930, MMA.

22. An account of the sinking of the Tahiti appears in the "Board of Trade wreck report for 'Tahiti,'" which was created by the Great Britain Board of Trade, November 12, 1930.

23. The story of "Zupatina" was shared by Selina Hastings in a personal conversation in Monterey, California, on January 30, 2014.

24. "British Lord and Lady Visitors in Monterey," *San Francisco Examiner*, November 9, 1930.

25. The story of Lord Hastings's relationship with Diego Rivera was shared by Selina Hastings in an e-mail on November 5, 2013.

CHAPTER SIXTEEN: LIVING ON BORROWED TIME

1. "Auto Blast Injures Gouverneur Morris," *New York Times*, January 21, 1931.

2. "May Cooper Dazed, Patient at Hospital," *Times* (San Mateo, CA), March 2, 1931.

3. "Edna Cooper Just Can't Find Those 5 Days," *San Francisco Examiner*, March 3, 1931.

4. "Edna Cooper's Memory Fails," *Los Angeles Times*, March 3, 1931.
5. "Aviatrix Still Mystified," *Los Angeles Times*, March 4, 1931.
6. "Evelyn 'Bobbi' Trout, 97; Record-Setting Aviatrix of the 1920s," *Los Angeles Times*, January 30, 2003.
7. Dan Miller and Di Freeze, "Bobbi Trout: 'Just Plane Crazy,'" Airport Journals, http://www.airportjournals.com/bobbi-trout-just-plane-crazy/.
8. Patrick Marnham, *Dreaming with His Eyes Open: A Life of Diego Rivera* (New York: Alfred A. Knopf, 1998), 234–269.
9. Bertram D. Wolfe, *The Fabulous Life of Diego Rivera* (New York: Stein and Day, 1963), 284–293.
10. Pete Hamill, *Diego Rivera* (New York: Harry N. Abrams, 1999), 145–249.
11. "Rivera Limns Industries in Great Fresco," *San Francisco Chronicle*, May 31, 1931.
12. "Gouverneur Morris to Be Center of Home Mural," *San Francisco Examiner*, May 1, 1931.
13. Letter from Frida Kahlo to Cristina Hastings, September 2, 1931, from the private collection of Selina Hastings.
14. Letter from Frida Kahlo to Cristina Hastings, November 21, 1931, from the private collection of Selina Hastings.
15. Letter from Diego Rivera to Lord Hastings, January 6, 1932, from the private collection of Selina Hastings.

CHAPTER SEVENTEEN: THE HARD-LUCK GIRL

1. "Mrs. Morris, Miss Gump with Three Pets Sail for South Seas," *San Francisco Chronicle*, July 9, 1931.
2. "President's Wife, Dean Smith in South Seas," *Southern California Trojan*, August 7, 1931.
3. Grace Kingsley, "Patsy Ruth Miller Travels," *Los Angeles Times*, August 4, 1931.
4. Star's Role Brings Nothing but Grief to Lila Lee," *Cumberland Times*, July 5, 1930.

5. "Fate Blacks Out a Hidden Scene in the True-Life Drama of Lila Lee," *Portsmouth Times*, January 12, 1936.

6. Helen Hayward, "Lila Lee," *American Weekly*, November 27, 1949.

7. "Rest Cure Taken by Lila Lee," *Los Angeles Times*, July 9, 1930.

8. "Breaking New Grounds for Divorce," *Motion Picture*, September 1930.

9. "Screen Favorite Battles Disease," *Los Angeles Times*, December 8, 1930.

10. John Farrow's trips to see Lila are mentioned in *Motion Picture*, February 1931.

11. "Lila Lee Back; Plans Early Film Return," *Los Angeles Times*, April 16, 1931.

12. More about Lila's time in the sanitarium is mentioned in *Motion Picture*, June 1931.

13. Patsy Ruth Miller, *My Hollywood: When Both of Us Were Young* (O'Raghailligh Publishers, 1988), 123–142.

14. "Morris' Tastes Blamed for Cost," *San Francisco Examiner*, November 6, 1931.

15. The details of the lawsuit against RWM and GM are found in *Union Supply Co. (A Corporation), Resondent, v. Gouverneur Morris et al., Appellants. S.H. Hooke et al., v. Gouverneur Morris et al., Appellants.*

CHAPTER EIGHTEEN: HOLLYWOOD—THE SEQUEL

1. "'Zeppo' Marx Home Robbed," clipping from unidentified newspaper, August 23, 1932.

2. "Gang Blamed in Marx Theft," *Los Angeles Times*, August 23, 1932.

3. Ruth Morris, "Capra Foresees Satirical Cycle: Many Subjects Ripe for Ridicule," *Variety*, February 1932.

4. Gossip about RWM and Lila Lee at the Brown Derby is found in "February 24, 1932," Hollywood Heyday, November 22, 2008, http://hollywoodheyday.blogspot.com/2008/11/february-24-1932.html.

5. Grace Kingsley, "Hobnobing in Movie Land," *Los Angeles Times*, May 22, 1932.

6. Glenn Fowler, "Colleen Moore, Star of 'Flapper' Films, Dies at 85," *New York Times*, January 26, 1988.

7. Eve Golden, *Golden Images: 41 Essays on Silent Film Stars* (Jefferson, NC: McFarland, 2001), 100.

8. Letter from executive at MGM to Zeppo Marx, June 7, 1932, from the private collection of Shirley Newcomb.

9. Zeppo Marx and Gouverneur Morris, *Tom, Dick and Harry*, an unproduced script.

10. Gouverneur Morris, "Diego Rivera," unidentified Los Angeles newspaper, circa 1932.

11. Glenn Kershner, "Cameraman-Artist-Musician Brings Back Fond Memories of Land and Water Where Food Is Least of Mankind's Worries," *International Photographer*, January 1933.

12. Letter from GM to Gene McComas, August 12, 1932, HL.

13. Letter from GM to Lord Hastings, November 17, 1932, from the private collection of Selina Hastings.

14. "Gouverneur Morris at 'U,'" *Los Angeles Times*, November 28, 1932.

15. Letter from Clifford Wight to Lord Hastings, circa October 1933, from the private collection of Selina Hastings.

16. Richard Gump described how GM got him a job in Hollywood during a long interview he provided to Suzanne B. Reiss at the University of California at Berkeley in 1987.

17. "Noted Movie Art Director Gibbons Dies," *Los Angeles Times*, July 27, 1960.

18. The story of how GM discovered Ayn Rand appears in "The Lee Side o' L.A.," *Los Angeles Times*, March 11, 1936.

19. "Audience to Play 'Jury,'" *Los Angeles Times*, October 22, 1934.

20. "Playwright Also Pens for Screen," *Los Angeles Times*, October 18, 1934.

21. "'Woman on Trial' Proving Popular," *Santa Ana Register*, November 6, 1934.

22. "Morris, Author, Sued by Hotel," *Los Angeles Times*, November 14, 1932.

23. "Autos Take Two Lives," *Los Angeles Times*, May 1, 1935.

24. "Morris Pays Traffic Fine," *Los Angeles Times*, July 10, 1935.

25. "Gouverneur Morris Fined $500," *New York Times*, July 10, 1935.

26. Alec Waugh, *So Lovers Dream* (London: Bloomsbury Publishing, e-book, 2011).

27. The poem "Exile" by Ernest Dowson copied in pencil by RWM, HGARC.

CHAPTER NINETEEN: DEATH AT THE MANSION

1. "Mystery Shooting," *Los Angeles Examiner*, September 26, 1936.

2. "Conflicting Clews Hamper Death Probe," *Los Angeles Examiner*, September 27, 1936.

3. "Beach Killing Held Suicide," *Los Angeles Times*, September 27, 1936.

4. "Threat Made in Death Case," *Los Angeles Times*, November 11, 1936.

5. "Second Probe of Mysterious Death Ordered," *Los Angeles Examiner*, November 13, 1936.

6. "Novelist to Appear in the Russell Case," *New York Times*, November 13, 1936.

7. "Called for New Inquiry," *Los Angeles Times*, November 14, 1936.

8. "Mrs. Morris' 'Suicide Bet' Investigated," *Los Angeles Examiner*, November 14, 1936.

9. "Police to Reenact Fatal Shooting at Gouverneur Morris Home," *Los Angeles Examiner*, November 15, 1936.

10. "Morris Writes Poignant Letter to Mrs. Russell," *Los Angeles Examiner*, November 15, 1936.

11. "Morris, Wife Questioned on Death," *Los Angeles Times*, November 15, 1936.

12. "Russell's Death to Be Re-Enacted," *New York Times*, November 15, 1936.

13. "Lila Lee Tells of Note," *New York Times*, November 15, 1936.

14. "Author's Wife in Collapse at Probe of Youth's Suicide; Says She Burned Note," *Milwaukee Journal*, November 15, 1936.

15. "Mrs. Gouverneur Morris Burned Note Left by Friend Shot on Her Lawn, She Says," *Syracuse Herald*, November 15, 1936.

16. "Policemen Lost Bullet, Says Lad," *Los Angeles Examiner*, November 16, 1936.

17. "Mrs. Morris Recalls Suicide Bet; Tells Events Prior to Tragedy," *Los Angeles Examiner*, November 16, 1936.

18. "Russell Inquiry Will Continue," *Los Angeles Times*, November 16, 1936.

19. "Friends Reveal Russell Love Affair in Mystery; Police Reenact Shooting," *Los Angeles Examiner*, November 17, 1936.

20. "Body May Be Exhumed," *Los Angeles Times*, November 17, 1936.

21. "Evidence Shows Murder, Is Claim," *Los Angeles Examiner*, November 18, 1936.

22. "Rumors Hit by Lila Lee," *Los Angeles Examiner*, November 18, 1936.

23. "Russell Body to Be Examined," *Los Angeles Times*, November 18, 1936.

24. "Racketeering Ring Linked to Russell Case," *Los Angeles Examiner*, November 19, 1936.

25. "Mrs. Morris Flouts Love Slaying Theory," *Los Angeles Examiner*, November 19, 1936.

26. "Query Stirs Mystery," *Los Angeles Times*, November 19, 1936.

27. "Reid Russell's Body Exhumed; Bruise Found," *Los Angeles Examiner*, November 20, 1936.

28. "Russell Arms Plot Hinted," *Los Angeles Times*, November 20, 1936.

29. "Customs Agents Aid Russell Quiz," *Los Angeles Examiner*, November 21, 1936.

30. "Gay Russell Party Bared: Jovial Host with Plenty of Money," *Los Angeles Examiner*, November 21, 1936.

31. "Russell Bank Funds Aired," *Los Angeles Times*, November 21, 1936.

32. "Reid Russell's Clothes Hunted," *Los Angeles Examiner*, November 22, 1936.
33. "Russell Death Garb Found," *Los Angeles Times*, November 22, 1936.
34. "Russell Bank Funds Aired," *Los Angeles Times*, November 22, 1936.
35. "Russell Death Clews Fading," *Los Angeles Times*, November 23, 1936.
36. "Reports on Bloodstains Awaited in Russell Case," *Los Angeles Times*, November 24, 1936.
37. "Morris, Wife Call Russell Probe Asinine," *Los Angeles Examiner*, November 24, 1936.
38. "New Mystery Angles Enter Russell Death Case," *Los Angeles Times*, November 25, 1936.
39. Cecilia Rasmussen, "D.A. Fitts Was Good Match for Scandalous '30s," *Los Angeles Times*, September 19, 1999.

CHAPTER TWENTY: SUNSET IN THE SOUTH SEAS

1. Details of the New Mexico home of RWM and GM appear in Ernie Bulow, "'Big Indian' and the Casa Del Navajo," *Gallup Journey*, December 2011.
2. GM discussed the reasons for moving to New Mexico in a letter to Gene McComas, July 10, 1939.
3. "Francis McComas Succumbs Today," *Monterey Herald*, December 27, 1938.
4. Telegram from GM to Gene McComas, January 6, 1939, from the private collection of Gary and Jane Gasperson.
5. Details about RWM's physical condition at the time of her death are contained in a letter from Bay Morris to AW, June 26, 1940, HGARC.
6. "Wife of Writer Is Dead," *Gallup Independent*, April 20, 1939.
7. Many of the details about RWM's life and death in Coolidge, New Mexico, come from an interview with Shirley Newcomb that took place on September 4, 2013, in Gallup, New Mexico. Ms. Newcomb is the one source for this book still living who

knew RWM when she was alive and could describe the rasp in her voice and the color of her hair from personal experience.

8. The nature of RWM's death is hinted at in a letter from AW to Gene McComas, March 27, 1940, HL.

9. "Gouverneur Morris," *Fifty-Year Report—Class of 1898—Yale University*, p. 80, from the private collection of Shirley Newcomb.

10. Alec Waugh, *Hot Countries* (New York: Literary Guild, 1930), 298–299.

EPILOGUE

1. The line that inspired the title of this book is contained in a letter from GM to Gene McComas, April 24, 1939, HL.

2. Gouverneur Morris, "Bright Wings Are Folded," *Good Housekeeping*, February 1936.

3. AW's reaction to RWM's death is contained in a letter to Gene McComas, June 5, 1940, HL.

4. Bosley Crowther, "Island in the Sun," *New York Times*, June 13, 1957.

5. "Mrs. Lulu Newcomb Dies at Home in Pacific Grove," *Santa Cruz Sentinel*, July 25, 1940.

6. Louis Bonsal Osler, GM's grandniece, confirmed in an e-mail that neither Bay nor Patsey had children but that Patsey had two stepchildren, February 24, 2012.

7. "Lila Lee, Valentino, Chaplin Love, Dies," *Long Beach Independent*, November 14, 1973.

8. "James Kirkwood, Author of Book for Musical 'Chorus Line,' Dies," *New York Times*, April 22, 1989.

9. Six original watercolors by GM are part of the Gene McComas papers, HL.

10. "Gouverneur Morris," *Fifty-Year Report—Class of 1898—Yale University*, p. 80, from the private collection of Shirley Newcomb.

11. Shirley Newcomb shared her vivid memories of GM's death in an interview on September 4, 2013, in Gallup, New Mexico.

BIBLIOGRAPHY

Atherton, Gertrude. *Adventures of a Novelist*. New York: Blue Ribbon Books, 1932.

Baerlein, Henry. *Belmonte: The Matador*. New York: Harrison Smith and Robert Hass, 1934.

Baker, Carlos. *Ernest Hemingway: A Life Story*. New York: Charles Scribner's Sons, 1969.

Beauchamp, Cari. *Without Lying Down: Frances Marion and the Powerful Women of Early Hollywood*. New York: Scribner, 1997.

Berg, A. Scott. *Goldwyn: A Biography*. New York: Riverhead Books, 1998.

———. *Lindbergh*. New York: G. P. Putnam's Sons, 1998.

Blake, Michael F. *Lon Chaney: The Man Behind the Thousand Faces*. New York: Vestal Press, 1993.

Blesh, Rudi. *Keaton*. New York: MacMillan, 1966.

Boon, Kevin Alexander. *Script Culture and the American Screenplay*. Detroit: Wayne State University Press, 2008.

Brookhiser, Richard. *Gouverneur Morris: An Independent Life.* New Haven: Yale University Press, 2014.

Buller, Richard P. *A Beautiful Fairy Tale: The Life of Actress Lois Moran.* Pompton Plains, NJ: Limelight Editions, 2005.

Carey, Gary. *Anita Loos: A Biography.* London: Bloomsbury, 1988.

Carpenter, Elizabeth, ed. *Frida Kahlo.* Minneapolis: Walker Art Center, 2007.

Chaplin, Charlie. *My Autobiography.* New York: Simon and Schuster, 1964.

Conway, J. D. *Monterey: Presidio, Pueblo, and Port.* Charleston, SC: Arcadia, 2003.

Curtis, Margaret. *Planter's Punch.* New York: Appleton-Century-Crofts, 1962.

Davies, Marion. *The Times We Had: Life with William Randolph Hearst.* New York: Ballantine Books, 1975.

Dennis, Jan. *A Walk Beside the Sea: A History of Manhattan Beach.* Manhattan Beach, CA: Janstan Studio, 1987.

———. *Manhattan Police Department.* Chicago: Arcadia, 2003.

Edmonds, Andy. *Frame-Up!: The Untold Story of Roscoe "Fatty" Arbuckle.* New York: William Morrow, 1991.

Eisner, Lotte H. *Murnau.* Berkeley: University of California Press, 1973.

Feiner, Muriel. *Women and the Bullring.* Gainesville, FL: University Press of Florida, 2003.

Golden, Eve. *Golden Images: 41 Essays on Silent Film Stars.* Jefferson, NC: McFarland, 2001.

———. *John Gilbert: The Last of the Silent Film Stars.* Lexington, KY: The University Press of Kentucky, 2013.

Goldman, Emma. *Living My Life,* vol. 1. New York: Alfred A. Knopf, 1931.

Goldwyn, Samuel. *Behind the Screen.* New York: George H. Doran, 1923.

Guild, Caroline. *Rainbow in Tahiti.* London: Hammond, Hammond, 1951.

Hall, James Norman. *My Island Home.* Honolulu: Mutual Publishing, 2001.

Hallett, Hilary. *Go West, Young Women!: The Rise of Early Hollywood.* Berkeley: University of California Press, 2013.

Hamill, Pete. *Diego Rivera.* New York: Harry N. Abrams, 1999.

Helms, Cynthia Newman, ed. *Diego Rivera: A Retrospective.* New York: W. W. Norton, 1986.

Hemingway, Ernest. *The Sun Also Rises.* New York: Charles Scribner's Sons, 1926.

Hemingway, Valerie. *Running with the Bulls: My Years with the Hemingways.* New York: Ballantine Books, 2004.

Joshi, S. T., ed. *From Baltimore to Bohemia: The Letters of H. L. Mencken and George Sterling.* Madison, WI: Fairleigh Dickinson University Press, 2001.

Karman, James, ed. *The Collected Letters of Robinson Jeffers*. Stanford, CA: Stanford University Press, 2009.

Kemm, James O. *Rupert Hughes: A Hollywood Legend*. Beverly Hills: Pomegranate Press, 1997.

Kershaw, Alex. *Jack London: A Life*. New York: St. Martin's Press, 1997.

Kert, Bernice. *The Hemingway Women: Those Who Loved Him—the Wives and Others*. New York: W. W. Norton, 1983.

Kurth, Peter. *American Cassandra: The Life of Dorothy Thompson*. Boston: Little, Brown, 1990.

Kyvig, David E. *Daily Life in the United States, 1920–1940*. Chicago: Ivan R. Dee, 2004.

Labor, Earle. *Jack London: An American Life*. New York: Farrar, Straus and Giroux, 2013.

Larsen, Stephen, and Robin Larsen. *Joseph Campbell: A Fire in the Mind*. Rochester, VT: Inner Traditions, 2002.

Lasky, Jesse L. *Whatever Happened to Hollywood?* New York: Funk and Wagnalls, 1973.

Lebow, Eileen F. *Before Amelia: Women Pilots in the Early Days of Aviation*. Washington, DC: Brassey's, 2002.

Lee, Anthony W. *Painting on the Left: Diego Rivera, Radical Politics, and San Francisco's Public Murals*. Berkeley: University of California Press, 1999.

Leider, Emily W. *Dark Lover: The Life and Death of Rudolph Valentino*. New York: Faber and Faber, 2004.

Lingeman, Richard. *Sinclair Lewis: Rebel from Main Street.* New York: Random House, 2002.

Loeb, Harold. *The Way It Was.* New York: Criterion Books, 1959.

Loos, Anita. *Cast of Thousands.* New York: Grosset & Dunlap, 1977.

Marnham, Patrick. *Dreaming with His Eyes Open: A Life of Diego Rivera.* New York: Alfred A. Knopf, 1998.

Maugham, W. Somerset. *The Trembling of a Leaf: Little Stories of the South Sea Islands.* New York: Doubleday, Doran, 1921.

McCarthy, Todd. *Fast Women: The Legendary Ladies of Racing.* New York: Hyperion, 2007.

McLain, Paula. *The Paris Wife.* New York: Ballantine Books, 2012.

Mellow, James R. *Hemingway: A Life Without Consequences.* New York: Houghton Mifflin, 1992.

Mencken, H. L. *Thirty-Five Years of Newspaper Work: A Memoir,* ed. Fred Hobson, Vincent Fitzpatrick, and Bradford Jacobs. Baltimore: Johns Hopkins University Press, 1994.

Merritt, Greg. *Room 1219: The Life of Fatty Arbuckle, the Mysterious Death of Virginia Rappe, and the Scandal That Changed Hollywood.* Chicago: Chicago Review Press, 2013.

Meyers, Jeffrey. *Scott Fitzgerald: A Biography.* New York: Harper-Collins, 1994.

Miller, Patsy Ruth. *My Hollywood: The Memories of Patsy Ruth Miller.* O'Raghailligh Publishers, 1988.

Milton, Joyce. *Tramp: The Life of Charlie Chaplin.* New York: HarperCollins, 1996.

Morris, Gouverneur. *The Penalty.* New York: Charles Scribner's Sons, 1913.

Omer, Harold L. *Where They Raced: Auto Racing Venues in Southern California, 1900–2000.* Chatsworth, CA: Harold L. Osmer, 2000.

Rice, Elmer. *Minority Report: An Autobiography.* New York: Simon and Schuster, 1963.

Rinehart, Mary Roberts. *My Story.* New York: Farrar and Rinehart, 1931.

Schorer, Mark. *Sinclair Lewis: An American Life.* New York: McGraw-Hill, 1961.

Schroeder, Theodore. *Free Speech for Radicals.* Riverside, CT: Hillacre Bookhouse, 1916.

Shearer, Stephen Michael. *Gloria Swanson: The Ultimate Star.* New York: St. Martin's Press, 2013.

Sheean, Vincent. *Dorothy and Red.* New York: Fawcett, 1963.

Shields, Scott A. *Artists at Continent's End: The Monterey Peninsula Art Colony, 1875–1907.* Sacramento: University of California Press, 2006.

Slide, Anthony, ed. *They Wrote for the Fan Magazines: Film Articles by Literary Giants from E. E. Cummings to Eleanor Roosevelt, 1920–1939.* Jefferson, NC: McFarland, 1992.

Starr, Kevin. *Endangered Dreams: The Great Depression in California.* New York: Oxford University Press, 1996.

Stevenson, Robert Louis. *Across the Plains*. London: Chatto and Windus, 1915.

———. *In the South Seas*. London: Chatto and Windus, 1908.

Stewart, Donald Ogden. *By a Stroke of Luck!: An Autobiography*. New York: Paddington Press, 1975.

Waugh, Alec. *The Best Wine Last*. London: W. H. Allen, 1978.

———. *The Early Years of Alec Waugh*. New York: Farrar, Straus, 1962.

———. *Hot Countries*. New York: Literary Guild, 1930.

———. *Kept*. London: Bloomsbury, 1996.

———. *Nor Many Waters*. London: Chapman and Hall, 1928.

———. *So Lovers Dream*. London: Bloomsbury, 1931.

Waugh, Alexander. *Fathers and Sons: The Autobiography of a Family*. New York: Broadway Books, 2004.

Waugh, Evelyn. *Vile Bodies*. London: Little, Brown, 1930.

Wolfe, Bertram D. *The Fabulous Life of Diego Rivera*. New York: Stein and Day, 1963.

INDEX

ABOUT THE AUTHOR

A California native, John A. Greenwald is a graduate of UC Berkeley and a former copywriter for several major advertising agencies. He later became a teacher and began helping high school students learn how to write. He lives with his wife, Carol, in Monterey.